BEYOND THE SCOREBOARD

An Insider's Guide to the Business of Sport

Rick Horrow

Karla Swatek

Human Kinetics

Library of Congress Cataloging-in-Publication Data

Horrow, Richard B.
  Beyond the scoreboard : an insider's guide to the business of sport / Rick Horrow, Karla Swatek.
     p. cm.
  Includes index.
  ISBN-13: 978-1-4504-1303-9 (soft cover)
  ISBN-10: 1-4504-1303-X (soft cover)
  1. Sports--Economic aspects. 2. Sports administration. I. Swatek, Karla. II. Title.
  GV716.H67 2011
  338.47796--dc22

                              2011010436

ISBN-10: 1-4504-1303-X (print)
ISBN-13: 978-1-4504-1303-9 (print)

Copyright © 2011, 2010 by Rick Horrow and Karla Swatek

This book is a revised edition of *Beyond the Box Score: An Insider's Guide to the $750 Billion Business of Sports,* published in 2010 by Morgan James Publishing.

The web addresses cited in this text were current as of June 2011, unless otherwise noted.

Acquisitions Editor: Myles Schrag; **Developmental Editor:** Julie Marx Goodreau; **Assistant Editor:** Tyler Wolpert; **Copyeditor:** Patricia L. MacDonald; **Indexer:** Alisha Jeddeloh; **Permissions Manager:** Martha Gullo; **Graphic Designer:** Nancy Rasmus; **Graphic Artist:** Julie L. Denzer; **Cover Designer:** Keith Blomberg; **Photographer (cover):** Tom Pennington/Getty Images; **Photographer (interior):** © Human Kinetics unless otherwise noted. Photo on page 35 © Christopher Dodge/fotolia, page 67 © Best Images/fotolia, page 113 © Outstyle/fotolia, page 159 © pressmaster/fotolia, page 183 © Bobby4237/fotolia, and page 213 © David Wood/fotolia; **Photo Asset Manager:** Laura Fitch; **Photo Production Manager:** Jason Allen; **Art Manager:** Kelly Hendren; **Associate Art Manager:** Alan L. Wilborn; **Illustration:** © Human Kinetics; **Printer:** United Graphics

Human Kinetics books are available at special discounts for bulk purchase. Special editions or book excerpts can also be created to specification. For details, contact the Special Sales Manager at Human Kinetics.

Printed in the United States of America   10   9   8   7   6   5   4   3   2   1

The paper in this book is certified under a sustainable forestry program.

Human Kinetics
Website: www.HumanKinetics.com

United States: Human Kinetics
P.O. Box 5076
Champaign, IL 61825-5076
800-747-4457
e-mail: humank@hkusa.com

Canada: Human Kinetics
475 Devonshire Road Unit 100
Windsor, ON N8Y 2L5
800-465-7301 (in Canada only)
e-mail: info@hkcanada.com

Europe: Human Kinetics
107 Bradford Road
Stanningley
Leeds LS28 6AT, United Kingdom
+44 (0) 113 255 5665
e-mail: hk@hkeurope.com

Australia: Human Kinetics
57A Price Avenue
Lower Mitcham, South Australia 5062
08 8372 0999
e-mail: info@hkaustralia.com

New Zealand: Human Kinetics
P.O. Box 80
Torrens Park, South Australia 5062
0800 222 062
e-mail: info@hknewzealand.com

                                                                        E5515

For Sally, who put the fanatic in sports fan

CONTENTS

FOREWORD

by Paul Tagliabue

I'm not big into images. I'm into reality.
The reality is that as the world changes, so does the business of sports.

In our homegrown American sports, sweeping changes are evident. Until the middle of the last century, Major League Baseball did not have teams on America's West Coast—no San Francisco Giants or Los Angeles Dodgers—until the late 1950s. Before that, the "far western" teams were east of Lawrence, Kansas—in Chicago and St. Louis.

Today, Major League Baseball in the United States draws from a global talent pool and plays its games against global competition, most notably in the successful World Baseball Classic. In recent seasons, about 25 percent of the players on MLB rosters have come from foreign lands. Baseball fans all know the great Japanese players in the major leagues—Hideki Matsui, Ichiro Suzuki, Tadahito Iguchi, and Daisuke Matsuzaka. The Dominican Republic and other Latin nations continue to be hotbeds of baseball talent.

In basketball, the NBA's player ranks currently feature some 75 international players from 32 countries and territories. Many of these players competed for their nations in the Olympic basketball competition in Beijing, and the embrace of global talent was evident: At the U.S.–China men's game, I photographed young Chinese fans draped in China's flag and sporting pins with Chairman Mao's portrait but wearing the NBA uniforms of LeBron James, with Cleveland then and now with the Miami Heat, and the L.A. Lakers' Kobe Bryant.

As a result, the NBA is planning a major investment in China in what may be a 12-team professional basketball league fueled by Chinese talent.

2010 was an extraordinary year for sports. For the first time in history, an international mega event, in this case, the FIFA World Cup, took place on an African stage. On the home front, the most expensive stadium ever built, the $1.6 billion Meadowlands Sports Complex, opened outside the financial capital of the world, New York City. Collective bargaining disputes continue to threaten America's big four sports leagues; as its former commissioner, I naturally take a heightened interest in the outcome of bargaining sessions between the National Football League and the NFLPA.

Of course, the paramount question of our current times remains: How do sports institutions pull themselves from the depths of the recession to remain both relevant and fiscally viable?

As fans, we invest more in sports than in the stock market. We have a right to understand what happens at league HQs and in team front offices. And especially in today's turbulent economy, we should have an idea of what tomorrow will bring the sports world.

That's why *Beyond the Scoreboard* is needed now more than ever.

If anyone should write this book, it's "The Sports Professor," Rick Horrow. I've worked with Rick for more than 15 years, since his days as the official facilities consultant for the NFL. Rick always draws from his real-world experience to put the business of sports into context for the casual and avid sports fan alike; I've followed with interest as he's found his voice as a growing television authority on the subject.

That voice also rings true on the printed page, as you'll find when you delve into the world of sports business put on display in *Beyond the Scoreboard*.

Paul Tagliabue

Former Commissioner,
National Football League
January 2011

ACKNOWLEDGMENTS

Good thing a printed page allows for more than the 30 seconds celebrities get to thank the people who helped get them to the podium at the Academy Awards and the Grammys. Because we have a lot of people to thank.

For starters, this book would not have happened without the dozens of people we interviewed who carved time out of their packed days to talk to us. Thanks to Paul Tagliabue, commissioners Gary Bettman, Roger Goodell, and David Stern, NASCAR chief Brian France, Steve Bass, Mike Caponigro, Jerry Colangelo, Barrett Davie, Michael Dennis, John DiCiurcio, Bob DuPuy, Dick Cattani, Gary Cypres, Don Fehr, Ted Ferris, Buffy Filippel, Pat Gallagher, Dave Howard, Jim Irsay, David Kohler, Mark Lamping, Lynn Lashbrook, Joe Leccese, Jeffrey Lurie, Peter Luukko, Pat Lynch, Mike McGee, Tom McGovern, Dan Migala, Jeff Moorad, Howie Nuchow, Neal Pilson, Tony Ponturo, Pat Rooney Jr., Jim Ross, Steve Ross, Chris Russo, Chad Sheckel, Jim Steeg, Leigh Steinberg, Harlan Stone, Peter Sullivan, Frank Supovitz, Doug Thornton, Marc Trestman, Ron Turner, Randy Vataha, Richard Weiss, and Dennis Wellner.

At Horrow Sports Ventures, Betty Curbelo and Brian Finkel offer their constant help and support at all hours; ditto our terrific team at CSE: Ned Simon, Leann Boucher, Robin Applebaum, Christy Duffner, Stephanie Butler, and David Newman—and Mark Lazarus, who now heads up NBC Sports.

We're indebted to Ray Katz and Greg Allocco at the Leverage Agency, who contributed much of the substance on sports marketing and branding. At *Bloomberg Businessweek*, Charles Dubow keeps us in line with our weekly column and features there.

At HKS, Bryan Trubey, Ralph Hawkins, Trish Martineck, and Mark Williams have always lent their support, as have Jim Maiwum, Fred Nance, Stephen Lerner, John Nisky, and Drez Jennings at Squire, Sanders & Dempsey LLC. Paul Weiler and Stephen Greyser at Harvard inspire.

Lauri Romaniello keeps us on the move; Michael Lipman keeps us well stocked with premium sports tickets; Barb Sumner at Office Central kept those perfect transcriptions coming. Student support came from David Eisenberg and Cindy Sue Kelley (through SMWW).

In the publishing world, we're grateful we've found such partners as the good people at Human Kinetics, especially Brian Holding, Myles Schrag, Julie Marx Goodreau, Maurey Williamson, and Jim Schmutz; and at Morgan James, especially David Hancock, Rick Frishman, Margo Toulouse, and Jim Howard. John Willig is a terrific agent, editor, and friend. Ditto David Hahn, Jared Sharpe, and the gang at Planned Television

Arts. David Thalberg keeps us entertained whenever we're in New York. Without Steve Viscusi, we would have never met. And then there's the guy at the Parker Meridien New York who lent Rick his pants. (Don't ask.)

On the Eastern home front, thanks to Terri, Caroline, Katie, and Steve for putting up with Rick. On the Left Coast, in Oklahoma, and elsewhere, Mike, Andrew, Dad, Michael, Wendy, assorted nephews and a niece, TP, Jessa, Carlita, and the wonderful women at Bobby Riggs Tennis Club, Karla owes you about two years of undivided attention. Thanks for your patience and encouragement.

INTRODUCTION

Looking at the World Through Rose Bowl–Colored Glasses

Welcome to the new era of sport—powered by the fan.

In 2011, fans are the designated drivers of the $750 billion business of sports. The digital age and its endless menu of options, from coverage of obscure fringe sports to prolific online fantasy leagues and sophisticated interactive video games, have fragmented the audience for major sporting events like never before.

American football players locked out? I'll just sample some Aussie rules football online. No NASCAR races on a Tuesday? No problem—I'll just play the latest motor sport video game on Xbox Live and compete head-to-head, in real time, with other drivers all over the world.

These days, fans are also participating in the management of leagues and teams, from voting players into All-Star contests via Twitter and text messages to influencing business decisions by way of powerful online fan forums and in some cases being directly involved in the ownership of a team. If you're a fan, however, unless you're that oddball subscriber to the *SportsBusiness Daily*, you're not getting the full business picture from your favorite sports talk radio host or Twitter feed. The casual fan is kept in the dark about to what degree this pastime is an incredibly complex multinational operation on par with the biggest Fortune 100 companies and small governments.

Beyond the Scoreboard: An Insider's Guide to the Business of Sport takes a comprehensive look at how the ever-growing professional sport industry really works. What are the real components driving this multibillion-dollar industry? Who are the true movers and shakers? What affects the price of your ticket, where you're able to take in a game, and what you see on *Sports Center*? What is the undercurrent of technology that now shapes everything that develops in the industry—as it increasingly does in all our lives?

Sport business is lucrative, intense, and largely undocumented. But where is its library of lessons? And how does the entrepreneurial reader learn to think like the skybox exec or superstar to whom victory means the development of brand and bankroll?

Consider the valuations of the world's top sport properties, as estimated by *SportsPro* magazine. Other industry sources consistently confirm these numbers. Not surprisingly, the National Football League ranks as the world's most valuable sport property at an estimated $4.5 billion (all numbers U.S.). Ranked under the NFL are the other three biggest American professional sports: Major League Baseball ($3.9 billion), the National Basketball Association ($3.35 billion), and NASCAR ($1.9 billion).

Interestingly, the next property on the list is only three years old—the Indian Premier League (cricket), valued at $1.6 billion. On the individual franchise side, the highest-rated team property is the English Premier League's Manchester United at $1.5 billion. The Dallas Cowboys are the top-rated U.S. franchise at close to $1.3 billion. Despite troubles revealed at the end of 2009 and stretching throughout the 2010 season, Tiger Woods tops the athletes' list at an estimated fortune of $1.25 billion, bolstered by his golf course design business and off-course business deals.

Despite these sky-high valuations, is sport—as jaded pundits increasingly suggest—now synonymous with entertainment, nothing more than an athletic reality show with no end purpose staged specifically for the amusement of fans and the convenience of advertisers? Philadelphia Eagles owner Jeff Lurie, also a veteran executive in the motion picture industry, hardly thinks so: "I think sports is a subset of the entertainment industry," he says. "If you take global entertainment, it's involving movies, live theater and concerts, live sports and televised sports. So it's really a huge segment of the entertainment industry, with a lot of the same priorities.

"If you own a team in the sports sphere, that business shares a lot of characteristics with the traditional entertainment industry because you want to put the best possible product out there," Lurie continues. "You have to deal with the representatives of the talent. You want the fans to love what you're doing in terms of the performance of the team, which certainly applies to a movie or concert. You don't want predictability, you want a fast-pace product, and you want to work with partners who can work well together as a team as opposed to just hiring the biggest movie star in the world and then throwing the movie out there in a disjointed fashion.

"Finally," Lurie says, "you're increasingly dealing with a global audience, not just domestic. Hopefully, you're also thinking years ahead, how the game or whatever you're producing can be increasingly accessed and understood around the world."

Regardless of all the fragmentation in sports, live televised sporting events—the original reality TV—remain the signature opportunity for sponsors and advertisers to capitalize on a mass audience, as evidenced by the staggering sums that media companies are willing to pay for content. NBC's $4.3 billion deal to televise the Olympic Games through 2020; the collegiate Pacific 12 Conference's new media rights agreement with Fox and ESPN, worth $3 billion over 12 years; and the NCAA's college basketball deal with CBS and Turner, announced at nearly $11 billion over 14 years for the rights to broadcast on TV, the Internet, and wireless devices all top the list.

There's no doubt, however, the recession that knocked out the global economy in the mid-2000s has lengthened the industry's injured-player roster. NASCAR, the darling of the 1990s and the early 2000s, has seen the desperation-driven consolidation of most of its top race teams as well as plummeting TV ratings and massive speedways so devoid of human traffic that you hardly need earplugs.

Nine of baseball's 30 teams are currently over Major League Baseball's prescribed debt ratios, and the ownership of two of its cornerstone franchises, the New York Mets and the Los Angeles Dodgers, is in serious jeopardy, the former due to the Wilpon family's all-in investment in Bernie Madoff's Ponzi scheme of a financial institution, and the latter due to the Hollywood-style greed and hubris of owners Frank and Jamie McCourt.

At press time, the NFL and the NBA are mired in labor stalemates not seen in decades. The NFL, whose owners locked out its players after the 2010 season over pay and benefits, a rookie wage scale, and expansion of the season to 18 games among other issues, could be only days away from signing a new collective bargaining agreement and salvaging the 2011-2012 season. The NBA, claiming $300 million in losses for the season just ended, locked out its players after that CBA expired on June 30. The two sides are far apart on revenue sharing and player salary reductions, and with no agreement in sight, the 2011-2012 season is in jeopardy.

In the sport industry, however, the wins column is typically much longer than the losses, and the current era is no different. Because sport is still appointment TV, billion-dollar sponsors—insurance companies, automobile manufacturers, quick-serve restaurant chains, and breweries—have largely stayed the course despite the recession and continue to align their brands with sports. The recession also produced value packages that helped fans stay in their stadium seats; those who can no longer afford to attend watch more sports at home on their 40-inch high-definition TVs.

While *Beyond the Scoreboard* focuses primarily on football, basketball, and baseball at the professional level—the biggest revenue-generating segments of the sport industry—we also include case studies, lists, and factoids from all sports as they are relevant. So we can't help but notice the lively new franchises in Major League Soccer and the professional National Lacrosse League that are attracting a new generation of fans from America's coasts into the heartland. Golf and tennis have never been more popular; all of their respective majors titles are currently held by foreign nationals, and prestigious tournaments are finding homes in Beijing, Shanghai, and Dubai.

As for us, *Beyond the Scoreboard* also serves as a companion in print to Rick Horrow's regular segments on Bloomberg Television, www.FoxSports.com, and *PBS' Nightly Business Report,* to name a few. *Beyond the Scoreboard* also ushers in a new series of books we are developing with Human Kinetics. The Sport Business Insider series, premiering in 2012, breaks the industry down by specific subject. Each stand-alone title focuses on one aspect of the industry, such as branding in sport, globalization, investing in sport, and deal making.

Sport is indeed the ultimate reality show—and it's a dream job for those of us fortunate enough to work in the industry. But at the end of the day, or more aptly at the end of the game, it is the ultimate mega-business.

1

The Mega Master Super Series XLXL

▶ The bar set by the Super Bowl serves as the primary catalyst for most decisions made in all sports throughout the professional sports year, including advertising and marketing budgets and TV rights deals—not as its end point.

▶ The economic impact of the Super Bowl averages $300-$400 million in each community that hosts the game.

▶ Preparing for the Super Bowl and other sports mega-events is a years-long process.

▶ The NFL has transformed the Super Bowl's visibility and appeal into a year-round must see mind-set, comprising the NFL Combine, the NFL Draft, the NFL Kickoff, the international series based in London, and the Pro Bowl.

the Super Bowl is the culmination of the sports calendar—the unofficial secular national holiday at the end of America's signature season—think again.

The Super Bowl, the crown jewel of all sports championship events, really marks the beginning of the professional sports year, setting into motion a trickle-down effect of ticket pricing, marketing campaigns, hospitality plans, advertising rates, facilities upgrades, and special merchandise design. What's more, all of the event-related elements of the Super Bowl—a lengthy bid process, a top-rated destination, a fan fest, and abundant corporate hospitality—have become staples in all other professional sports and the Olympic Games. Even the Academy Awards closely follows trends that come to the forefront during the NFL's big day.

The Super Bowl is also the starting point for the billion-dollar business decisions made by the gold standard National Football League itself and for other leagues as well. The event has essentially become the sports industry's biggest convention, drawing upwards of 30,000 executives, vendors, and athletes who conduct business in the host city the week beforehand but don't even stick around for the game.

Author Michael MacCambridge puts it well. "At some point the Super Bowl no longer became a game, but it became a show," he claimed in a *Wall Street Journal* review. "And from that, football no longer became a game, it became show business."

It's hard to believe that the first AFL–NFL World Championship Game, as then-NFL commissioner Pete Rozelle called the January 15, 1967, event between the Kansas City Chiefs and the Green Bay Packers, didn't even sell out the Los Angeles Coliseum. (The *Super Bowl* tag came courtesy of Chiefs owner Lamar Hunt a couple of years later.) From the game's most memorable moments—Broadway Joe Namath's 1969 victory guarantee, the Dolphins' cap to their perfect 1972-1973 season, Janet Jackson's 2004 halftime flash of flesh—the Super Bowl is the most watched party for big business each year, just as it is for most Americans. In 2011, 111 million people tuned in to watch at least part of Super Bowl XLV in North Texas, becoming the most watched American television broadcast of all time, besting by a good margin Super Bowl XLIV, which in 2010 took over the spot held for 27 years by the 1983 *M*A*S*H* finale (that event drew 106 million viewers).

Even though there was about a 20 to 25 percent recession-driven reduction in ancillary events starting in 2009 in Tampa Bay—even *Playboy* canceled its uberexclusive annual party—a significant premium will always be attached to the NFL's championship game, and regardless of greater economic conditions, the premier event's host communities will always benefit.

The Super Bowl will always be the Super Bowl.

Super Bowl Economic Impact

The broadly defined sports travel market, according to *SportsTravel*, generated about $182 billion a year in the latter part of the last decade. Twenty-seven percent of all round trips of 100 miles (160 km) or more taken annually were sports related, generating $177 billion in travel spending.

On average, economic research places the financial windfall from hosting a Super Bowl for host cities and regions at $300 to $400 million—a figure that is continually and hotly debated. How do event organizers arrive at that number?

Economic impact studies, whether conducted by independent agencies or regional academic institutions, take into account key postevent indicators and metrics: game and related event attendance, the number of out-of-town visitors, average hotel room rates, tax receipts, and event management spending. The studies also factor in the effect of multipliers (dollars circulating through a community more than once) and displacement (the level of spending in the region at the time of the event had it not been held).

Results for the Super Bowl, of course, vary from location to location and year to year. The last Super Bowl to be held in South Florida before the 2010 event, the 2007 Super Bowl XLI in Miami, was estimated by the Sport Management Research Institute to have a total economic impact of $463 million, the sum of visitors' spending and $183 million in indirect spending, most of that by local businesses. The report indicated that about 112,400 visitors flocked to the region for the event, staying for four or five days and spending $668.80 per day.

However, PricewaterhouseCoopers forecast a financial windfall of only $150 million in direct spending for Tampa Bay in 2009, down 20 percent from previous years as a result of the economy. And while Super Bowl XL in Detroit surprised some by bringing more than 120,000 visitors to the Motor City, including 3,000 media members, and a stated $300 million windfall, figures released afterward by the Michigan Department of Treasury revealed that the event had little overall impact on the state's economy, with state sales tax receipts up only 2 percent over the year before.

By comparison, the MLB All-Star Game at Detroit's Comerica Park the previous summer brought $50 to $70 million in economic impact and 30,000 visitors to the region. The NBA All-Star Game in New Orleans in 2008 gave that city a $100 million boost, while the same event a year later brought closer to $80 million into the Phoenix metro area.

The typical budget for a Super Bowl host committee to put on the game is $12 to $15 million ($30 million for the supersized 2011 event at Dallas Cowboys Stadium in North Texas); on average, it costs the NFL around $60 million for its share.

Rodney Barreto, four-time Miami Super Bowl Host Committee chairman, enthuses about the Super Bowl's long-term relationship with South Florida. "Corporate America comes for the best restaurants, best hotels, and best beaches," Barreto says. "The NFL has realized we're the best destination, and that's why Miami has hosted 10 Super Bowls."

The addition of the Pro Bowl to the weeklong slate of events in 2010 did the South Florida region one better. If a region can turn 7 out-of-towner days (Monday to Sunday) into 14 (the Pro Bowl–Super Bowl combination in 2010), it can add 40 to 60 percent more economic impact to the region because of that second week.

South Florida economic impact numbers are skewed by sheer fact, however: Snowbirds and tourists flock to the region on Super Bowl weekend, with or without the game being held there (just as they're drawn to Las Vegas). And hotel rooms would be mostly full without the Super Bowl events. South Florida tourism peaks during Spring Break season in March, but February is almost always the second busiest month.

Speaking of Vegas, that city's more than 170 sport and race books always benefit from Super Bowl weekend. More bets are laid down on the Super Bowl than any other American sporting event—even the NCAA basketball tournament. In 2007, the Las Vegas Convention and Visitors Authority estimated that 287,000 people visited Las Vegas on Super Bowl weekend, producing $109.5 million in nongambling economic impact, almost equal to the total handle for the game.

Reeling In a Mega Event

Taking their cue from the long tradition of the Olympic Games, North American cities vying to host the Super Bowl, an All-Star Game, a regional component of a nationwide event (the NCAA tourney, the World Cup, the World Baseball Classic), or the Olympics themselves must go through an elaborate bid process. Outside of the Olympics, none is as mired in precision and politics as the bidding process for a Super Bowl.

Each November, the NFL issues a 200- to 300-page bid book to cities looking to host the game. Draft bids are due in April, and the NFL's 32 owners vote on the location at an owners' meeting sometime thereafter. Baseline hosting requirements, according to *SportsBusiness Journal*, include the following:

- A 70,000-seat stadium or one that can be expanded to at least that size
- At least 19,000 hotel rooms that require three- or four-night minimum stays, including rooms for both teams and NFL personnel

- A range of nearby facilities or spaces to house the media and accreditation center for more than 4,000 media representatives, the NFL Experience, the NFL Tailgate Party, and the like
- An average daily temperature of 50 degrees Fahrenheit (10 °C) or above the week of the game, or a climate-controlled indoor facility
- Provision of police, fire, ambulance, and other infrastructure services at no cost to the NFL

Over the years, insiders indicate that the politics of the bid process have ratcheted up considerably—as have the perks. The 2007 Miami bid committee threw in the use of a yacht for each of the 32 owners, while Tampa offered all the teams free golf. The 2011 North Texas group went green instead, offering the NFL an additional $1 million to cover game-day expenses at Cowboys Stadium, enticing enough as that new facility is on its own.

The bid process is also "shrouded in secrecy, like someone had found the Holy Grail," says Ted Ferris, chairman of the Arizona Sports and Tourism Authority, the regional agency in charge of University of Phoenix Stadium in Glendale and an organization heavily involved in the roll-up to Super Bowl XLII in 2008.

"Our former chairman, John Benton, gave an apt description of what our role was in the bid process," Ferris says. "We were working with the Bidwill family [the Arizona Cardinals' owners], and information was getting passed back and forth. But we never saw the entire bid document. As Benton said, if you view the bid as the plans for an airplane, we were given only the plans for a wing—the stadium and what the authority would commit to do for the NFL. We had no clue what the airplane looked like. We just knew what the wing looked like."

But it wasn't always that way. Jim Steeg, who spent 33 years with the NFL, including 26 in charge of the league's special events department, says when he first was put in charge of the Super Bowl, the bid specifications were "maybe two pages long."

"We didn't go through all of this," Steeg says. "When I first got involved, the bids were very Chamber of Commerce. Then the ante was upped in March 1979. We were in Hawaii, and we were looking for sites for the Super Bowl in '81, '82, and '83. Detroit really wanted the '81 game, which New Orleans ended up winning. But Detroit came in—this was how crazy it was—and made a presentation, and it had a slide show, a video, and all this stuff up there. And all these owners, who you think are really tremendously sophisticated, were looking at this presentation and just going on and on. That's how Detroit got it [the 1982 Super Bowl]. Their presentation materials were so far ahead of everybody else's."

The Silverdome may have won the day in 1982, but that Motor City facility would never pass muster these days. The quality of Detroit's newer Ford Field and the $505 million public–private financing partnership that enabled a weatherproof roof to be built over it (chronicled in my book *When the Game Is On the Line*) were among the primary reasons chilly Detroit was chosen to host Super Bowl XL in 2006. XL provided the biggest of international stages upon which to showcase downtown Detroit's rebirth—and in hindsight, it may have helped stave off the precipitous crash of the auto industry for a year or two.

The new stadium trump card Detroit played before the NFL to earn Super Bowl XL also paved the way for Glendale in 2008, North Texas in 2011, Indianapolis in 2012, and New Meadowlands Stadium in 2014. San Diego, formerly a popular stop in the so-called Super Bowl rotation, knows full well it will never see another Super Bowl without building a new stadium to replace aging Qualcomm (the city may lose the Chargers for that reason as well). Even NFL favorite Miami has been told that unless it completes renovations to Sun Life Stadium, including additional seating capacity and suites and at least a partial roof, it will no longer be allowed to compete with cutting-edge venues such as Cowboys Stadium.

Corporate America Loves Sports

What's the quickest way for a company's stock to rocket in value? According to a University of Missouri study of 53 national corporations, companies gained an average of $257 million in stock value and $13.6 billion in total economic value in the first trading week after announcing sponsorship deals with the NFL, NBA, NHL, MLB, or PGA Tour. What's more, products "seen as more relevant to the sports" had an 11 percent stronger return than products "without a clear-cut connection."

Three major sports sponsorship categories stood at the millennium: automotive, beverage, and finance. By 2010, sponsorship marriages

Sponsorships in the Millennium

- Focus on activation rather than on passive sponsorship
- Feature relationships that are more fully integrated (e.g., naming rights)
- Apply the "everything is sponsorable" rule—modules are broken down into small increments to maximize revenue
- Are moving away from individual athletes endorsing products (endorsement and sponsorship contracts are shorter, smaller, and easier to terminate)

morphed from a gut decision reflecting the personal preferences of ego-driven chairmen to a highly sophisticated science, reliant on fan avidity and consumer preference studies.

The past couple of years have created an interesting environment for sports marketing case studies. Congressional representatives vilified banks for taking Troubled Asset Relief Program (TARP) funds while spending lavishly on corporate hospitality. The New York Mets opened their new stadium with the richest naming rights deal in history, a $20 million-per-year pact with Citi. However, spending money doesn't necessarily guarantee success. Despite the $12 billion spent on player endorsements, 2009-2010 reminded us that even our favorite athletes, people such as Tiger Woods, Michael Phelps, and LeBron James, have their flaws. Clearly, sports marketing's incredible exposure comes at an even more incredible expense, which is why future contracts will be shorter and easier to terminate.

The Super Bowl, however, continues to break all practical sports marketing rules. Regardless of which teams are in the championship game, the Super Bowl has always been appointment viewing for America and the world, drawing by far the single largest television audience of the year to whatever network has been fortunate enough to land the rights, meaning that between 80 and 90 million Americans are tuned in to the Super Bowl at any given time, with peaks of 140 million or more. By contrast, the January 2009 inauguration of President Barack Obama was watched by 37.8 million viewers, spread over more than a dozen network and cable outlets.

Even in a recessed economy, an audience of this size is too big for corporate sponsors and advertisers to pass up—never mind the $100,000-range price tag just to sponsor a seven-figure VIP Super Bowl party, or the $3 million per 60 second price tag FOX charged for ads in 2011. Total ad spending on network TV was $16.4 billion the year before XL; NBC took in a record $261 million from Super Bowl XLIII. By comparison, an ad during a regular-season Sunday night *Football Night in America* game on NBC cost $434,792, according to the network.

"The Super Bowl is essentially the beginning of the year, and you want to get the year off right," says Tony Ponturo, former vice president of global media and sports marketing at Anheuser-Busch/InBev, which holds exclusive rights to the alcoholic beverage ad category during the game and scored the highest-rated Super Bowl ad in *USA Today*'s Ad Meter poll for 10 years in a row. "[In] beer sponsorship and sports sponsorship, particularly in today's cluttered environment and [with] all the choices we as consumers have, it's tough to dominate anything. In the U.S., the majority of us stop on Super Bowl Sunday and say, 'We're going to watch the Super Bowl.' Over time, it was '*and* we want to see the commercials.' It was an easy decision for us to say this is a place where we're going to get a lot of impact.

"Yes, they're $2 to $3 million commercials," he continues, "but we're reaching 50 percent of our consumer base, and thanks to the press and the media, we're getting a month of PR prior to the Super Bowl and then at least 7 to 10 days after it. If you're going to spend $20 million, then you better make sure you have creativity that can stand up to the $20 million asset."

And stand up it had better. A survey released by Nielsen reveals that 51 percent of respondents prefer the ads that air during the Super Bowl to the game itself and that ads running early in the game are better remembered than those airing later. Further, TNS indicates that about 20 to 25 percent of Super Bowl advertisers each year are first timers, and the "average tenure for advertisers is three or four years before dropping out."

Traffic to advertiser websites also spikes the day after the Super Bowl; in general, Web traffic to Super Bowl broadcaster sites and sports-specific sites broadly increased over the last four years, mostly thanks to advertisers' online promotions and their slow but steady migration online. According to a recent case study, PepsiCo, a 23-year Super Bowl ad veteran, chose to sit out Super Bowl XLIV in favor of less expensive digital campaigns including social networking sites such as Facebook. (And this only a year after the beverage and food giant created enormous buzz in the ad community by offering $1 million in prize money to anybody who could create a Super Bowl ad for its Doritos brand that trumped all other ads in viewer rankings during the game.)

FACT An estimated 30 million pounds (14 million kg) of snack foods are consumed on Super Bowl Sunday.

But the Super Bowl being the Super Bowl, exposure for corporate sponsors and advertisers remains unparalleled. Outside of Anheuser-Busch, brokerage firm Raymond James estimated its overall media exposure in Tampa Bay in 2009 to be $37.3 million, according to a Joyce Julius & Associates study, because its name was front and center on the stadium where Super Bowl XLIII was played.

First-time advertiser Denny's valued its ad coverage during the same event at $50 million, largely thanks to its single ad's offer of a free Grand Slam breakfast at Denny's stores nationwide the Tuesday after the game. Denny's continued the promotion in 2010 but decided to pass in 2011. Why? As Denny's chief marketing officer Frances Allen told *Ad Age*, "We have done the Super Bowl for the last two years, and it has accomplished the objective of reintroducing the Denny's brand to America and giving back to our guests. The Super Bowl is a big splash and a way of getting noticed, but we've really found that our guests want consistent appreciation over time. We are giving back to them every day; we didn't feel the need to do the one-hit wonder for the Super Bowl in 2011."

Customer perceptions count. Some advertisers receiving federal bailout funds, such as General Motors, sidelined themselves from Super Bowl advertising for a time, primarily to prevent taxpayer and stockholder backlash. Despite receiving $45 billion in bailout funds, Bank of America continued to spend tens of millions to put its name on the NFL Experience. The bank claimed it was legally required to fulfill its contract and called the expenditure a "business proposition" and "growth strategy."

FACT When the Daytona 500, NASCAR's biggest annual celebration, celebrated its 50th anniversary in 2008, the race averaged 17.8 million viewers, with 33.5 million Americans watching at least part of the race coverage on FOX.
Source: Nielsen Media Research

More All-Stars and Grand Slams

One-third of the country usually tunes into at least part of the Super Bowl, which echoes Harris Interactive surveys indicating 30 percent of Americans regularly choose pro football as their favorite sport, compared to 15 percent who prefer baseball and only 4 percent preferring the NBA.

Numbers for mega events in those pro team sports shake out accordingly and provide an interesting comparison to the Super Bowl, as do the grand slams of top individual sports golf and tennis.

MLB All-Star Break

On New Years' Day 2010, the city of Anaheim's float design in the 2010 Tournament of Roses Parade promoted the 2010 MLB All-Star Game at Angel Stadium. The $150,000 float featured a baseball, two bats, and the Angels logo. That's just the tip of the floral iceberg on what communities are willing to do to attract other big events besides the Super Bowl—and to keep them coming back.

The growth of its ancillary events is one of the main reasons that the MLB All-Star break is now consistently over a $100 million extravaganza, far beyond the World Series, which has seen attendance and ratings drops over the last few years. (Of course, it's not a fair comparison, since World Series matchups and locales are decided only days before the event commences.)

In St. Louis, the four-day 2009 MLB All-Star break put up more impressive numbers than the Home Run Derby participants themselves. The *St. Louis Post-Dispatch* estimated that 45,000 to 50,000 people attended Saturday's MLB All-Star Charity Concert headlined by Sheryl Crow. Further, according to MLB, an announced crowd of 36,311 attended Sunday's XM All-Star Futures Game at Busch Stadium.

Major League Baseball Advanced Media (MLBAM) recorded 68.6 million votes for the four-day Final Vote push for the Tuesday MLB All-Star Game, an all-time high.

The average ticket price to the All-Star Game was down by more than half, to $679, while ticket prices to Monday's Home Run Derby were up more than 9 percent, to $491.

Which Sport Has the Best All-Star Weekend?

5. **NFL:** The only All-Star Game that comes at the end of a season, Pro Bowl rosters are consistently filled with apathetic players trying to avoid injury. Although the game has been played at Aloha Stadium every year since 1979, the 2010 edition took place the week before the Super Bowl in Miami. The 2011 contest returned to Hawaii, and the play was more pathetic than apathetic—the game saw six AFC turnovers before that squad scored the final touchdown on a 67-yard pass play that included two laterals and, moments later, a failed two-point conversion.

4. **NASCAR:** Unlike most NASCAR races, the Sprint All-Star Race has a more selective field and a unique segmented format. With a $1 million winner-take-all prize, drivers often make reckless moves that result in frequent crashes. However, off the track, the All-Star Race does little to differentiate itself from a typical NASCAR Sunday. The season-opening Daytona 500 and end-of-season Homestead (Miami) Chase for the Championship get most of NASCAR's special event focus.

3. **NHL:** In addition to the actual game, the NHL's All-Star Weekend holds the Young Stars contest for rookies and the Skills Competition. Growing in popularity is the NHL's outdoor New Year's Day Winter Classic, along with the league's outdoor Heritage Classic game in Canada.

2. **MLB:** A bit of an exception to the All-Star Weekend rule of thumb, the Midsummer Classic takes place during the week. From its inception in 1985, the Home Run Derby is one of the most beloved All-Star events in all of sports, while the Futures Game and Celebrity Softball Game round out the Classic. The winner of the All-Star Game now receives home field advantage in the World Series.

1. **NBA:** Undoubtedly, the premier All-Star Weekend belongs to the NBA. With countless events including the Slam Dunk Contest, Three-Point Shootout, Skills Challenge, and Shooting Stars Competition, it is the only All-Star Weekend where the actual game takes a back seat. And what other sport could pull off having its most recognizable player dance with the JabbaWockeeZ?

Advertisers bought the entire 73-unit ad inventory on FOX about "two weeks ahead of last year," according to *USA Today*. MLB sponsor PepsiCo is the All-Star Game's biggest advertiser; Anheuser-Busch had its Clydesdale horses and beer wagon on the field during the pregame.

The biggest booster of in-game ad prices the summer of 2009 was none other than the First Fan himself. President Obama not only threw out the ceremonial first pitch at the All-Star Game but also stuck around to do an in-booth interview with FOX anchors Joe Buck and Tim McCarver. *USA Today* reports Obama's presence "helped FOX get a 30 percent premium on its unsold pregame ad slots." Before the game, Obama and former presidents Bill Clinton, George W. Bush, George H.W. Bush, and Jimmy Carter appeared in a video honoring the 30 winners of MLB and *People* magazine's All-Stars Among Us contest, marking the first time all living U.S. presidents took part in a ceremony at a sports event.

The NBA Jams

Of all the All-Star breaks in pro sports, the NBA's annual weekend is the most attuned to providing signature opportunities for all of its fans, even if they can't get into the game or All-Star Saturday Night, highlighted by the wildly popular Slam Dunk Contest. Jam Session, the NBA's fan fest, now spans five days and seems to take over the whole convention center in whatever city is hosting the events. In 2009, the league also premiered the NBA All-Star Block Party, a free outdoor festival primarily aimed at local fans, featuring player appearances, video game pavilions, and live music.

Like the Super Bowl, the NBA All-Star Weekend provides a major jumping-off point for NBA sponsors and other businesses associated with the league. Last year, a record 25 sponsors planned activities pegged to All-Star Weekend, according to NBA executive vice president of marketing partnerships Mark Tatum, including FedEx, McDonald's, and Hewlett-Packard. According to league sources, All-Star Game host teams typically see an influx of three times more people than those holding game tickets, a mixture of NBA vendors and avid basketball fans.

On television, however, the NBA All-Star events don't fare as well as the NBA Finals, especially since their migration to cable on TNT. The NBA Finals is also a major international attraction—the league routinely provides television feeds to 215 countries in 42 languages and attracts more than 250 international journalists to the Finals' two host cities.

Professional Golf's Top American Extravaganzas: The Masters and the U.S. Open

Under the canopy of Augusta National's tall pines, all is much the same as it's been for 75 years, as the Masters is perhaps the only sporting event in America to remain economy-proof. The tournament lists only three major corporate sponsors: AT&T, ExxonMobil, and IBM Corp.—all of which are more visible on the tournament's website than they are on the grounds.

The Augusta Convention and Visitors Bureau estimates the tournament pumps more than $100 million into the city's economy; the surrounding region also fares well. By comparison, the Ryder Cup, held every four years in the United States, injects $114 to $150 million into the economies of significantly larger metropolitan areas.

Linda Rooney, owner of Linda's Bistro in nearby Aiken, South Carolina, says Masters week business has never been busier. "We start getting calls for reservations early in March, in February, even," Rooney says. Lodging in the region is booked up every year, and 40,000 people make their way to Augusta National each day for the practice rounds, Wednesday's Par 3 Contest, and the main event.

U.S. Open Golf: Fast Facts

- More than 120,000 hats are sold during the U.S. Open, an average of 16 hats per minute.
- More than 140,000 transactions are processed during the 123 hours the event's enormous merchandise pavilion is open.
- More than 50 golf merchandise vendors are represented in the pavilion; prices range from $2 to $1,395.
- 55,000 spectators per day are expected on-site. According to U.S. Open officials, about 42,500 tickets are normally sold for each day of the tournament, 75 percent of which are sold to out-of-towners. In 2008 at Torrey Pines in San Diego, face value on the sold-out tickets ranged from $40 for practice rounds to $100 for rounds one through four.

U.S. Open Tennis

With a record 2009 attendance of 721,059, and 2010 numbers only marginally below that, America's premier tennis event continues to grow. According to the USTA, revenues for the event near $208 million, with profits of $110 to $115 million; overall attendance averages around 675,000 tennis fans.

Despite the economy, all 85 suites within the Billie Jean King National Tennis Center were sold out last year, with only a few long-term sponsors, such as financial giant JPMorgan Chase, reining in hospitality. Outside of Arthur Ashe Stadium suites, most U.S. Open corporate hospitality centers around the National Tennis Center's indoor tennis facility, which also serves as the stage for the family-oriented SmashZone and fans willing to spend $475 to $1,500 to be entertained.

In 2009, ESPN televised the U.S. Open for the first time, with coverage spanning ESPN2, www.ESPN360.com, and ESPN Mobile TV and backed by sponsors including IBM, DirecTV, American Airlines, Lexus, and Miller Genuine Draft 64. If that wasn't enough, Tennis Channel aired more than 70 hours of live tournament coverage.

Prep Work

As it nears its half-century mark, the Super Bowl has evolved from a relatively simple sports championship to a weeklong extravaganza that emphasizes the participation of the local community on business, educational, and charitable fronts, not just sporting ones.

After a city lands a Super Bowl and before all that revenue comes rolling in are four years' worth of planning sessions, fund-raising, sponsor wooing, and volunteer wrangling—in the Super Bowl's case, to the tune of about 8,000 local residents pulled in for operational help. Broadcast agreements must be negotiated—the Super Bowl is the cornerstone of the NFL's TV deals now worth $4 billion a year. Stadiums must be built-out and team practice sites identified. Citywide transportation and security measures must be put in place. And then there are all those parties to plan.

After the NFL secures the city, the stadium, and several thousand hotel rooms from the close to 20,000 a city must guarantee, it partners with the full-time host committee staff to educate local businesses on how they can capitalize on the game. The NFL's Emerging Business Program, introduced by Jim Steeg, gives small minority- and women-owned businesses a chance to bid on service contracts that support the game and all the ancillary events going on around town. Local restaurant and hospitality associations hold educational seminars on ways businesses can benefit from the influx of fans. Steeg was also the driving force behind most NFL-sponsored charity events, including the league's Youth Education Town Center and the Taste of the NFL, which have raised more than $55 million for host communities over the past 25 years and positively affected thousands of families.

Days before the Super Bowl, the planning process funnels down to specific tasks. The NFL takes over the facility, with access closely controlled and security measures tightened. The TV crew eases into place the 75 3-D and HD cameras, 25 digital replay sources, 20 handheld cameras, multiple

Jim Steeg's Super Bowl A to Z

A. Ambush marketing—corporate fulfillment

B. Business opportunities—emerging business

C. (1) Charities; (2) Communication, the most important key to success

D. Decorations—logo and theme art—airports, streets, hotels, stadium

E. (1) Escorts—security, police (city, county, and state), FBI, Secret Service, postal inspectors, ushers, and ticket takers; (2) Events

F. (1) Field preparation; (2) Family trip

G. Groups—corporate hospitality, Stadium Club

H. (1) Host committee; (2) Hotels house teams, media, networks, sponsors, affiliated groups, fans, assign more than 16,000 and use more than 35,000

I. (1) Invitations—parties and events; (2) International

J. JumboTron, Scoreboard, and Stat program

K. Koncerts

L. Licensed products

M. Media—credentialing, schedule, registration, and work areas

N. Numbers—staffing-team help, consultants, and New York staff

O. (1) Off week; (2) Offices—NFL, teams

P. (1) Parking—traffic, FAA, and lots (show plans)—driving directions; (2) Preplanning; (3) Pregame shows—anthem, coin toss, and flyovers

Q. Quest for the best possible experience for all attendees

R. Radios—telephones, cell phones, and faxes

S. Stadium—refitting—power, TV, media, and teams

T. (1) Teams; (2) Television; (3) Tickets

U. Unity—city, host committee, and NFL working for common purpose

V. Volunteers

W. Workers—the tens of thousands who work events and game day at the stadium

X. Xs and Os

Y. (1) Youth clinics; (2) YET (Youth Education Towns) Centers

Z. Halftime (ZZ Top once performed)

robots, and 100 microphones they'll use to broadcast the event around the world. Medical personnel construct temporary hospital facilities on the grounds, where staff are capable of treating anything from an ankle sprained during a fall to an industrial accident or stroke. And military sharpshooters scout out the posts where they'll be hidden away during the game, prepared for the worst possible scenario the event could produce: an attack on the fans or a singular dignitary in the crowd.

Other preparations are a lot more fun. *Playboy* and *Maxim* party planners pore over their guest lists, and Taste of the NFL celebrity chefs ready their kitchens and sharpen their knives.

Premier ticket broker Michael Lipman, founder and CEO of Miami-based Tickets of America, has a different sort of Super Bowl planning dilemma to dice out. "I had an NFL player playing in the Super Bowl, I won't give any names, but football players tend to have this problem," Lipman says. "He needed three single tickets in three different areas of the stadium. His wife we put on the 50-yard line behind his bench. We gave his girlfriend who flew into town a good seat in one end zone—and we gave his other girlfriend a seat in the opposite one.

"We had to be careful," Lipman grins. "We couldn't mix up the FedEx envelopes. When we booked their hotel rooms, same thing. He wanted his wife in the Players Tower and his girlfriend within walking distance. The other girlfriend? We put her in the next county over."

University of Phoenix Stadium Takes Its Seat at the Big Event Table

For some of the world's biggest sporting events, such as the Olympics and the World Cup, host cities opt to erect temporary disposable arenas. At about $6 to $7 million, they're cheap compared to building from the ground up, and they don't run the risk of sitting empty, bleeding money, after all the fans go home.

In America, the NFL prefers to house its premier event in a permanent venue—preferably the biggest, most cutting-edge building possible, such as the giant silver spaceship that appeared on the west edge of Phoenix shortly after the millennium.

The first of the new wave of millennial sports facilities to hold a Super Bowl, University of Phoenix Stadium in Glendale, Arizona, opened its doors in 2006, hosted Super Bowl XLII in 2008, and is run by facilities management giant Global Spectrum.

Among other amenities, including its famous roll-in field tray of natural grass, the stadium seats 63,400 fans, with additional seating capable of bringing that total to 73,000, all with uninterrupted sight lines. The retractable roof is made of translucent fiberglass that fills the stadium

The University of Phoenix Stadium with the roof open.
© Gene Lower/Southcreek Global/Icon SMI

with natural light even when the roof is closed. And the full utility grid embedded in the stadium floor gives trade shows and promoters another off-season venue option in the region, guaranteeing additional revenue streams to the community and the team.

The savvy that Global Spectrum brings to the table is a key reason why the Arizona Sports and Tourism Authority brought the group in years before University of Phoenix Stadium actually opened, a bold departure from common practice. "We spent like $2.5 million before we had our first event, just making sure that we had a staff that was ready to hit the ground running. We also asked them to review the stadium design from an operational standpoint and to point out things that we were overlooking or missing that we ought to address," the Arizona Sports and Tourism Authority's Ferris says.

"Ten, twenty years from now, if someone drives up to this stadium, they're still going to go, 'Wow!'" says Peter Sullivan, general manager, University of Phoenix Stadium. "I just love bringing people here and witnessing that first impression."

Like any multimillion-dollar multiuse facility today, the building, and its management, had better be ready for anything. To them, hosting the Super Bowl was just another day at the office. With a few extra people around. And a few extra chairs.

Sullivan and his staff had the foresight to plan for an extra 10,000 seats for mega events, bringing the stadium's capacity up to 73,000 from the 63,400 normally available for Cardinals games. Unlike most other stadiums, these temporary seats are a permanent part of the facility—they're owned by the building and stored there, not an inconsequential detail.

"When Global Spectrum got here," Sullivan says, "everybody was talking about 10 percent more seats for big events. It took us almost three years to figure out how to do that. It was a huge task, because in this building you not only have to get the seats up in 48 hours, you have to be able to take them right back down in the same amount of time.

"Our hypothetical perfect storm," Sullivan continues, "is a late home Cardinal game, December 29th, where we're going to have 63,000 seats. On January 1 you have the Fiesta Bowl, which is 73,000 seats. Five days later, you could have a home Cardinal playoff game, 63,000 people. Three or four days after that, you could be sitting at the BCS National Championship game, which requires space for 73,000 fans. Had anybody ever thought about it? No. That's where we come in."

Why not just leave the extra 10,000 seats in place throughout that span, even during the games where they're not required? "You would be thinking reasonably and logically if you did that," Sullivan replies, "and that has no bearing on the operation of a stadium. No one is willing to take the chance that those 10,000 seats are going to show up largely empty on a national TV broadcast."

To store those extra seats, Global Spectrum helped the Cardinals design a 40,000-square-foot (3,700 m2) underground storage facility that is the envy of stadium managers everywhere. "We've had most of the NFL's stadium guys here," Sullivan says. "I don't think there's one who hasn't walked into that 40,000 square feet of storage space and started crying."

The Global Spectrum staff might have already weathered its perfect storm. In a 13-day span in October and November 2006, University of Phoenix Stadium hosted four totally different major events, each of which saw more than 150,000 people stream through the building. Among them was the 160,000-square-foot (15,000 m2) International Motorcycle Expo trade show on the building's field level. That was immediately followed by the Rolling Stones, the largest traveling concert known to man, who agreed to coexist with the bike expo during setup.

"The Stones: 90 18-wheeler trucks, 40 buses, 20 half trucks," Sullivan ticks off. "A stage 205 feet [62 m] wide and nine stories tall. Yet, the Stones finished their show on a Tuesday night at 11:30. By Wednesday at 4:00 p.m., you would not have known the Rolling Stones were here. That's a testament to how the building was designed.

"It was unbelievable," Sullivan enthuses. "In my 25 years in the business, I have never seen cooperation like that. I mean, it's the Rolling Stones—the greatest rock and roll band of all time! Mick Jagger is a musician first, but he's also a businessman. They knew they were going to be the first concert in the newest NFL stadium at the time, and they said it was the greatest venue they'd ever played, production-wise. We were very proud of that, and so were they."

Immediately after the Stones concert, the stadium hosted a major international soccer tournament, in front of 40,000 screaming Chivas fans, and then a sold-out Cardinals game against the Dallas Cowboys.

"We made it happen," Sullivan says, "and if there's another stadium in the U.S. or abroad that could have done that, I'd like to know where it is."

The Mega-Event Hospitality Scene

It became a well-rehearsed mantra starting in the 1990s—"The Super Bowl is just for suits. Real fans can't get anywhere near the game." With the Super Bowl, the line rings pretty much true.

At the Super Bowl, regardless of the city in which it's being held, nearly 80 percent of the seats go to some corporate relationship—sponsors, NFL partners, vendors, consultants, or companies shelling out millions to entertain their best customers. More than 25 percent of the game's attendees are board members of midsize or large corporations.

Before the Sunday finale, these corporate types spend their days on the golf course, in lavish hotel suites and conference rooms, and at parties. Big parties, boasting top bands, premium food and liquor, hundreds of Las Vegas escorts who typically fly in for the game, and A-list celebrities and athletes looking to party-hop and schmooze. (Regulars include the likes of Bill Clinton, Paris Hilton, Donald Trump, and Sean "P. Diddy" Combs.)

The constellation of star athletes, music superstars, Hollywood elite, and Beltway power brokers has party planners charging six-figure fees for mostly downtown venues, and the most exclusive parties, such as those held by *Playboy* and *Maxim* and Victoria's Secret lingerie, can rack up final tabs into the millions.

Finding sponsors such as Red Bull and Sprint willing to underwrite these lavish evenings because of the exposure to influencers and key decision makers helps, but the cost of entry is creeping up as well—at many parties, VIP tickets routinely go for $350 or more. (That many of the events support athletes' and local charities aids those filling out expense reports.)

Other sports' All-Star Weekends and top golf and tennis events have historically been synonymous with extravagance. But after Sarbanes–Oxley legislation mandating corporate transparency passed in 2002, in the wake of the Enron meltdown, and after the government and the media cracked down on corporations receiving recession-driven federal bailout funds but still throwing lavish events—Northern Trust Bank, for instance—companies have scaled back on entertaining around All-Star celebrations.

Helping to downplay the excess are the leagues themselves, who tout the community service aspects of their events, such as the NBA's All-Star Day of Service.

The scaling back has a trickle-down effect on local restaurants and clubs looking for a windfall and on other service providers, too. In 2009, limo company owner Ed Palladini complained to the *Los Angeles Times* that many of his luxury cars were gathering dust on a Tampa lot. Executives coming into town for Super Bowl XLIII, he said, "want Town Cars or SUVs or 15-passenger vans. They don't want to be seen in stretch limousines."

Michael Lipman is another mega-event vendor who's seen his business drop in the last couple of years. But Lipman isn't particularly worried—in his 20 years in the ticket and hospitality business, he's witnessed every conceivable fluctuation.

Lipman parlayed entrepreneurial lessons learned hustling Red Sox tickets during his years at the Boston University School of Management into launching one of the first home food delivery services in Coral Gables, Florida. It was right before the 1995 Super Bowl, pitting the San Francisco 49ers against the San Diego Chargers, that he saw the full potential of selling tickets and hospitality services to mega events.

"One of my food delivery drivers broke down in front of a townhouse in Coconut Grove," Lipman recalls, "and the dispatcher calls me up and says, 'Can you help the driver with his delivery to the Grand Bay Hotel,' the only five-star hotel in the area at the time. So I picked up the food, delivered it to the Grand Bay; I walk in and see the concierges wheeling and dealing Super Bowl tickets.

"I know the guys well from my food delivery business, so I walk over to see what's going on. They explain, 'Well, Michael, the face value is like $200 to $300 a ticket and they're going for $1,800 apiece.' 'Really!' I said. So I called up a Miami Dolphins executive who was a client of mine. He said, Michael, these Super Bowl tickets are really expensive. Club seats are going for $300. I'd have to charge you $600.' I said, 'How many?'

"I'm in the cash business, so I drive over, buy 10 tickets from this executive and drive back to the Grand Bay. The concierges settle for around $1,400 because they could get $1,800 for the tickets. I made a nice little $8,000 profit just putting A and B together, and that's what the ticket business is. Putting A and B together and delivering people's dreams to go to an event such as the Super Bowl."

Lipman has since expanded his business internationally, and while he claims that a VIP ringside seat at the Tyson–Louis fight in the Pyramid in Memphis, Tennessee, was the most expensive single ticket he's ever sold—it went for $16,500—even in a down economy he still does a healthy business at the Super Bowl.

"We're a niche player. It's always been my philosophy to seize opportunities to expand and build from quality, not quantity," Lipman says. "I deal with A-list celebrities, NFL players, entertainers as well as successful businesspeople. Everyone wants to sit courtside. It's always fascinated me that the guy who owns 20 gas stations in Iowa is willing to spend $5,000 to sit center court for the Final Four. Corporate America would only ever spend about $2,000 to $2,500 per person, especially after Sarbanes–Oxley passed."

By 2009, for the first time, some Super Bowl tickets also came with a face value price of $1,000. About 17,000 of those club and suite section tickets were distributed by the league; 53,000 more with a face value of $800 were split up among the participating teams (35 percent); the Tampa Bay Buccaneers (5 percent); the other 29 NFL teams (1.2 percent); and 25.2 percent to the NFL for sponsors, business partners, charities, and the media. Acknowledging the recession, the NFL also set aside 1,000 tickets with a $500 face value.

Super Bowl Ticket Surge

Outside of the tens of thousands of dollars ticket brokers and secondary market sellers are able to get for Super Bowl tickets, prices at face value have risen significantly since the first Super Bowl was held. Here's how face value prices have risen over the years:

Event	Year	Price
Super Bowl I	1967	$6-$12
Super Bowl XV	1981	$40
Super Bowl XXII	1988	$100
Super Bowl XXX	1996	$200-$350
Super Bowl XXIII	1999	$325
Super Bowl XLI	2007	$600-$700
Super Bowl XLIII	2009	$500-$1,000
Super Bowl XLIV	2010	$600-$1,200
Super Bowl XLV	2011	$600-$1,200*

*Due to the economy, the NFL chose to keep prices the same.
Source: Associated Press

The Art of the Year-Round Sport: The NFL Updates Its Calendar

The NBA, the NHL, and certainly Major League Baseball have a leg up on the NFL in their ability to make their sports year-round attractions, simply by virtue of their volume of games: 82 apiece in the NBA and NHL and 162 in baseball. With only 16 regular-season games to play, each NFL team must make every single game count, and the league must work extra hard to keep fans engaged during the long off-season.

In the act of playing catch-up, the NFL has surged ahead.

Enter Frank Supovitz, NFL senior vice president of events, sometimes still referred to as "the new Jim Steeg." In this role, Supovitz stages the most widely viewed sporting events in the world, up there with the Olympic Games and the World Cup.

Within the NFL, Supovitz is responsible for the Super Bowl, the Pro Bowl, and the NFL Draft. He joined the league in January 2005 after 13 years in a similar role for the NHL and just in time to receive the baton passed from Steeg at Super Bowl XXXIX in Jacksonville. One of Supovitz's primary responsibilities is seeing to it that the NFL's other events throughout the year become appointment happenings for NFL fans, mini mega events in their own right.

Supovitz's first Super Bowl experience came in San Diego in 1988, when Radio City Music Hall, where he served as director of special events, was tapped to produce the Super Bowl XXII halftime show. That extravaganza, titled "Something Grand," featured performances by Chubby Checker, the Radio City Rockettes . . . and pianists on 88 Kimball grand pianos.

Of his Radio City background, Supovitz says, "I've often been credited with placing the NFL Draft there, but the objective was not to return to Radio City. We were looking for a new home after several years spent at Madison Square Garden.

"Quite literally, I found out that I had to move the draft by reading the newspaper and *Sports Illustrated,* which said that 'Frank Supovitz is taking over Special Events at the NFL and his first job is to find a place for the draft in April.' I was like, 'Okay, I guess I should ask if that's what I should be doing.'

The draft moved to the Javits Center for a short time, but the NFL was really looking for what Supovitz terms "an identity home." He explains: "We decided Radio City was a neat television spot for it; it was a big enough facility, 5,000 seats. We officially opened up the building on draft day at about 10:00 a.m., but by 6:00 a.m. we were sending people home—we just didn't have enough room for them. So we commandeered 51st Street, closed it to the public and to traffic, put a giant JumboTron on the 7th Avenue side, called it Draft Fan Central, and had 15,000 people in there on draft day.

"What we're doing with the draft is creating tent pole events that have a broader influence than just the event itself," Supovitz continues. "The Super Bowl's very much like that, where the game is the most important thing, but there's a lot of tonnage around the game that's promoting football and the NFL and this great unofficial American holiday. With the draft, we're starting to grow a number of educational programs and clinics, even potentially an awards show.

"For now, it's important for the brand to keep the NFL Draft in New York," he adds. "We were very close to leaving New York and touring, but city officials came back to us and said, 'We'd like to keep it here and we'd like to be your partner.' The public educational programs, the street banners, the billboards, you'd never get anything like that without the city's involvement."

FACT In its 2010 debut as prime-time programming on ESPN and the NFL Network, the NFL Draft averaged nearly 10 million viewers.
Source: Nielsen Co.

After cementing the NFL Draft on sports fans' calendars—2009 coverage drew a combined viewership of 6.3 million on ESPN and the NFL Network, according to Nielsen—Supovitz and his staff began to further develop the NFL Kickoff at the beginning of every season, the NFL Combine, and the increasingly popular International Series at Wembley Stadium in London in late October (partnering with the NFL's international division). The Thursday night NFL Kickoff, held in the home market of whichever team wins the Super Bowl earlier that year, includes a free concert and other public celebrations in addition to the league's first regular-season game. The concert alone regularly draws more than 100,000 people.

Supovitz terms the NFL Combine as "significant in terms of the public consciousness . . . now it's become a media event. International media can peek in, which they have never been allowed to do before." And live coverage of the once-obscure event on the NFL Network draws five million viewers, according to the league.

The NFL's Pro Bowl is also evolving—the event the week before Super Bowl XLIV in Miami being case in point, rounded out by free concerts and fireworks shows on Miami's South Beach and in Fort Lauderdale.

"Every time it has evolved, it has been exciting," Supovitz says about that game. "The event had been in Hawaii since 1980. It really took off locally after we partnered with the City of Honolulu and the Waikiki Business District. We developed a block party for Kalakaua Avenue, the main drag through Waikiki, and closed the street. The night before the game 60,000 people were on the street. We had five stages, including a sports talk stage, cheerleaders, and all kinds of other stuff going on. It was off-the-charts successful because it was a good blend of Hawaiians and tourists and in fact was larger than the Aloha Festival, the local annual festival. We were really encouraged by that.

"We realize that we've got all these events that happen during the Super Bowl, and the public is generally not able to take part in any of it except the NFL Experience," Supovitz says. "We wanted to create a more accessible schedule of events for fans, have buzz around the Pro Bowl in the vein of 'Oh, my God, the All Star game is here. What a great opportunity for us to be a part of the Super Bowl experience.'

"The Super Bowl is already an American cultural celebration," Supovitz summarizes. "How do we make a whole city be the epicenter of all of this celebration, whether you are a corporate client, a fan of a particular team, or just a fan of NFL football? The Olympics provide us with a really good laboratory of how an event can take over an entire city, so that regardless of where you look, you know where the Olympics are. We have to continue to move that forward in the NFL. I think that's the ultimate expectation."

While the Pro Bowl returns to Honolulu's Aloha Stadium in 2011 and 2012, plans for future sites are uncertain. There was quite a lot of grumbling among two very powerful NFL lobbies—the players and the owners—about the 2010 game in Miami. Why? For one thing, holding the Pro Bowl before the Super Bowl means that there's no chance that Pro Bowl selectees on the Super Bowl teams will play in the game. For another, it's a not-so-well-kept secret in the raucous world of pro football that the Pro Bowl is the girlfriend game. Athletes and owners take their families to the Super Bowl . . . but their mistresses accompany them to the more secluded beaches of Hawaii.

A Win-Win Proposition for Teams, and for Business

The NFL is intensively working with the Dallas Cowboys, Indianapolis Colts, and New Orleans Saints to create new and unique high-tech, on-site experiences to complement their Super Bowl events, such as integrating Cisco Systems' TelePresence videoconferencing systems to allow fans to talk directly to their favorite players. Major improvements incorporated right into stadium designs mean that the NFL, teams awarded Super Bowl games, and the league's technology partners must begin planning years in advance of scheduled Super Bowl games, such as the 2012 contest in Indianapolis, the 2013 event in New Orleans, and the 2014 return to a cold-weather site at New Meadowlands Stadium.

Speaking of Indy, a few months after his Indianapolis Colts won Super Bowl XLI in 2007, owner Jim Irsay was asked, "What has winning the Super Bowl meant from a business perspective?" Here's what the spiritual Dylan Thomas and Grateful Dead–loving Irsay had to say:

"I don't think it's changed how you run the business at all. Winning the Super Bowl is primarily a great blessing. Before we went down to Miami, I crowded my office with Tony Dungy and players such as Peyton [Manning] and Marvin Harrison, Bob Sanders, Dwight Freeney, Adam Vinatieri. I said, 'Look, this is about going down and winning this game, so that 20, 30 years from now when I see you and when I pass away and you're at my funeral, we are champions.'

"I knew that we were 100 feet from the top of Mount Everest. It was the hardest game I have ever been through by far because you are watching history crawl, you are literally seeing it. You're witnessing what people will be talking about 10, 20, 100 years from now. Parade plans are either going to be hoisted up or they're going in the garbage can in three hours. However, it's still an earthly thing, so you keep it in perspective.

Indianapolis Colts owner Jim Irsay hoists the Lombardi Trophy after the Colts' 2007 Super Bowl win.

Courtesy of Indianapolis Colts

"It's my job to be of service and to be the caretaker," Irsay continues. "I'm talking about 36 years and a father and a son chasing it. Coming through it you know from a business standpoint that it is going to give you short-term, immense sales success, marketability, and help your brand. But our brand was already very strong. It's a little different if all of a sudden you come out of nowhere and you're in the Super Bowl and you win it, it's like an explosion, but we have been building our product for a very long time. It was the last missing piece."

This is what Irsay wrote and read on the Colts' ring ceremony night:

Once upon a time
Oh, what a time it was.
A time that moved within us,
The seeds of our humble beginnings.
We would gather in our circles and
Pray together on sore bended knees,
Holding hands to keep our dreams,
From escaping from our hearts.
We had heard about a time,
A time that might be ours,
A time that the spirit might deliver,
When long tired days were shared
Within those rooms.
And we would lose some along the way,
But we would honor them with the gift
Of conviction and faith.
We would hold on when nothing
Was left within us,
Except the will that says,
Hold on.
We would cry and we would laugh,
We would suffer and we would rejoice.
We would get angry
And we would meet sadness.
But we would always find our circles
With clenched hands and heads bowed
And ask for the courage
When the distance seemed too far.
Then, on a rain-drenched windy night,
Hiding deep inside a magical Florida winter,
We finally walked softly into our time.

Roger Goodell, NFL

Roger Goodell, elected NFL commissioner in 2006, embodies the sports league equivalent of working one's way up from the mailroom—he started his NFL career as a public relations intern in 1982. The son of former New York senator Charles Goodell, political savvy is in the current commissioner's blood. He captained his football, basketball, and baseball teams in high school and planned to play college football at Washington & Jefferson College until an injury sidelined those aspirations.

Goodell served as former commissioner Paul Tagliabue's right-hand man for the better part of 17 years and as NFL chief operating officer since 2001. He was named the NFL's ninth commissioner after owners voted him in over outside counsel Gregg Levy. Since his appointment, Goodell has established a hard line on player behavior through a strict personal conduct policy that was evident in the 2007 suspensions of Chris Henry, Terry "Tank" Johnson, Adam "Pacman" Jones, and Michael Vick. He also levied record fines on the New England Patriots and their coach Bill Belichick after evidence surfaced in the fall of 2007 that the team had spied on opponents' practices, a blatant violation of league policy. In December 2010 Goodell slapped legendary quarterback Brett Favre with a $50,000 fine after Favre was found to have sent lewd photos via text to a Jets hostess during his brief tenure with the team.

In 2011, Goodell faced his biggest challenge yet as leader of the U.S.'s biggest sports concern. On March 4, the league's existing collective bargaining agreement with the NFLPA, its players union, expired without a new agreement in place. One week later, the NFL officially announced a lockout of players by team owners following the move by the players' union to dissolve and pursue court action against the league.

With a $9 billion business hanging in the balance, the league and the NFLPA worked tirelessly to get a deal done. Both parties spent extensive time in Washington and elsewhere working with federal mediators and filed a near-ceaseless series of motions in federal court. Primary issues on the table included an 18-game regular season, a rookie wage scale, benefits for retirees, and dividing league-wide revenue.

As negotiations dragged on into the summer, making the cancellation of 2011 games a real threat, Goodell emphasized that scratching even the offseason and preseason would result in a $1 billion loss of revenue. The NFL's 32 teams began to plan accordingly for this gridiron doomsday scenario.

Q: Leading the NFL comes with great power and great responsibility. You come from a political family—to what degree are you a politician as opposed to a sports guy?

RG: The political skills are helpful. I don't know if I would define my job as political. I've often heard it said that a commissioner's job, because we work on the basis of getting three-quarters vote out of 32, in some ways is more relevant to a Speaker of the House than it is to being a CEO.

I wouldn't take that perspective, necessarily. It is true that that's how we function, but I think if you can present a strong business case for what you're trying to accomplish, the votes follow behind that. We work very closely with the owners to do just that.

The role of commissioner is complex in that it involves a lot of different requirements to perform the job effectively. Political skills are beneficial, but you have to understand the game; you have to understand business; you have to understand how to communicate properly across various platforms including with your owners, your fans, your players, and the coaches. I think you have to be curious enough to be interested in all the different aspects that can affect your business.

Q: To be commissioner of a major sports league, is it a huge benefit to have come up from within that organization rather than be hired from the outside?

RG: For me, the answer is unequivocally yes. I think when you have relationships, you understand how the league operates from the inside, you've got experience in a variety of different areas, you bring a perspective that can only benefit you. There is a potential that it can harm you if you don't understand that you're no longer in those other positions. You're now commissioner. You have to now take a broader perspective and a commissioner's perspective rather than as a chief operating officer, or head of marketing, or CFO–any other position that you may have held. You have to understand that perspective.

Q: When NFL team owners diversify their interests and buy either controlling interest or a smaller percentage in teams in other sports, do you feel it strengthens the NFL or dilutes their focus on their NFL teams?

RG: We just try to ensure that the owners are singularly focused on doing the best possible job representing the NFL. The other thing that is somewhat unique in sports today is not allowing anyone with media interests that could be a conflict of interest. We don't allow corporate ownership as an example, because again, we're chartered to promote the NFL, promote the game, its players, and its coaches to the broadest possible audience, and we want owners singularly driven by doing the best possible job with that objective.

Q: In regard to working with the NFLPA, there are so many agents– the Tom Condons of the world–whose power seems to be growing year after year. How is the balance of labor evolving? Is it a good balance between the league and individual athletes?

RG: Owners and players are in a better place than we have ever been in our history with respect to the relationship between the two parties. That's

> CONTINUED

because of the recognition of both of those parties of the importance of the other party. I think the owners recognize the importance of players, what they contribute to the success of the game, and they've been rewarded handsomely for that and appropriately.

On the other hand, I think the players also have a great respect for what the owners do. As owners, they take significant financial risk, they have shouldered the responsibility to make sure the game continues to grow and flourish, and the players have benefited from their wisdom and the way that they've managed the business. So we're in a position like never before where there's great respect and understanding of the value of both parties and the fact that by working together you can continue to grow the game successfully, and each party benefits. That is always the trick in labor management negotiations. How do you continue to grow the business so all parties benefit fairly? That's our objective.

A series of things will happen if we're not successful. There will not be free agency, which will impact the players. There will be a number of things that I'm sure both sides will consider, that, strategically, I believe will move us away from the negotiating table rather than toward the negotiating table. I have frequently said, and I will be as clear as I can on this, this will get resolved at the negotiating table. All of the other public relations, litigation strategies, congressional strategies, this is about a negotiation. We have to address the issues and find solutions.

Q: There seems to be a massive disconnect between the owners and labor, and trust seems to not exist or at least exist in a very scant amount. Why should fans trust either side when it's looked at as billionaires arguing with millionaires?

RG: I think at this point, what I hear from fans is that they just want football, and the fans aren't forgotten here. We want to bring more football—better football—to our fans. And that's the focus I think both sides have to keep their attention on because we need to get an agreement that works for everybody, that's fair to everybody, but also continue the great game that we have for our fans. I think they care about just getting an agreement. They don't care about the details. They just want to make sure that their football is going to appear on Sundays and Mondays and Thursdays. They want to make sure they have the great game they love. That's our responsibility, and I don't think anyone is going to feel sorry for any one of us, including yours truly, if we're not successful at doing that.

Q: **Given the rate of injuries we're seeing during the regular season, how is the push for an 18-game schedule consistent with the concern you express for the long- and short-term health of the players?**

RG: We are still staying within our 20-game format. We are not playing 22 games, which is permitted in the current collective bargaining agreement, by the way. We are taking the 20 games that we are looking at, and we are proposing and working with the union and figuring out the best way to do that, and if we can't do it right, we won't do it. But consistent with the safety issues, you always have to keep safety as a priority, under any format. Injuries occur in preseason games, so you have to try to look to see what you can do in the off-season. We've talked very extensively about this: Do you alter the OTA (Organized Team Activities, or offseason workouts) structure, and what happens within the OTA structure? Do you alter the training camp period? What happens in the regular season? I think all of those things have been addressed by the ownership for the last couple of years. Our committees have been focused on this. All of this is going to help us make better decisions and the right decision to make the game as safe as possible.

Q: **In early February 2011, Anschutz Entertainment Group announced a 30-year $700 million naming rights deal with Farmers Insurance. Keeping in mind there have been no stadiums started since 2006, can you look ahead and tell me what a naming rights deal, which would be the largest in history, would mean to bringing football back to Los Angeles? Is this a game changer?**

RG: I think it's obviously a positive development because it's an important revenue stream, but even with that positive development the financing of the stadium in Los Angeles is still a very difficult proposition. We have to get the collective bargaining agreement addressed in such a way as to make it a smart investment that can be financed to create the kind of economic activity in Los Angeles that I believe can happen if we're successful, whether it be in downtown or out in the City of Industry. There are some great opportunities for us to continue to grow the game, but we have to recognize that cost is associated with that and address it in a way that incentivizes everyone to make those kinds of investments. I think this is a positive thing for the league, for the players, for the game, and for, most importantly, our fans in Southern California.

> *CONTINUED*

Q: As NFL tickets have gotten more expensive, and most fans are really priced out of tickets for games, is the televised game really the heart of what the NFL product is these days? Are you spending more energy on the television product than you did before?

RG: Well, I agree and I don't agree with you. Where I don't really agree is that we've priced our average fan out. I think NFL tickets remain affordable, they're priced from a market standpoint that varies from market to market and section to section, so I don't believe that our fans are priced out of that.

What I do agree with is that the media are incredibly important because most fans experience NFL football through some type of media device, obviously television being the primary, with radio, online, and increasingly mobile devices. This is the best time in my lifetime to be an NFL fan because there is so much media coverage and there is so much focus around NFL football and information around NFL football, and I think that's great for the fans. We also continue to focus on broadcast policies that make our games available to the largest possible audience. That serves us well, and we'll continue to have a focus on that. Some pretty big markets don't have access to cable television or satellite television. So it's paramount to us that we continue to have our product available on free network TV.

Q: What are some of the innovations that you envision with respect to the NFL's digital media and overall technology future? For instance, iPads, graphs being used during games to diagram plays, and iPads used in games by team personnel to receive X-ray results. For ownership, perhaps some password-protected apps for showing and sending confidential league business information, and perhaps for fans, the ability to purchase special helmets allowing them to listen to quarterback huddle plays while the quarterback is talking?

RG: You talk about something that is critical to the National Football League, and that's innovation. The National Football League has had great success, but to continue that success, we have to innovate everything we do. That means the game of football, that means the experience for our fans in the stadium, it means the experience for our fans at home. One of the great things about technology is it has made the game greater for our fans. They have new ways of experiencing the game of football. I think one of the greatest innovations in television history, frankly, is the RedZone. It's an extraordinary product that is now going to be available at some point on iPads and on your telephone. That's a great thing for fans. There has never been a better time to be a fan of the NFL because you can get football, more football, to so many other platforms.

But it also creates challenges. The experience at home on a high-definition television with super slo-mo and that great technology, that makes that experience wonderful. We're also trying to get people to come into our stadiums and enjoy the game in the stadiums. So we have to put money into stadiums to make sure that the digital opportunities that you're talking about are available to fans in the stadiums so *that* experience can compete against the experience at home. That's a challenge for us going forward. I think it's a challenge for all the sports. But we can meet that challenge because we have a great product. This is why I'm so optimistic about the future of the NFL. All these devices are going to just allow people to engage with the NFL more deeply. When that happens, there are more fans, the game continues to grow, and the popularity of the game continues to grow. That's a great thing for all of us.

Q: What's the view on fantasy football at the league level?

RG: In the fantasy following of the NFL Draft, who would have ever thought that you'd get the kind of audience, the kind of interest that you have in the NFL Draft? You know, when I first started in the NFL, we had the draft in the fall, over in a hotel, and there was very little interest, and what happened? Now, it's one of the highest-rated programs in sports television, bar none.

But that's the other thing that we're trying to build. Around these mega events, there becomes such an extraordinary interest in, you know, part of it's reality television, part of it's the anticipation of the event itself, part of it is trying to make your best guess at what's going to happen. That's what makes sports great, and I think that's why people love to get inside and see how people build a football team. They love to follow their team and debate about whether they've made a good decision or a bad decision on a draft-eligible player—that's all part of getting our fans closer to the game and engaging them.

Q: How much time do you personally spend with fans? Do you convene roundtables? When you go to games, do you ever go up in the cheap seats and talk to people?

RG: Yes, I do. I think it's very important. At the AFC Championship game up in New England, I went with my 14-year-old niece, and we sat in two different locations, one for the first half at the top of the stadium and then the second half in the end zone. Last week, I was in Buffalo and we walked out into the parking lot to see what was going on in the pregame period; they're quite famous for their pregame partying there in Buffalo. When I go to games, I try to get out and see the fans. I walk the corridors with everybody else, and people have comments, and I make comments, and that's great for us. We want the fans to know we listen to them.

> CONTINUED

Q: What is the pro football business going to look like 10 years from now?

RG: I think it's going to develop from a media standpoint primarily. Digital media, new technologies, are going to make the delivery of our games and the information around our games so much more accessible. Growing up in the *Get Smart* era where people used to laugh about Maxwell Smart for talking into his shoe, look at it. Now people are talking on telephones the size of your palm. And as video becomes more and more prevalent on those devices, it's great for fans. It's going to give fans ever-increasing ways to engage with the NFL and sports in general and news in general. Our fans might even be in danger of becoming oversaturated with information.

Q: Is the NFL going to expand?

RG: I don't know. Going on 10 years, it's tough to say. Our international business continues to expand; I think we're being very calculated and focused on how we do that from both our strategy and execution, and I would not at all be surprised. I'm not sure about a 10-year horizon, but it's possible that we would have an international franchise.

Our success with the games we stage in London now each year continues to amaze me. Coming off of a first game, you always wonder whether it was just the novelty of the event. It wasn't. These are hard-core, sophisticated fans who understand the game and who I think had a wonderful time. The demand for tickets was extraordinary. We had a tailgate party with 20,000 people, and we were turning people away before the game. There was a parade. The game was outstanding, and the fans knew how to react. I think we have a very sophisticated fan base over there that I think potentially could support an NFL franchise.

Q: What about Latin America? Is that an important growth market for you as well?

RG: Absolutely. The Hispanic base, the Latin American fans—we think it's got a lot of promise for us, and we put a lot of focus on those markets, in particular Mexico, but as you look farther south, down into Latin America, we think there's a great deal of potential there as Steve Ross is pointing out.

Q: What will your legacy look like—will you be remembered as the law and order guy?

RG: I've got to tell you, I don't spend three seconds thinking about my legacy. No one who's doing a job should be thinking about their legacy. You're not doing your job properly. So from my standpoint, that's something to be answered when I get to the end of my career and I move on, 'cause let's face it, this is a temporary job. The focus right now is for me to do the best job that I can and have the greatest impact on the game. When you leave, then people will have their own determinations about what your legacy is.

2

Remote-Controlling What You See on Sports TV

- ▶ Sports TV is the most lucrative sector of the sports industry today.

- ▶ The rise of such cable entities as ESPN and FOX Sports has changed the rules of the media game for good.

- ▶ Most professional sports leagues have also established their own TV networks to maximize revenue and control content.

- ▶ Technology rules all 21st-century sports content delivery.

major league sporting event was televised, a Cincinnati Reds–Brooklyn Dodgers doubleheader aired live from Ebbets Field on August 26, 1939, sportswriters bemoaned the end of the baseball experience as they knew it. No one, the pundits said, would opt to attend a game if they had the option of watching it from the warmth and comfort of their own home.

Fast forward 70 years, when a new crop of pundits is predicting the collapse of attendance at Major League Baseball, National Football League, and National Basketball Association games and most other pro sports events because now people not only have the option of watching Reds–Dodgers games on television but can do so on a 66-inch (168 cm) plasma model while uploading player stats for their fantasy league onto the high-def big screen from the Internet, catching a grid of six more games live on www.MLB.com on their nearby laptops . . . and text messaging their Dodger-hating buddy across the city. In less than a century, sports television has gone from being a New York–region cottage industry to one in which an eight-year contract for NFL football broadcast rights costs $8.8 billion.

That attendance collapse has yet to happen—NFL crowds have been stable over time, MLB reached all-time high in 2010, and even hockey now averages 93 percent of capacity. Sports fans clearly understand that the television experience is one type of viewing opportunity, and attending an event is, quite literally, a whole different ball game.

What's more, NFL Network head and former ESPN chief Steve Bornstein has been overheard as saying to never underestimate a viewer's desire for sports programming. "There's almost no such thing as market saturation when companies have great products," he would argue. "Has that stopped Starbucks from being on every corner of America?"

Sports television, and all of its attendant technology, is clearly the most lucrative sector of the sports industry today. It's certainly no coincidence that 18 out of 100—almost 20 percent—of *BusinessWeek*'s inaugural Power 100 most influential people in sports were sports television executives, nor that the *Sporting News*' annual Power 100 lists 20 to 25 TV executives on its list every year.

The valuation of regional sports channels and the rights fees paid for major properties continue to grow, notwithstanding that so many sports are available and fans have so much access to any given sport. What we are experiencing today is that major franchises of major sports continue to grow in value, despite the fractionalization of the audience. The reason is relatively simple: The franchises are more important in the thousand-channel universe than they are in the three-channel universe because there is a historic guarantee that 50 years from now, people

Early Sports Television

May 17, 1939	First sports telecast, a baseball game between Princeton and Columbia at Baker Field in New York, on W2XBS
June 1, 1939	First heavyweight boxing match televised, Max Baer versus Lou Nova, from Yankee Stadium
Aug. 26, 1939	First Major League Baseball game telecast, a double-header between the Cincinnati Reds and the Brooklyn Dodgers at Ebbets Field, Brooklyn, on W2XBS
Sept. 30, 1939	First televised college football game, Fordham versus Waynesburg, at Randall's Island, New York, on W2XBS
Oct. 22, 1939	First NFL game televised by W2XBS: The Brooklyn Dodgers beat the Philadelphia Eagles 23-14 at Ebbets Field

Source: *U. S. Television Chronology, 1875-1970*

will be watching these same sports, and they will be watching them on televisions. This is true with the NFL, it's true with the NBA, and that's why those franchises, because of the element of scarcity in an otherwise prolific market, retain value, and in many instances, increase in value.

Also continuing to grow, of course, is the seemingly endless array of content delivery and distribution options afforded to sports fans by the warp-speed advance of new media technologies. Increasingly, it's not so much the message that matters in the sports TV world—it's the medium. And that medium is putting the control of sports TV ever more firmly in the remote-ready hands of the fans.

The Rise
of Cable and Satellite Sports TV

Over the last three decades, the growth of sport-specific channels on cable television and satellite TV has provided an electronic cornucopia for sports fans. From sport-specific channels (Golf or Tennis Channel) to Regional Sports Networks featuring teams from discrete geographic areas to league-run offerings such as the NFL Network and NBATV, these days, whatever your sports viewing passion, it's only a click of the remote away.

And it all started with ESPN.

The Network Perspective: A Conversation With Former CBS Sports President Neal Pilson

Neal Pilson, former president of CBS Sports, joined CBS in 1976 from the entertainment side of television. When he joined CBS, he was head of business affairs and negotiated the contracts for programming, eventually ending up as president of CBS Sports in 1981.

"When I joined CBS," Pilson says, "it was 1975-1976. Ironically, major issues in boxing, tennis, and skiing, all of which occurred within a two- or three-year span, led CBS to put a lawyer in charge of the business operation at CBS Sports, not in charge of making program deals, but in charge of approving all the business arrangements. They wanted a legally trained person to monitor the activities of the division, as an oversight function. I was that lawyer, and I dealt with these issues of sports as news, which it is, and sports as entertainment, which it also is.

"I often describe sports as a pendulum," Pilson continues. "It swings between principles regarding news and principles regarding entertainment. We just have to be very careful that we maintain a balance of objective coverage of major sports events, keeping in mind that in terms of fan interest and volume of interest, we're very close to the entertainment sides. Fans want to be entertained, but they want to be entertained by events where the outcome is not predetermined or where the outcome is not skewed by unknown elements that if known might change the entertainment value."

ESPN

When ESPN was formed in 1979, television sports reporting was limited to clips on local newscasts. ESPN changed that and, in so doing, also changed the way the sports industry was covered, society's viewing habits, and sport itself.

Launched by father and son sportscasters Bill and Scott Rasmussen on September 7, 1979, out of a small studio in Bristol, Connecticut (and aided by seed money from Getty Oil), the network is now available in more than 100 million homes in the United States and more than 150 countries and territories via ESPN International. The Rasmussens originally planned to launch a regional cable television network focused exclusively on covering sports in the state of Connecticut but upgraded to a 24-hour satellite feed when they realized that was less expensive.

ESPN unofficially refers to itself as "the Worldwide Leader in Sports;" the slogan appears on nearly all company media. Early broadcasts comprised mostly the cheaper sports events networks didn't deign to cover, including professional wrestling, boxing, Davis Cup tennis, Australian rules football, and lower-tier college football and basketball games.

In 1983, the United States Football League (USFL) debuted on ESPN and ABC and marked ESPN's first foray into original sports broadcasting content. Four years later, in August 1987, ESPN signed its first deal with the National Football League, an agreement that continues though today, first via *ESPN's Sunday Night Football* and now through its takeover of *Monday Night Football* games from parent ABC in 2006. (That deal currently extends through 2013.) Baseball came in 1990; the network's current deal with that league extends through 2011. Contracts with NASCAR extend through 2014, MLS through 2014, and the FIFA World Cup also through 2014.

SportsCenter, the network's signature program, debuted with the network in 1979 and aired its 35,000th episode in 2009. *SportsCenter* produces three primary broadcasts each day, at 6:00 p.m., 11:00 p.m., and 1:00 a.m. EST.

ESPN2 premiered in 1993, followed by ESPN News in 1996, ESPN Classic in 1997, and its channel devoted to collegiate sports, ESPNU, in 2005. In the early 1990s, ESPN International was established to take advantage of growth markets in Latin America, Asia, and Africa. ESPN Deportes, the network's Spanish-language channel (and a separately held business venture), debuted in 2005.

In 1984, ABC made a deal with Getty Oil to acquire ESPN. ABC retained an 80 percent share and sold 20 percent to Nabisco. The Nabisco shares were later sold to the Hearst Corporation, which still holds a 20 percent stake today. In 1986, ABC was purchased for $3.5 billion by Capital Cities Communications. In 1995, Disney purchased Capital Cities/ABC for $19 billion and picked up an 80 percent stake in ESPN at that time. After 1996 ESPN was closely integrated with ABC Sports, and 10 years later, ABC Sports' operations were merged with ESPN's. As a result, all of ABC's sports programming is now called *ESPN on ABC*.

High definition television telecasts came to ESPN in June 2004.

ESPN has ventured into scripted programming, most notably with the controversial *Playmakers*, a behind-the-scenes look at a fictional professional football team—anger management issues, steroids, mistresses and all—that so infuriated the NFL that the league threatened to pull all rights to their programming off the network if the show continued. As a result, *Playmakers* aired only 11 episodes from August to November 1993.

And thanks to ESPN Original Entertainment, a separate production company that develops original programming for ESPN, we now can see *Around the Horn*, *Pardon the Interruption*, *Jim Rome Is Burning*, miniseries such as *The Bronx Is Burning*, and such movies as *The Junction Boys* and *A Season on the Brink*.

ESPN has also moved into ancillary products, including *ESPN The Magazine*, ESPN Books, the annual ESPY Awards, and ESPN Zone restaurants throughout the United States. The company has also dabbled in licensing, including Mobile ESPN, a cellular phone–based sports information service offered in conjunction with Verizon Wireless, and a line of greeting cards, stationery, and wrapping paper with Hallmark Inc.

FOX Sports

As the *Washington Times* noted in September 2008, "It's hard to think of TV sports today without a permanent score box in a corner of the screen, without a constant blitz of digital sound and high-end graphics or without cameras and microphones in previously unheard of spots like inside a base or a catcher's mask."

Those innovations all started with FOX Sports, which in 1993 acquired NFC football television rights and ended a CBS stranglehold that had lasted more than three decades.

Added the *Richmond Times-Dispatch*, "Of all the networks FOX leads the way in being . . . shall we say, full of itself. From the leader of the pack, David Hill, to FOX Sports president Ed Goren on down, there is an attitude that's unmistakable on and off the air. If they didn't invent sports television, the Foxies certainly upgraded it. Nobody does it better. Just ask them."

Though a relatively short time ago, now an established and highly regarded operation, FOX Sports began as perhaps the most ridiculed and scrutinized sports TV entity ever.

In the early 1990s, FOX Television's primary TV properties were *The Simpsons*, *Married . . . With Children*, and *Beverly Hills, 90210*, programs that at the time drew neither the ratings nor respect of the big three networks of ABC, NBC, and CBS. FOX Sports, however, quickly proved itself up to the challenge of earning respect through two major attributes: an eagerness to spend money and a mantra to be different by all means possible.

At its inception, FOX Sports paid the NFL a then-record $395 million a year, totaling $1.58 billion over four years, for the NFC broadcast package, upping what CBS had previously paid by $400 million (nearly 50 percent). Acquiring the NFL gave FOX credibility it had never had before. Encouraged by network chairman Rupert Murdoch, FOX successfully lured away key CBS sports talents, including executive producer Ed Goren, popular announcers John Madden and Pat Summerall, and studio host Terry Bradshaw. Three dozen affiliate stations quickly transferred to the upstart FOX Sports network.

Hill knew he wanted to inject a more energetic and theatrical feel to the game productions. He went to work to develop a unique look and feel to the NFL broadcasts, extending the Sunday pregame show to a full hour; encouraging his hosts to engage in lively, sports bar–style debates; and even putting a mini football field on the set to demonstrate plays.

"It couldn't just be 'same old, same old,'" Hill said. "I looked around at what had been done for years, and it was all very serious. My belief has always been that sports is the greatest entertainment there is. With sports, you could have the world's worst job, but you can be taken away to another place for two or three hours when you're watching a game. We kind of did that."

Terry Bradshaw tells this story about what it was like in the early days working for FOX Sports chairman David Hill.

In 1994, FOX's first season carrying NFL games, the cast of *FOX NFL Sunday* decided it needed to be more serious. During the first half hour of one pregame show, the panel threw out all the football Xs and Os that viewers could handle.

"We were so proud of ourselves," Bradshaw recalled.

During a commercial break, David Hill, at the time the FOX Sports Television Group chairman, walked into the studio. "He quietly put his hands [on the desk]," Bradshaw recounted, "and said, 'Listen, you SOBs, we didn't hire you to do this. I want to see some personality, the [stuff] we hired you for.' Then he walked out.

"We sat there in shock. We just had our butts chewed out royally. The second half of the show was so over the top, it was ridiculous."

When the show ended, Hill told Bradshaw, James Brown, Howie Long, and Jimmy Johnson, "That's what I'm talking about!"

Viewers responded favorably, and the network's adventurous spirit continued. FOX landed the broadcast rights to the NHL in 1994—albeit losing tens of millions in the process. More recently, NASCAR received an entirely more modern and graphic-heavy treatment through its broadcast partner FOX, including mounting cameras directly behind drivers in cars for (at times) a horrifyingly scary race view.

Major League Baseball came to FOX in 1996, and the network's high-energy coverage of the sport contrasted sharply with the more cerebral presentation seen for years with NBC.

Never a network to be complacent, FOX in 2004 dug into its tech bag of tricks during an early-season game between the New York Yankees and Boston Red Sox that featured a series of on-screen graphics that sought to alter how we watch baseball.

The game, as recounted by the *Boston Times*, saw the debut of Ball Tracer, which showed a comet trail–style path of pitches from the mound to the plate, and High Home Camera, which displayed the trajectories of home runs as well as gauging the leads of runners at first base with what looked like a multicolored tape measure. And in easily the most bizarre move, viewers were introduced to Scooter, a talking baseball that sought to explain the nuances of certain pitches to children.

Why the renewed technological arms race? The need and desire to keep pushing forward and engaging younger viewers stands firmly intact. Many of FOX's new ideas emerged from commissioner Bud Selig's innovative marketing task force. That committee, composed of players, executives, academics, and union leaders, is charged with an open-ended task of improving fan interest in baseball.

Predictably, the results with the new graphics were mixed. Ball Tracer was a runaway success, but Scooter, voiced by Tom Kenny (aka Sponge-Bob SquarePants), was a disaster. Hill acknowledged Scooter and the rest of this new technology ultimately may not work. "He's still a work in progress," Hill said. "If it works, it'll be a demonstration. If it doesn't, it'll be an experiment."

FOX Sports delivered its first full high-definition broadcasts beginning in the third quarter of 2004. Between July 2004 and February 2005, FOX carried NASCAR's Pepsi 400 from Daytona International Speedway; MLB's 75th anniversary All-Star Game from Houston, playoffs, and World Series; regular- and postseason NFL coverage including Super Bowl XXXIX from Jacksonville, Florida; and the Daytona 500. In February 2011, FOX's coverage of Super Bowl XLV in North Texas included the first 3-D broadcast intended for home consumption.

Even as the ratings for its Sunday NFC games now routinely top those for *Monday Night Football* and FOX's innovations have boosted

Stats Hype Doesn't Help

"I think the real culprit in all the controversy about steroid use and baseball records is Major League Baseball's overuse of statistics. Try watching or listening to a baseball game any day of the week on any network or station. Every pitch produces an endless array of statistical information meant to enhance one's every waking moment and somehow make the game better. Baseball cards, announcers, and TV screens are filled with stats. It's time we realize that comparing statistics between the various eras in baseball—or in any other sport for that matter—is for the hopeless boozers in sports bars."

–Ron Kershner, Hagerstown, Maryland

Source: Letter to the Editor, *USA Today*

NASCAR to the number two regular-season sport (behind the NFL) and helped MLB remain the number two postseason sport, the last few years have been challenging for FOX. In 2001 the network wrote down nearly $1 billion in fiscal losses from big-time sports. Over the next few years after that, the World Series posted its worst ratings ever. FOX Sports Net, the network's cable entity, despite establishing an innovative system of regional sports networks under its corporate umbrella, never has found a formula to compete fully with dominant ESPN.

However, FOX Sports' success also led to the acquisition and growth of Speed Channel, FOX Sports World, FOX Sports en Espanol, www.FOXSports.com, FOX Sports Radio Network, FOX Sports Sky Box sports bars, and FOX Sports Grill restaurants.

The Rights Landscape

The NFL, long considered the gold standard of American sports programming, earns close to $4 billion in rights fees annually by selling its football games to the likes of CBS, NBC, and ESPN/ABC. The gargantuan rights fees have allowed NFL team owners to pay their stars salaries such as the $98 million over seven years that Colts quarterback Peyton Manning is reportedly guaranteed.

In 1987, ESPN shocked the sports world by obtaining the rights to eight NFL games per season in an unheard-of three-year $153 million deal. The agreement helped the development of *ESPN's Sunday Night Football*, which would later pave the way to the cable channel's assumption of the *Monday Night Football* mantle from ABC Sports in 2006.

The cost of the deal, plus a healthy margin, was passed on to the cable carriers . . . and then, of course, on to the viewers. Eleven years later, their cable bills gained weight when Bornstein agreed to pay the NFL $4.8 billion over an eight-year span. That single deal helped ESPN boost the ransom cable companies were forced to pay to the sports net over 20 percent annually for years on end.

While the strategy was hugely successful for ESPN, it was a major headache for cable and satellite operators and their end users. Currently, cable companies pay ESPN more than $3 each month for every household that gets their signal, compared to roughly 50 cents a month for such fare as CNN and MTV.

In New York, roughly 20 percent of an average customer's cable bill goes to sports channels—regardless of whether that viewer is a sports fan.

In the 1990s, the NFL introduced *Sunday Ticket* along with its existing Sunday and Monday night game packages. *Sunday Ticket* allowed viewers, for a fee, to watch up to 14 games every Sunday. The package was sold to satellite television operator DirecTV for exclusive carriage on their satellite system packages. Viewers could now have the convenience of a sports bar right in their own living rooms.

But *Sunday Ticket* clearly wasn't the only ticket for the NFL.

The Leagues Just Do It for Themselves—The NFL Network, MLBTV, and the MLB Channel

At first, it was all bells and champagne. The NFL Network, now led by Bornstein, who had left ESPN/ABC in 2002, launched in November 2003, by means of a unanimous vote by the league's 32 owners only eight months earlier and a generous $100 million dowry from the league. The honeymoon lasted only until the first regular-season broadcast in September 2006, when Cablevision Systems and Time Warner Cable, America's two largest cable providers, yanked the network out of millions of homes after a bitter carriage battle. After years of budget crunches caused by the escalating cost of football games, cable executives—and, they claimed, the viewers they served—had had enough.

The NFL Network had projected to have 50 million subscribers after its first two broadcast seasons but had closer to 35 million—even though satellite companies such as Dish Network and DirecTV and telecommunications companies such as AT&T and Verizon offer the NFL Network on broad packages.

If the network was able to convince Comcast to carry its programming, the 24 million viewers on Comcast's basic tier alone would push the subscriber number over projections.

Throughout 2007 and 2008, Dallas Cowboys owner and NFL Network committee head Jerry Jones negotiated with Comcast CEO Brian Roberts in an attempt to get Comcast to once again embrace the NFL Network.

Average Monthly License Fee for a Sampling of Sports Channels, per Cable Subscriber*

ESPN	$3.26
YES Network	$2.15
CSN Chicago	$1.90
NFL Network	$0.80
NBA TV	$0.36
Tennis Channel	$0.27
Golf Channel	$0.24

*2007 prices.

Source: *Wall Street Journal, SNL Kagan*

The two entities were contentious since January 2006, when the NFL announced that it was placing its late-season game package on NFL Network after Comcast was certain it had been awarded the package for its OLN (now Versus) channel. The NFL sued Comcast at the end of that year after the cable giant announced that it was moving NFL Network to a sports tier (so that only people who wanted to receive it had to pay for it). The NFL staunchly maintained its channel should be on digital basic cable so that more fans would have access to it.

When negotiations came to a standstill, Comcast asked the Federal Communications Commission (FCC) to allow an arbitrator to determine if and how cable operators should carry the channel. Yet it wasn't until May 2009 that the league and the cable giant finally compromised, signing a long-term agreement for the cable company to carry the NFL Network as part of a package available to approximately two-thirds of Comcast's digital customers. Comcast also agreed to carry the NFL's popular new RedZone Channel, which constantly shifts between continuous live action and drama from Sunday games.

Looking forward, the NFL maintains that despite thousands of hours of pro football coverage, viewers are still insatiable. Each year since its debut, the NFL Network has increased the number of regular-season games and nonleague content it broadcasts, including college football bowl games.

"The 32 NFL team owners are unified in our basic commitment to the network," claimed Jerry Jones in a Reuters interview. "It's so important to our future. The NFL, because of its visibility and credibility, will attract other football content. It is in [other football proprieties'] best interest to be on the NFL channel alongside a lot of our programming."

The NFL is far from alone in its tussles with cable networks and other sports content providers. Major League Baseball's seven-year $700 million deal with DirecTV for its Extra Innings package, announced early spring 2007, included a last-minute provision that allowed In Demand and Dish Network the continued right to carry Extra Innings if they matched financial and basic tier carriage terms.

The Extra Innings package, similar to the NFL's Prime Ticket, debuted in 1996. Approximately 500,000 fans subscribed a decade later, paying $179 for up to 60 regular season out-of-market games a week. By 2006, a little more than half of all Extra Innings subscribers were DirecTV customers.

Thanks to Massachusetts senator (and avid Red Sox fan) John Kerry, MLB was now firmly on notice that if it didn't provide adequate access to the consumer, Congress stood ready to oversee the league's broadcast deals. While consumer choice was the surface driver behind the tweaking of the de facto exclusive deal, the new provision was seemingly in direct response to FCC commissioner Kevin Martin's ongoing investigation (prompted by Kerry) of the surrounding distribution and accessibility issues. Pennsylvania senator Arlen Specter had also asked his staff to investigate whether the DirecTV deal might constitute an antitrust violation.

MLB hoped that the increased access would deflect the controversy to cable operators, following the same strategy as the NFL Network did in the fall of 2006.

On the other hand, In Demand and Dish Network both called the arrangement anticompetitive—including conditions for carriage that MLB and DirecTV designed to be impossible for cable and Dish to meet. In Demand CEO Robert Jacobson even went as far as to call the proposed deal "stunning in its disregard for baseball fans."

The new deal also increased the burden on technologists to generate additional access, creating a viable option for people who geographically couldn't get a satellite signal, residents of apartment and condo buildings that didn't allow satellite dish installation, and homeowners who love baseball but didn't want an ugly dish on their roof.

That's where www.MLB.com came in.

What got somewhat lost in that controversial shuffle, however, is how much www.MLB.com stood to gain in the new arrangement. In 2006, more than 300,000 subscribers paid $79 to watch any out-of-market game they chose through that site's MLB.TV service. In 2007, the price rose to $89.95 for the standard service or $119.95 for the premium service, which allowed viewers to watch any six live games simultaneously, along with Player Tracker, Clickable Linescore, and other related functions.

The success of MLB.com also helped to pave the way for a warm fan reception to the MLB Channel, which debuted in January 2009.

Regarding the NFL and MLB in-house networks, Neal Pilson says, "The NFL appears to be staying with their format, which is obviously putting the eight games on the NFL Network and foregoing anywhere from $300 to $350 million in additional revenues which they might otherwise secure by licensing those games to a national cable channel or to broadcasters.

"Ours is a business that doesn't allow you certitude until we have a five-year perspective," he continues. "When you're in the middle of the process, it's very hard to say whether it's the right balance or the right decision. Motivation and strategy are easily explainable. Success is a more difficult measurement, but what we have today is unparalleled access by sports fans to football and baseball, near constant availability. I would say that's a form of success."

Technology Rules All 21st-Century Sports Content Delivery

According to David Hill, only one issue matters in the new universe of global media. Just one. "The Internet and piracy," he says. "It's like we're living in [Gutenberg] weeks after Europe discovered movable type—a seismic change in the media world—and how that plays out is going to create the media frame of reference." Combating piracy is key, Hill says, because unless it's corralled, "the fiscal ability to create world-class entertainment is removed."

Time-shifting viewing habits are changing the way TV shows are rated and marketed. DVR ratings lag behind a couple weeks, so networks can't rely solely on the traditionally overnight numbers to gauge how a show is performing. DVR use is starting to have a significant impact on viewing, including sports (although it's not as prevalent in sports because most viewers still prefer to watch sport contests live). By February, 2011, DVR penetration had reached 39.7%, according to Nielsen data. That meant millions more people were skipping commercials—which could spell disaster for the broadcast networks.

Realizing that their audiences are more niche oriented, broadcast and cable channels alike began to push a myriad of new media marketing techniques, driving people to websites with endless statistics, blogs, and original content, offering streaming and downloading options.

And then there's 3-D.

Imagine you're a hockey goalie trying to stop an Alex Ovechkin slapshot. Or, maybe you're a running back in the open field, hoping to elude a Troy Polamalu tackle. Now you can live moments like these from the comfort of your own living room.

The future is now for sports media, as a handful of entities launched 3-D television in 2009-2010. Besides the Super Bowl, among the events that have to date aired in 3-D are World Cup matches, the Summer X Games, and the MLB All-Star Game.

Regardless of how thrilling 3-D TV is, work must still be done. First, consumers need a special, likely expensive TV to watch 3-D broadcasts, and for live sporting events, stadiums and arenas will have to be outfitted with new cameras and equipment. However, once mainstream, 3-D TV could have an adverse impact on ticket sales, as the home viewing experience will suddenly rival a day at the ballpark.

But, no matter how great or evolutionary 3-D TV ends up being, there is still one advantage to actually attending games. You don't have to wear those silly glasses.

Glasses aside, FOX Sports has begun a major push to develop 3-D television technology that will revolutionize the sports-viewing experience. "3-D is going to be the next big thing," FOX's Hill emphasizes. And while he thinks high definition is "great for what it is," he doesn't seem to feel it could change the success of a sport. 3-D, he predicts, will revolutionize.

"3-D will re-create boxing as a major sport," Hill concludes.

Five Sports Television Innovations Fans Can't Live Without

1. **Instant replay:** introduced in 1955 during a Canadian Broadcasting Corporation broadcast of *Hockey Night in Canada*.

2. **BlimpCam:** aerial cameras mounted on Goodyear (1960s), Fuji (1984), MetLife (1987), Budweiser (1993), and other blimps. Under arrangements with TV networks and cable, blimps carry the camera and reciprocally receive free on-air publicity.

3. **Corner score box:** relatively unobtrusive digital graphic projecting the game score and time clock.

4. **1st and Ten line:** digital yellow first down marker developed by Sportvision in 1998.

5. **K-Zone:** graphic developed by ESPN in 2001 to show if pitches were or were not strikes.

And one that didn't make it: the **glowing hockey puck**, developed by FOX in 1996 and retired in 1998.

3

Not Far From the Madden-ing Crowd

► Professional sports in the digital age have expanded well beyond the playing field to become an everyday agent of change for fans.

► We have become a nation of avid video game players, with sports-themed games and others accessible in almost every home; video game software alone is more than a $18 billion industry.

► Fantasy sports participation now provides a major point of connection among sports fans, played online and largely outside of the control of sports leagues and teams.

if not digital Play-Doh? It's formative and multihued, and it solidifies with age. For consumers, it's a relatively cheap source of creative expression, providing hours of interaction and almost never producing the same experience twice. The Internet is many things to many people—news source, encyclopedia, photo album, concert hall, shopping mall. For the sports industry—just as it is to politics—it's the ultimate Monday morning water cooler after a weekend's worth of games, the fans' chance to interact with their teams and leagues and with each other, celebrating, venting, jawing, second-guessing, handicapping the next matchup.

More than anything else, however, the Internet lets fans control their own sports experience, whether they're passionate about football, hockey, figure skating, cricket, or golf. Through fantasy sports, the Internet even lets them create a league of their own—and, sometimes, be highly compensated for it. In January 2008, FLW Outdoors unveiled a fantasy fishing league to run alongside its televised fishing tour. Fantasy league participants "formed teams of 10 anglers from the FLW Tour," according to the Los Angeles Times, and earned the same points as the real fishermen did in each tournament. The fantasy league winner netted a cool $1 million—at the time, the top prize money in any fantasy sport.

The new media impact on sports, of course, is by no means limited to the Internet. Ever since Atari first sucked us in with Pong in 1972, three generations of video gamers have spent untold billions of hours in front of arcade, TV, and computer gaming screens. The Madden NFL series first unleashed in 1989 continues to dominate the sports video game landscape, but others have their addicts as well. We get new media sports content on our cell phones and an endless supply via customized satellite radio channels in our cars. (And, of course, on satellite and cable television, as covered extensively in chapter 2.)

Many of these elements come together in what is perhaps an early pinnacle of fan new media involvement. NFL Call the Play, an NFLPA-sanctioned play-calling competition that debuted in fall 2007 on www.AirPlay.com, an interactive gaming site, allows fans to follow live NFL football games and predict every play in real time before it unfolds on their computers or Sprint cell phones. These cybercoaches compete with other players, transforming football, says the site, from "a sit-back experience to a more engaged, connected, and event-driven atmosphere." AirPlay "delivers a compelling multiplayer game experience based on television's most popular programs." The site also allows participants to "interact" with NBA and college football games, and with such nonsports programs as the Emmy Awards and Deal or No Deal on ABC.

For the pro sports leagues, what video games, fantasy sports sites, and good old-fashioned sports card trading are really about is great fan development. These products get the next generation of fans excited about the games, absorbing nuances from an early age, and capture fans who might prefer consuming a sport in front of a computer screen or joystick to sitting in a ballpark or watching on TV.

As leagues continue to jockey for ways to develop new revenue streams, interpersonal communications between fans online are going to increasingly carry more weight within the industry and beyond.

Sports as a Social Change Agent: Participatory Media

From their advent, social networking sites have rapidly morphed into sophisticated sports marketing tools, with virtually all teams in all sports expanding their reach via uniquely crafted, personalized websites. As Web traffic to these sites increases, Web marketers welcome unprecedented advertising and sponsorship opportunities to tap into this highly engaged audience. Industry watchdog eMarketer estimates that U.S. advertising spending on sports-related websites will grow from $407 million in 2006 to $1.1 billion in 2011.

Major League Baseball reported traffic of more than 61 million unique monthly visitors on its www.MLB.com site during the summer of 2007; after its relaunch by Sports Illustrated with new features linked to the magazine, the new FanNation received close to three million page views in its first two days. The blogosphere has created a user-generated sports media platform, where anyone can become a commentator or critic, a de facto sports journalist. Sports social networking sites have even fostered real sports team ownership, as covered in chapter 6. What does all of this have in common, and how does it affect the future of the sports business?

If there's one point the surging popularity of sports social networking sites has driven home, it's this: The $750 billion sports business, along with every other media-based enterprise, now relies on fans communicating with each other more than ever before.

The value of such sites is certainly not lost on such esteemed entrepreneurs as Pierre Omidyar, founder of eBay. Since he retired from the day-to-day operations of eBay years ago, Omidyar explains in a 2007 Wall Street Journal interview, his investment fund, Omidyar Network,

Blogletes and Tweeters

Besides maintaining MySpace and Facebook pages and their own websites, more and more athletes, coaches, and owners are using their personal online journals and Twitter to connect with fans on a weekly, and sometimes daily, basis. Among the most popular are the following:

Gilbert Arenas NBA.com/blog	Kobe Bryant kb24.com	Tiger Woods tigerwoods.com
Chad Ochocinco @OGOchoCinco	Lance Armstrong @lancearmstrong	Mark Cuban @Mcuban
David Beckham davidbeckham.com	Serena Williams serenawilliamsblog.com	
Shaquille O'Neal @THE_REAL_SHAQ	Natalie Gulbis @natalie_gulbis	

has backed a wide array of Web-based networking sites, including considering more than 20 investments in participatory media, "more than doubling that part of their portfolio."

Omidyar explains why he thinks participatory sites are the future of media, "even if it won't always be profitable. . . . eBay created all these social benefits by connecting people with shared interests. That led us to think: 'How can we find other opportunities to do the same thing?'" The content people are sharing doesn't really matter—it's the interaction that's critical.

Sports executives are taking heed. Among the dozens of sports social networking sites to launch since 2006 are a handful that truly illustrate the promise of the genre. The NBA's first team-based social networking site, the Portland Trail Blazers' www.iamatrailblazersfan.com—no doubt overseen by the team's owner, Microsoft genius Paul Allen—has relationships with more than 10,000 registered users, allowing the team to exponentially expand its relationship with title sponsor Cricket Communications and allowing fans to join with each other to get behind the team. Fan support is one reason cited for the Blazers' return to the top of the Western Conference in 2007-2008—even without injured star draft pick Kevin Durant.

In Cincinnati, the Bengals' website was the first in the NFL to deploy an online widget, created for them by a company called Gydget. The device loads on to fans' personal Web pages and links to a Bengals season schedule, a video profile of star wide receiver Chad Ochocinco, an RSS news feed of Bengals-related articles and team videos, and the online store and fan forum on the team's home site. Only weeks into its activation, Andy Ware, Bengals director of new media, reported that the widget had been downloaded about 6,000 times. The widget also serves as a means of staying connected with the team's most loyal fans during the off-season. "It is a neat fan-affinity concept," Ware says, "and a good way to market ourselves virally and get free advertising." The NHL was not far behind, announcing in November 2007 a partnership with Gydget to provide free widgets for all 30 NHL teams on www.NHL.com.

Sports industry leaders are also using social networking sites as business networking tools—BusinessWeek reported that Tiger Woods and Seattle Seahawks and Trail Blazers owner Allen are among the 250,000 members of A Small World, an invitation-only social networking site that founder Erik Wachtmeister calls "a high-end Zagat's and Monster Jobs rolled into one."

Insta-Poll: Fans Don't Wait to React to MLB Choice

In January 2008, when MLB owners voted unanimously to extend commissioner Bud Selig's contract by three years, in the wake of (good) the league's first $6 billion season and (bad) the Mitchell Report, sports fans in online forums reacted swiftly. And surely. And hotly.

Within the first hour of the announcement, a survey of fan forums on four popular online sports sites revealed that out of a total 152 initial comments, only four posters—or 2.6 percent—supported the MLB owners' decision; 97.4 percent were adamant that Selig be replaced.

On www.FOXSports.com, 32 fan comments appeared, all highly critical of the decision. Comments ranged from "I really do hope this is just a trip through the twilight zone. When I re-enter reality, Bud's retirement party is still planned for next year" to "I can only pray that ANYBODY from MLB's front office will read these reactions and see what the public clearly wants. Selig, do us and baseball (and Congress) a favor and STEP DOWN!!!"

On www.SportingNews.com, only one reader expressed support of Selig. On www.ESPN.com, out of 99 initial reader comments, only three supported the Selig contract extension. Perhaps one frustrated fan said it best: "The sad thing is that there are only 30 people in the entire country who believe Selig has done a good job . . . but they are the only ones who get to vote."

A popular blogger on AOL's Fanhouse added "That decision is on par with Britney Spears' recent choice to have another kid on the intelligence scale."

Wii Are Gamers

Just as it's sometimes difficult, when you glance at a screen from Electronic Arts (EA) Sports' Madden NFL 10 game, to tell whether the real Adrian Peterson or cyber AD is carrying the ball, so too has the line between stick and ball sports and cybersports blurred.

Right now, at any time on any day, more than two million Americans are playing video games, either online or via gaming systems such as Microsoft's Xbox 360, Sony's PlayStation 2 and PS3, and Nintendo's Wii. But that's a drop in the cyberbucket compared to countries such as South Korea, where cybersports trump stick and ball games to the point that the country's two 24/7 video game cable television channels—one of which has been around for eight years—attract 4.5 to 5.5 million viewers nightly during prime time.

Along with consumer fascination with video games, professionals—cyberathletes—have taken up the challenge. Again, America lags far behind South Korea, where pro gaming is a source of national pride, and professional gaming leagues flourish. But slowly in the United States, what started with a tiny tournament in 1983 in Ottumwa, Iowa, has taken e-flight as the Cyberathlete Professional League, which now attracts corporate sponsors and cities vying for its annual championship just like the NBA and NFL. More importantly, many cybersports and cyberathletes are attracting the same sponsors and endorsements that traditional sports have enjoyed. Sony, Intel, Red Bull, Sierra, and Circuit City, among others, have jumped into the e-ring, and clearly more big-time sports sponsors will follow.

Today, the video game industry is perhaps the most dynamic entertainment development since Philo Farnsworth loosed the television on the world in 1928. Video games are accessible in almost every home in America via gaming consoles, computers, or cell phones. Nielsen reported in 2007 that more than 50 percent of American homes had at least one dedicated gaming console. And more than 33 percent of all Americans played a video game in 2010, with somewhat surprising demographics. The Entertainment Software Association reported in 2007 that the average age of video game players nationwide is 33—and more than a quarter of all gamers are over 50. Women, the association asserted, make up 38 percent of all gamers; women 18 and older make up nearly a third of the entire gaming population, while boys 17 and younger come in at only 20 percent.

For years now, video games have given more traditional forms of entertainment a run for their money. In 2007, according to SportsTravel, the video game industry surpassed the music industry in terms of consumer spending. That extended to the motion picture industry as well—in 2006, Americans bought $13 billion worth of video game software, or about $3 billion more than they spent at the box office.

Advertisers have taken note. As reported in the Los Angeles Times, Michael Cai, an analyst with Parks Associates in Dallas, estimates that spending on in-game advertising will grow to more than $800 million in 2012, up from $90 million in 2007. Cai also estimates that by 2012, companies will spend $2 billion to "promote their products in all game-related settings, including sponsored tournaments, display ads on casual game websites, creating a presence in virtual game worlds such as www.there.com and Second Life, as well as product placement within games."

Peter Moore, President, EA Sports

He had retired from Microsoft a wealthy man. But when he got the call from the world's hottest interactive entertainment software company—video games to the jargon averse—Peter Moore jumped right back into the digital fray.

With net annual revenues of $3.654 billion in 2010 and more than 8,000 employees worldwide, Electronic Arts, Inc. develops, publishes, and distributes interactive software worldwide for video game systems, personal computers, cellular handsets, and the internet. In fiscal 2010, EA had 27 titles that sold more than one million copies and five titles that each sold more than four million copies, including FIFA 10, Madden NFL 10, Need for Speed SHIFT, The SIMS 3, and Battlefield: Bad Company 2.

Moore was appointed president of EA Sports, the video game giant's sports-specific brand, in September 2007, taking over strategic leadership of one of the most recognized brands in sports and entertainment.

In his role as EA Sports president, Moore is responsible for product development, global product management, marketing, and planning for all packaged goods and online offerings within the EA Sports brand, which includes blockbuster video game franchises such as Madden NFL, FIFA Soccer, NBA Live, Tiger Woods PGA Tour, NASCAR, and more. Moore's global operation of EA Sports, which includes the EA Sports Freestyle brand and development of more than 15 video game franchises, is anchored by studios in Vancouver, B.C. (EA Canada), and in Orlando, Florida (EA Tiburon).

Madden Nation

With apologies to the stout Mr. M himself, the 900-pound (400 kg) gorilla on the video game shelf is clearly the Madden NFL series, which debuted way back in 1989. Since its first incarnation, the Madden series has sold more than 60 million copies, generating global sales volumes north of $2 billion. Madden NFL 07 was the top-selling video game in North America in 2006, selling more than 7.4 million units. Its parent, EA Sports, followed that up a year later with an even better received version, selling 4.5 million units in its first fiscal quarter alone. (In contrast, FIFA Soccer 08 sold 2.9 million copies in the same reporting period.)

EA Sports and the Madden product line benefit tremendously from their exclusive licensing deal with the NFL and the NFLPA. EA is the only manufacturer able to use the names and images of real NFL players—augmented by periodic live updates by the NFL Network and ESPN. "Every year it's our goal—to get to the point where there's no difference from what you'll see on Sunday," emphasizes EA producer Ryan Ferwerda, as quoted by the Los Angeles Times. The game has even spawned the annual Madden Challenge, a nationwide tournament offering a $100,000 grand prize; Madden Nation, a regular series on ESPN; and a Spanish-language version of the series.

2010 Video Game Retail Sales: A Snapshot of $18.58 Billion in Revenue

In 2010, for the second year in a row, video game retail sales were down—the first time the industry has recorded back-to-back years of negative growth. These games topped 2010 sales:

1. Call of Duty, Black Ops (Activision)	9.4 million copies sold
2. **Wii Sports (Nintendo)**	**8.9 million**
3. **Wii Sports Resort (Nintendo)**	**7.3 million**
4. New Super Mario Brothers (Nintendo)	6.7 million
5. Halo: Reach (Microsoft)	6.1 million
6. Pokemon Heart Gold/Soul Silver (Nintendo)	5.9 million
7. **Wii Fit Plus (Nintendo)**	**5.8 million**
8. Super Mario Galaxy II (Nintendo)	4.7 million
9. Pokemon Black/White Version (Nintendo)	4.5 million
10. Red Dead Redemption (Rockstar San Diego)	3.6 million

Sports-related games in bold.

Alongside Sony's PlayStation and Microsoft's Xbox, the new kid on the hardware cyberblock, Nintendo's Wii, turns out to have an old soul—Nintendo was founded more than 100 years ago as a traditional Japanese playing card manufacturer. Yet the Wii, first introduced in 2006, captured young and old hearts alike. Shoppers snapped up 6.3 million of the lower-priced, lower-tech console, a huge December holiday seller, in 2006 alone. The hook? A novel remote control device that uses a motion sensor to allow players to use arm movements to control the action on the screen. The aerobic appeal of the device helped the Wii become a best seller with family units and even seniors—and since it is played by more people in more households, it means the product has a consistently better shot at selling more units.

The game has sold well ever since, with new models from Nintendo and competitors employing technology that eliminates the handheld motion sensors and effectively turns the human player into the gaming device.

Another boost for the Wii: While a typical PS3 or Xbox 360 game can cost more than $20 million to produce, and take more than a year because of its complex, high-level graphics, the simpler Wii games cost only $1 to $7 million and takes less than a year to finalize.

A final note on the impact of the genre: The fallout from England's failure to qualify for the European Championship in soccer in 2007, it seems, was blamed on video games. At least by Britain's goalkeeper Robert Green, who blamed the downfall of the national team on a generation of children parked in front of video screens instead of atop neighborhood pitches. "If you want to have the best national side on a longer-term basis," Green said, "you need to go into every household and throw away the PlayStation, Xbox, and video games. Maybe in 15 years' time you'd have the best national side."

The Evolution of Fantasy Sports

It's no secret that the Internet is the playing field of choice for fantasy sports fans. While fantasy sports competitions have been around for more than a decade, the Web's evolving social media tools, treasure trove of real-time statistics, and networking capabilities let fans research and form teams and compete against other fantasy team owners and managers based on the statistics generated by individual players and teams more effectively than ever before.

Simply put, fantasy sports sites allow people to join competitions based on the performance of pro athletes and teams. Participants choose a fantasy team within a league and pick players for each game or match. Points are then awarded—or deducted—throughout the season based on chosen players' performances.

The World Championship of Fantasy Football

The WCOFF is "this country's original high-stakes fantasy football league, the Super Bowl of the hobby," states author Mark St. Amant, writing in the New York Times. Every September, thousands of rabid fantasy footballers descend upon Las Vegas, paying a $2,000 entrance fee and spending six straight hours on a Saturday drafting players for the season. Payout if you win? A $300,000 top prize, accompanied by a trip for two to the NFL Pro Bowl in Honolulu.

The inaugural WCOFF in 2002 drew more than a thousand people, fielding 552 teams in 46 leagues. What started as a single-day event has turned into a four-day Las Vegas extravaganza, spawning subevents of its own and attracting—you got it—dozens of sponsors. It's lucrative for contestants, too: The 2011 event offers over $2 million in cash awards, with a top prize of $300,000.

The growth of the internet has fueled the increase in fantasy sports participation and the rise of fantasy football in particular, which in turn has helped fuel NFL ratings. In 2010, the estimated 29 million Americans who participated in fantasy football leagues, according to Liberty Media, helped the NFL achieve unprecedented television ratings across all of its broadcast platforms. Online, an entire media industry devoted to fantasy football has exploded, seeking to satisfy the thirst for stats on the league's 1,700-odd players among fantasy team owners.

The majority of fantasy participants are young and about 85 percent male, 15 percent female. The average fantasy player spends three to four hours online per week and has played for 10 years. Fantasy gaming is addictive—the industry is currently valued at $4.48 billion annually, with the average fantasy sports player spending more than $467.60 annually to participate. A study by the Kellogg School of Management at Northwestern University revealed the three main reasons people play fantasy sports: (1) the competition, (2) love of the sport, and (3) prizes and rewards.

As in any technology sector, the fast-growing fantasy sports and social networking start-ups have been ripe acquisition targets, and the industry segment is fast consolidating. In 2007 alone, Yahoo! acquired the popular college sports site www.rivals.com, Wikia purchased ArmchairGM, and Time Inc./Sports Illustrated snapped up FanNation, a move S.I. editor-in-chief Terry McDonell characterized as "almost tribal . . . www.FanNation.com will make everything in and about sports more interesting—including you." Like almost all of the sports social networking sites, FanNation is highly sponsor friendly; Cadillac, Vonage, and Sprint were among early advertisers on the site.

Sports leagues have been doing whatever they can to protect what they consider copyrighted material from free exposure on fantasy gaming sites. On October 16, 2007, the U.S. Eighth Circuit ruled that the First Amendment protected the use of player names and statistics on fantasy baseball sites established by C.B.C. Distribution and Marketing, Inc. That company had brought a declaratory judgment action against MLB Advanced Media to permit the unlicensed use of names and statistics of Major League Baseball players in connection with fantasy baseball products available online.

The district court granted summary judgment in favor of C.B.C. In affirming the district court, the Eighth Circuit espoused the proposition that the use of information in the public domain is protected by the First Amendment. The court also countered arguments that the use of statistics wasn't speech at all. One particularly interesting argument by the Eighth Circuit related to the protection of economic interests under the right of publicity, stating that "Major League Baseball players are rewarded, and handsomely, too, for their participation in games and can earn additional large sums from endorsements and sponsorship arrangements." Major League Baseball has appealed the ruling, and the case, years in the making now, may still go all the way to the Supreme Court.

Fantasy sports, of course, do have their detractors—naysayers claim that fantasy sports eat away at workplace productivity (40 percent of fantasy team management reportedly takes place at work) and that the focus on individual achievement is distorting the beauty and purpose of team sports. When asked by ESPN reporter Greg Garber his opinion on the rise of fantasy football, former Denver Broncos quarterback Jake "the Snake" Plummer replied, "I think it has ruined the game. There are no true fans anymore. . . . If I lost a game . . . no Denver fan was mad because I lost, but happy because I threw three TDs."

ESPN Sports Poll: Do You Play Fantasy Sports?

The ESPN Sports Poll, a service of TNS Sport, asked respondents age 12+ if they had played in a fantasy sports or rotisserie league in the past 12 months, and if so, in what sport. Following are the results from January 2009:

MLB	19.5%
NBA	12.0%
Soccer	8.6%
NASCAR	5.7%
College basketball	4.6%
Golf	2.3%
Other	20.5%

David Stern, NBA

David Stern celebrated his silver anniversary as NBA commissioner in 2009—although his association with the NBA started way back in 1966, when, as a newly minted Columbia University lawyer, he began providing outside counsel work for the league. Under his watch, the league has built 28 new arenas, added seven teams, and seen franchise values and TV rights soar. From the time I met Stern in the 1980s, it was clear that he had all of the necessary qualities to be an ideal ambassador for professional basketball. He's articulate, passionate, and maybe most of all, intelligent.

Stern became the fourth commissioner of the NBA in 1984, a golden age for the league with its "Showtime" Lakers, led by Magic Johnson; archrivals Larry Bird and the Boston Celtics; and star rookies Charles Barkley, John Stockton, Hakeem Olajuwon, and Michael Jordan. The stars' shoe contracts helped fuel NBA growth; under Stern, the league expanded from 23 to its current 30 teams, saw unprecedented globalization, launched the WNBA, and pressured more than a dozen cities to come up with public money to fund NBA-centric arenas.

Like Bud Selig, Stern has seen his share of controversy, most notably out-of-control player behavior as exemplified by the November 2004 "Basketbrawl" between the home team Detroit Pistons and Indiana Pacers, called by many the low point in NBA history. The incident was followed by denouncement of the game's prevailing hip-hop culture; dozens of player arrests; and an ugly, public sexual harassment suit against New York Knicks team president and former player Isiah Thomas in the summer of 2007.

Yet it was Stern's take-charge leadership of the gambling crisis surrounding NBA referee Tim Donaghy in the spring of 2007 that really defined his character. Says Phoenix Suns general manager Steve Kerr, "There's never a question who's in charge when there's a crisis in the NBA."

Like NFL commissioner Roger Goodell, Stern in 2011 faced the end of labor peace in the NBA, as that league's collective bargaining agreement (CBA) is set to expire. At the heart of the NBA's collective bargaining agreement issues is revenue sharing, with NBA owners bidding to impose a hard salary cap and slash players' salaries by $750 million to $800 million annually. Although Stern is a seasoned negotiator, a stalemate between the sides, coupled with the potential of the NFL going dark, would leave pro sports fans facing a true winter of discontent.

Stern, finally, has done a tremendous job making the NBA a global brand. Currently, the game is available in more than 200 countries; international customers account for nearly half of league merchandise and jersey sales; and for the first time ever, a team has a foreign-born owner. During the 2009 season, the NBA launched a new marketing campaign called "éne-bé-a," the Spanish pronunciation of NBA, and will pour $10 million into various Hispanic initiatives.

Q: The NBA has seen 10 arena and five franchise relocations since 1999. What's the deal with all the comings and goings?

DS: I really think it's a failure. I'm old school. . . . I grew up thinking that players should keep playing for their teams and franchises should stay in their cities. But, it's good that there are other cities that are willing to welcome us even though we haven't done that well for the city that preceded it.

Q: Speaking of journeys, in September 2009 the NBA welcomed its first foreign owner, in the guise of Russian oligarch Mikhail Prokhorov. Is this the beginning of a new phase in the globalization of your league?

DS: The deal closed in March, 2010, and so far, Prokhorov has focused almost exclusively on his team, the New Jersey Nets. Prokhorov's money isn't going to be what turns around the Nets. He's going to do it by hard work and good management. That's what works—drafting a good player that comes out of the lottery and the draft, by surrounding that player with other good players, and by making sure that people understand that he's committed to the entertainment experience at the Prudential Center.

Q: Here in the United States, the closest we get to basketball aristocracy is "King" LeBron James. Do you think that James is overhyped by the media, who, in some cases, also call him overrated?

DS: You know, he hasn't won anything yet, but he may be the best player ever to descend to this planet. It's a delight to watch him; it's a delight to watch him grow, to see his width and breadth, in terms of his interest and capacities. He's a great kid and a great player.

He may be the best player ever to have played. Michael [Jordan] might dispute that, but he has a lot of canvas yet on which to paint. I have no doubt the picture is going to be beautiful.

Q: In February 2010, the NBA All-Star Game was played in the 100,000-seat Dallas Cowboys Stadium. Are we now always going to see that event in domed stadiums that hold a lot of people but aren't necessarily conducive to basketball?

DS: No, absolutely not. We've elected to go to Los Angeles the year after. I'm talking about Orlando; my guess is New Orleans will somehow get back in at some point into a rotation. We talked about an application from a newly renovated Madison Square Garden; I'm sure there will be one from the new Brooklyn building. No it's not about domes, it's about cities and what the particularities are of each market.

I think it's going to be an event, and it's kind of neat. . . . many [spectators] are going to watch it on this spectacular scoreboard, and the one thing we know is that no shot from any place is going to hit the video board. We're feeling a sense of comfort about that.

> CONTINUED

Q: What mechanisms do you have in place to talk to the fans? Do you go sit in the cheap seats, do you do roundtables, what do you do to get directly involved?

DS: We have about 20,000 fans on an online survey, which is critical. We have our own polls, we have Harris, that's the way we do this. You listen, you observe, you read, you understand everything about it because you become steeped in it. But then again, that's not usually good enough because, you know, one person's view is getting to be less acceptable when companies such as Proctor and Gamble and Coca-Cola spend millions and millions of dollars to do research to understand what the consumer interaction is, and so we do that. You can go online and see what the bloggers are talking about.

When I joined the NBA as general counsel in 1978, my guess is that our gross income was about $75 million. Now I don't mean gross income at the league level, I mean network, local TV, and so on. Yet in the intervening years, and this is true of all sports, there's been a complete build out of the arena–stadium structure, which changed not only the economic model but also the arena–stadium experience. There was a time, and unbelievable as it may sound, when there was no ESPN, okay? Everyone born after a certain date thinks that on a certain date ESPN was invented, but it wasn't.

There's a third thing, and it has to do with licensing. I think in 1978 they were selling $80 million at retail as opposed to $3 billion. I mean, that was it! Sports marketing is a big deal because it makes your players bigger, and you can't spend enough money to equal what sponsors pay. You can't spend enough money to get the kind of promotion they're having with kids.

Q: What's your perspective on globalizing the NBA?

DS: I believe that you take advantage of opportunities because of the power of sports on a global scale.

Right now, we're focusing on Eastern Europe, the Middle East, and China. If you are a student of the world, you see these things are coming. We've sent a group that's been in discussions with Abu Dhabi and Dubai. We're talking to Russia; we're obviously going to investigate China because of the positive changes that are happening there. Following sports content is a global thing.

Q: What are the trends for the next 30 years?

DS: There are many trends that we anticipate. The first trend, of course, is additional trends. The opportunities to communicate online are boundless, and nobody's in a better position than sports to capitalize on that.

Q: You're the only pro team sport that has its own women's division, if you will. So how much marketing leverage does that give you with women?

DS: There hasn't been an extraordinary advantage yet, but on a long-term basis it will be because if you watch it, there's a fundamental change taking place. More high schools and colleges are having women's programming; it's a woman's community. Now it's not just Connecticut and Tennessee, but it's Stanford, and Baylor, and other schools all over.

Q: What's your biggest regret?

DS: One of my biggest regrets is the fact that we suffered a lockout in the 1998-1999 season. I don't know exactly what I would have done differently, but I just feel as though I didn't get my message through to the players. There has to be a better way than shutting down a sport to do that. That was terrible.

Q: What is your most significant accomplishment?

DS: I usually say that there are two. One is the fact that people said our sport was too black to succeed in America. Our players earned too much and did drugs. I said America is a lot better than that, and it turned out that America is a lot better than that. I love to have been part of the growth of the sport. I'm really highlighted by the Dream Team stepping up to the platform in 1992 representing America. The second highlight is really how we were part of Magic Johnson's announcing that he was HIV positive. In the aftermath of that, to ride along with Magic to educate the world and change literally the debate on HIV and AIDS, because now the patient was a beloved face to the world, that was something.

4

The Big Labinski

- ▶ Public–private partnerships have funneled more than $6 billion to cities and their sports facility projects.

- ▶ Today's sports facilities are mostly single-sport and built for one purpose: maximizing revenue generation.

- ▶ The lineage of virtually every modern sports facility's architecture practice can be traced back to Kansas City circa 1970.

- ▶ The essence of a fan's love for his or her team is what defines excellence in stadium design.

AROUND 2,000 YEARS AGO

Roman taxpayers rendered their gold coins to pay for the Colosseum, a multipurpose 45,000-seat stadium with a retractable canvas roof, luxury boxes for the emperor and his entourage, and a club level for senators and other imperial VIPs. To this day the Colosseum stands as one of the most recognizable landmarks in Rome—and while it's a crumbling monument now, it was put to active use for more than 500 years.

In 2011 America, we don't have a sparkling new Colosseum. We have dozens—with many more on the way. We also have an abundance of abandoned and crumbling sports palaces, some of which were built only within the last 20 years.

Public–private sports facilities' development partnerships and infrastructure branding has, to date, enticed more than $6 billion in corporate funding to cities and development projects. What's more, at least $15 billion, a good chunk of it public money, might be spent this decade on more than 75 stadiums and arenas for the four major sports leagues in the United States and Canada, as well as millions more on the racetracks of NASCAR.

More than 30 stadiums or arenas have opened since 1990, a handful more are under construction, and dozens more are desired by team owners or municipalities. Current prices range from about $200 million for an arena seating 15,000 to upwards of $1 billion for a 100,000-seat retractable-roof stadium with every high-tech and luxury feature imaginable. As the price tag for the buildings has gotten bigger, public financing has shrunken proportionately, meaning that even though more of the construction and operational costs are left in private hands, so, too, is more of the revenue.

Today's stadiums are built for revenue generation, with a sharp focus on corporate clients and the premium club-level fan base—as vital to the facilities' profitability as business travelers are to airlines. Proximity to the action is key: More of this premium seating can be found at field level, such as the 70 bullpen box seats the Chicago Cubs added along the third-base line at Wrigley Field and the end zone–adjacent suites at Lucas Oil Stadium in Indianapolis. And far more of the square footage is an open hospitality environment, perfect for networking, not carved up into isolated corporate suites.

No longer are most stadiums lone rangers in the midst of acres of tailgating-happy parking lots—even the University of Phoenix Stadium and its extensive grounds in Glendale, Arizona, are fronted by hotel, retail, and office space. Most are either the centerpieces of sophisticated mixed-use developments, such as the $2 billion Xanadu project across the road from New Meadowlands Stadium in Bergen County, New Jersey, or the keystone of a downtown revitalization zone and a highly visible symbol of community pride.

And no longer do stadiums have to juggle football and baseball schedules and seating configurations that favor neither sport. "Multipurpose stadiums are soon to become extinct," said Ron Labinski, senior vice president of HOK, a leading architectural firm for stadiums and arenas, in a *Chicago Sun-Times* interview in September 1995. "They were the result of poor planning in the first place, and that's why so many of them are being abandoned so soon. The whole notion of the multipurpose stadium in the '60s and '70s was flawed."

That's one reason why sports architects such as Labinski are anything but extinct. Thanks to seemingly endless renovations of these 1960s and 1970s buildings and new palaces whose size is rivaled only by the egos of team owners or the dreams of city councils, their design shops are booming.

And Labinski, the Marlon Brando of sports architecture, has been at the forefront of it all—as have the dozens of young sports architects he has mentored and who have moved on to create a high-profile, highly successful, and incredibly inbred sports architect family tree.

Roots of the HNTB, HOK Sport Venue Event, and Populous Architecture Tree

Between 80 AD, when Rome's best engineers completed the Colosseum under Emperor Titus, and the opening of the Dallas Cowboys Stadium in September 2009 under football czar Jerry Jones, architects, builders, visionaries of all nationalities, and even the church developed grand stages on which sporting events could unfold. And while it seems as if HOK Sport, now known as Populous, was around for the whole span, that division of Hellmuth, Obata & Kassabaum, Inc., has in reality been around only since 1983.

Labinski, once described by *Time* as the world's foremost stadium architect, is a native of Buffalo who attended the prestigious school of architecture and design at the University of Illinois. After serving in the Army for two years in the late 1960s, Labinski took a job with the Jackson & Smith architecture firm in Kansas City, which specialized in hospital complex design. However, crosstown competitor Kivett & Myers soon recruited him to help design Kansas City's Kauffman Stadium as well as Arrowhead Stadium, a project on which he served as lead designer, completed in 1972.

Ron Labinski at Kansas City's Arrowhead Stadium.

Courtesy of Populous

In 1973, Labinski and other local architects formed their own shop, Devine, James, Labinski & Myers (DJLM). One of their early hires was a young architect named Ron Turner, who soon became a catalyst for Labinski's departure from that firm.

"When I became a partner at DJLM," Turner recalls, "we had some partners that were not pulling their weight—one guy was drunk half the time, one guy never followed up. Since I was the greenhorn partner, I constantly found myself shoveling the poop after these guys." Turner, who had been recruited by another local firm of good repute, HNTB, then went to Labinski to resign.

"I went to [him] one day," Turner continues, "and said, 'You know, I'm no Goody Two-shoes, but I'm not going to do this anymore. I really like working with you, we've got a good gig going on here, but this, you know, we're both out of town a lot and nobody's at home watching the store. These guys are blowing it up, and that's not going to be good for us.'"

Turner joined HNTB to run their architecture division. The team won a high-profile project in Indiana, the Hoosier Dome; acquired Kivett & Myers in 1975; and thus was soon inundated with work. "So I called [Labinski] up," Turner says, and said, 'Ron, why don't you come over and run the sports group?' And so he did. So he came over and ran the sports group and grew it and it was great."

Labinski remained with HNTB until 1983, when he and the eight colleagues he took with him created the sports architecture practice at HOK, the world's second biggest architecture firm.

In the late 1960s, stadiums were hardly the multimillion-dollar civic centerpieces they are today. Most were hastily constructed, inward-facing concrete doughnuts with minimal luxuries and no views of the cities or vistas around them. Sharing two professional sports meant that the configuration was optimal for neither baseball nor football. Virtually all were owned by their cities, and, to the growing chagrin of team owners in Major League Baseball and the growing National Football League, their designs gave almost no thought to fan convenience or revenue streams.

"Baseball is a square game and football is a rectangular game, and they both were playing in a round stadium. The only thing that I know of that works in a round stadium is bullfighting," Labinski was famously quoted as saying years later during an industry conference keynote speech.

Plans for Arrowhead that Labinski refined and implemented were a major exception.

In 1967, the Chiefs played in the NFL's first Super Bowl, giving local fans and Kansas City leaders a major reason to support and showcase their top-notch team. Although the Chiefs lost to the Green Bay Packers, later that year, voters approved a $102 million bond issue to build two stadiums side by side, one for baseball and one for football—the first professional multisport complex in America.

"Architecturally, there was no historical precedent for NFL stadiums or what a football stadium might be other than as a collegiate facility and bleachers, so there was no real architectural context when we designed Arrowhead because it was the first stadium built specifically for a professional team," says Dennis Wellner, another of the founding HOK Sport architects. "But we understood that proximity to the field was important to fans—that's still one of the hallmarks of Arrowhead today."

Original plans called for the football and baseball stadiums to be constructed with a common roof that would roll between them. That design was scrapped when money and time intervened; Labinski's reworking of the plans produced the fan and home team–friendly close-to-the-action configuration that Arrowhead maintains today—even more so after its $375 million renovation was completed in 2010.

As Labinski and colleagues Chris Carver, Joe Spear, and Wellner made the move over to HOK, they compiled a target list of 17 stadiums that would soon need to be replaced and made the case to Jerry Sincoff, HOK vice chairman, that enough business was out there to support a sports-specific HOK division. Sincoff agreed, and the team got to work.

Joe Robbie, Camden Yards, and the Next Generation of Stadium Design

The fledgling HOK Sport's first project was an architectural study for Sullivan Stadium in Foxborough, Massachusetts, in late 1983, followed by a spring training facility for the Houston Astros in 1985. Then, HOK Sport landed what would prove to be one of its early signature projects and a model for many other NFL stadiums over the next two decades: Miami's Joe Robbie Stadium, headed by Wellner and opened in 1987.

A couple of major challenges awaited Wellner and his Kansas City team as they made their way to the palm tree–lined Miami Gardens site that would eventually be the home of Joe Robbie Stadium. First was the curmudgeonly Joe Robbie himself. Owner of the Miami Dolphins, at the time the only pro sports franchise in the state, the cantankerous Robbie was constantly at war with the city—not likely to make the construction permitting process any easier. He also had a widespread reputation as a skinflint who would rummage through the Dolphins locker room, counting towels, and wasn't exactly known to be gentle or collaborative with the people in his employ.

The second challenge facing HOK was a direct result of Robbie's miserly nature: While Robbie had approved HOK's initial blueprint, he still lacked most of the money needed to complete the $115 million project.

Labinski introduced an idea the architects had cooked up nearly a decade before, when they were working on a design for the Edmonton Eskimos, a Canadian Football League team: a 10,000-capacity luxury seating level, with its own entrances, an enclosed mezzanine, plusher seats, and better food and drink. The club seats, Labinski estimated, could be leased for $600 to $1,400 per year, depending on location, on a 10-year, prepaid basis, guaranteeing a huge influx of cash up front. Expanding on that concept, Labinski and his team also included in the design 212 executive suites, seating 10 to 16 people and ranging in price from $29,000 to $65,000 per year—also available only through a 10-year lease. The suite concept had been covertly introduced at the Houston Astrodome when it opened in 1965—although the Astrodome suites had no windows and thus no view of the game in progress. (The Astrodome did, however, pioneer another now-ubiquitous sports facility feature—synthetic turf, better known universally as AstroTurf.)

As even more revenue icing, HOK increased the size of Joe Robbie Stadium's nonseating areas throughout the building to squeeze in more concession stands, retail, and other attractions.

An average lease of $50,000 per suite for the 212 suites would produce an annual income of $10.6 million, or $100.6 million over the course of the 10-year lease. Add the club seats at an average of $1,000 per seat and you're looking at potential revenue of $9.27 million per year, or $92.7 million over the 10-year lease period. Fully leased, the Joe Robbie Stadium suites would generate $200 million in revenue over 10 years—without even considering profits from the remaining 61,000 seats, concessions, parking, local sponsorship deals, and each NFL team's share of the league's then multimillion-dollar television contract.

Not surprisingly, Robbie bought into the club concept and used the guaranteed leases as collateral to secure loans for the $90 million he needed to finish stadium construction. The club-level concept rapidly caught on throughout the NFL and the other pro sports leagues and can be found in virtually every sports venue HOK Sport and its progeny have designed since.

The next Miami Dolphins owner, Wayne Huizenga, assumed ownership in 1990 when he bought 15 percent of the team and 50 percent of Joe Robbie Stadium from Robbie's family at a cost of $168 million. The following year, Huizenga made good on his promise to bring major league baseball to South Florida; the Florida Marlins began playing there in 1993. In 1994, Huizenga became sole owner of the Dolphins; in 2008, he announced it was time for someone else to take control and sold the majority of the team to real estate mogul Stephen Ross.

On Huizenga's watch, the franchise signed a 10-year $20 million naming rights deal for Joe Robbie Stadium with Pro Player, subsidiary of Fruit of the Loom, only to take back the rights in 2000. In 2010 the building got its current Sun Life Stadium moniker as well as a privately financed $300 million facelift that helped to land Super Bowl XLI in 2007 and XLIIII in 2010. But it was Labinski's original design that played a key role in winning the record five Super Bowls the stadium has held to date.

After Joe Robbie Stadium opened for business, HOK Sport architects, their reputations made, began playing around with major changes in stadium design. Their next breakthrough was the $110 million Baltimore's Oriole Park at Camden Yards, opened in 1992, whose "retro" red-brick facade and layout conjured up nostalgic thoughts of the inner-city baseball parks of the 1920s and 1930s and was a romantic escape from the utilitarian Shea Stadiums and echoing Astrodomes that had since sprung up. What's more, with an old warehouse practically integrated into the park's right-field wall, Camden Yards seemed as if it had long been woven into the fabric of Baltimore itself.

The design prompted a wave of similar new baseball facilities; Ravens Stadium at Camden Yards was built years later as a companion piece and earned popularity of its own.

"It made a difference in the way people viewed possibilities with stadiums," said Spear, who served as the lead on the Oriole Park design team. "After that project, our credibility was much higher."

The urban design would be later repeated in other signature HOK projects, including the $175 million Jacobs Field (now Progressive Field) in Cleveland; the $300 million Comerica Park in Detroit; and San Diego's $450 million Petco Park, opened in 2004. "When we first started out, $100 million projects were the biggest thing going," notes Wellner. "Now, they're $1 billion projects."

Other HOK design elements help spectators get even closer to the action. The bull pens at San Francisco's waterfront Pac Bell Park (now AT&T Park), which opened in 2000, for example, sit directly in front of the seats along the first and third baselines. Aside from the players themselves, fans in those seats are the first to know when a manager is calling up another pitcher. And fans at the new Yankees Stadium are practically on the field.

At the end of the day, the design elements are still about making money for the owner of the venue. At Houston's Reliant Stadium, another signature HOK project, project planners installed one concession cash register for every 125 spectators—the highest concentration at that time in the NFL. If it's more convenient for fans, they'll spend more—which is much more convenient for the owners.

"Our success is built on the fact that we were the first," Labinski said in a *SportsBusiness Journal* interview not long after he retired in April 2000. "We were the first to recognize an opportunity in sports and in the market. We were the first architectural firm to specialize in sports, and we were the first ones to try to understand the business of sports clients. I think that [is what shaped our success] and by delivering. We delivered in terms of design, in terms of innovation and in terms of cost-effective buildings."

Not Your Father's AstroTurf: An Iconic American Brand Reinvents From the Ground Up

In the United States, a handful of brands, in consumers' minds, are synonymous with the product. Kleenex is one, Coke another, Windex a squeaky-clean third.

And then there's AstroTurf.

Invented in Research Triangle Park, North Carolina, and patented by Monsanto in 1965, AstroTurf is the world's first synthetic turf used as a sports playing surface, coming to fame—and its name—when it was put into the Houston Astrodome in 1966. Pro athletes were hardly the first target users of the synthetic turf: It was primarily invented to expand youth sports participation in urban areas where fields were limited after the Army realized that inductees living in rural areas of the country were in far better shape than urban recruits.

AstroTurf gained its first major worldwide exposure in 1974, when the Dolphins played the Vikings on the surface in Super Bowl VIII in Houston. The following year, the product was installed in the New Orleans Superdome and Detroit Silverdome; the Cincinnati Reds won the 1975 World Series playing on an AstroTurf field.

Through the 1980s and 1990s, AstroTurf's worldwide growth was matched only by its growing notoriety, as athletes complained of turf-related injuries ranging from rug burns to twisted knees and even concussions. That changed in 2004, when Textile Management Associates (TMA) of Dalton, Georgia, acquired the AstroTurf IP and manufacturing facilities, intent on remaking the brand. In 2006, TMA entered into a long-term licensing agreement with General Sports Venue (GSV), LLC, a sports facilities and turf specialty company, giving GSV exclusive rights to develop, market, and install synthetic turf products under the AstroTurf name in North America. In 2009, TMA purchased General Sports Venue outright and moved AstroTurf's headquarters back to the original plant built by Monsanto in the early 1970s.

"When we acquired the AstroTurf brand and manufacturing plant, our goal was to return it to its original incarnation: a cutting-edge category creator, representing the best in sports science and innovation," recalls Bryan Peeples, AstroTurf's president.

"We likened AstroTurf to Harley-Davidson, "he added. "Harley-Davidson was a category creator and iconic brand that later fell on rough times. That perception is gone—now, when you think of a Harley, you think high-end, high-value showpiece. That's the direction we're taking AstroTurf."

The new generation of AstroTurf systems are safe, are shock absorbent, and never affect the outcome of the game. AstroTurf is environmentally friendly (no mowing, water, or pesticides) and looks and feels like natural grass. "You shouldn't be able to tell it is synthetic," Peeples says, "unless you reach down and try to pluck it." And AstroTurf systems actually cost less than real grass—especially for heavily used stadiums and youth sports complexes. "Our fields pay for themselves in just a few years, when measured in terms of increased activity on the field, maintenance, and replacement costs," notes Peeples.

Central to the AstroTurf portfolio are its innovations. First, its "more fiber; less fill" designs reduce the need for rubber in the infill (also reducing rubber granule "fly-out," which players hate). Second, its Root Zone technology consists of a shorter fiber layer that keeps the infill locked in place, provides additional shock absorbency, and keeps its tall fibers upright, like blades of natural grass.

Third is astroflect, a technology that lowers surface temperature by increasing the amount of sunlight that the AstroTurf fibers reflect rather than absorb. "We are getting a 14 percent reduction in surface temperature now," explains Peeples, "but we are aiming at 30 percent and working with BASF and others to get there." The company has signed a comprehensive five-year R&D deal with the University of Tennessee to study issues surrounding grass and turf, including injury prevention and performance (shoe–surface interface).

Recently, after a thorough study, AstroTurf was selected as the Official Synthetic Turf of Major League Baseball. With new clients such as the St. Louis Rams, Rogers Centre in Toronto, the University of Oregon, and numerous colleges and high schools across the country, AstroTurf's resurgence is well under way.

However, the real success of an evolving AstroTurf can be found on its many youth sports fields—AstroTurf has now come full circle, providing kids with safer, more abundant recreation opportunities, especially in urban areas where playing space is extremely limited.

Branching Out From KC

In 1988, five years after HOK launched its sports facilities practice, five HOK architects left the firm to launch Ellerbe Becket, among them Turner and Michael Hallmark. With four thriving sports architecture firms now spread across the city—HNTB, HOK, DJLM (now Devine, deFlon & Yaeger), and the fledgling Ellerbe Becket—Kansas City soon cemented its place as ground zero for cutting-edge sports architecture. As Arrowhead begat Giants Stadium which begat Joe Robbie, HNTB and HOK begat virtually all of the leading names in worldwide sports architecture today.

In 1995, George Heinlein and Brad Schrock left HOK to found Heinlein Schrock Architecture. At HOK, Heinlein had served as lead project designer for Chicago's United Center, home of the Chicago Blackhawks NHL franchise and the Bulls, at the apex of the Michael Jordan era and covered on worldwide television every single day, providing phenomenal exposure for the building and its architect.

It was at the United Center that Heinlein mastered the concept of designing seating that would be equally as fan friendly for basketball as it was for hockey. The seating geometry for each sport was different enough that up to that point, sharing arena space had been a compromise for the teams and fans involved and had led to teams in many cities that shared such a facility threatening to build their own arena or to relocate.

Heinlein designed a system known as variable rise seating, which uses portable platforms to "pull in" the corners of the seating, creating a more proximate venue for spectators of both sports.

"Most dual sports arenas were not conducive to both sports," says sports executive Jay Cross in a January 2009 *SportsBusiness Journal* interview. "[Heinlein] pioneered a system that changed the slope from the sidelines to the end zones with steeper seats for basketball that could retract properly for hockey. It was very clever."

Working out of Schrock's basement, Heinlein Schrock was soon tapped to work on Safeco Field in Seattle, Air Canada Centre in Toronto, American Airlines Arena in Miami, and the new Giants and Jets stadium at the Meadowlands. In 2005, the firm became 360 Architecture after merging with CDFM2.

Over the years, Ellerbe Becket's portfolio expanded to include Chase Field in Phoenix (formerly Bank One Ballpark), Qwest Field in Seattle, TD Banknorth Garden in Boston (formerly Fleet Center), Quicken Loans Arena in Cleveland (formerly Gund), and the Scottrade Center in St. Louis (formerly Kiel Center).

For Turner, working at Ellerbe at the time was about as far as you could get from his first project right out of school, the much-derided 1973 renovation of Yankee Stadium—which he had shared with Labinski during their DJLM days. The project received widespread criticism for basically erasing the house that Ruth, Gehrig, and company had built, and on top of that, it was carried out at the height of New York's then-worst downturn since the Depression. "It was at a time when there was no construction going on in New York, so you couldn't get the contractors out of the building," Turner recalls. "It was just horrible. I'd walk down the concourse and they'd be shooting craps in the corner and stuff like that, you know, just not working at all."

The project, however, ultimately came with a major career boost for Turner. "The Yankees were playing at Shea Stadium during the construction," he says, "and George Steinbrenner had been suspended by Bowie Kuhn, so he couldn't go to the stadium or to the office or anywhere. He had a Brownstone in New York, and it was my job to go there every two weeks and make a presentation to George along with Gabe Paul, president of the team at that time.

"I'd have to go and make this presentation, and Gabe was seasoned enough to know better than to go in with me. George was at the height of his rage at that point, so most of his communication was carried out via screaming and yelling. I'd show him the latest slides of the project and bring him up to speed. It gave me incredible insight into what an owner wants, what's closest to his heart, the team facilities and his personal space—there must have been 20 different schemes for his office alone—all being paid for by taxpayer funds.

"I'd come out of there, I'd just be wringing wet and worn out and Gabe would put his arm around me and he'd say, 'Let's go out and get a beer.' He was Mr. Baseball. He was well liked and had been around for a long time, so that was pretty cool. So in strange way, it was fun. It set me off on a career. I've never done anything but sports since—at least 43 facilities.

Another project that clearly demonstrates the evolution of Turner's vision of stadiums as entertainment centers is the work he did on the stadium for the Olympic Games in Atlanta in 1996. "It was a very special time when [Ellerbe Becket] was awarded the Olympic Stadium," he says. "HOK had been working with the Braves and trying to convince Ted Turner that they could do a stadium. But after the cost overruns in Montreal during those Olympic Games, Turner never believed they could do it.

"So [Carl] Bunky Helfrich, Turner's right-hand man and an architect himself, called me and said, 'Okay, Ron, can you come down and have a meeting with Turner and talk about what your vision might be for something like this?' We won the Olympic Stadium and also had Turner convinced that we could turn it into a great ballpark for the Braves when the Games were done as well."

Sometimes, having the same last name as a local power broker pays off. "I always stayed in the Omni Hotel right there, where Ted Turner lived," Ron Turner says. "When I would check in, I'd go to my room, and it was always a suite and it was always covered with flowers and all kinds of other perks. They didn't want to take a chance."

The project, however, caused a rift with Labinski. "We always had this kind of 'why fight' pact," Turner says. "We'd never go after HOK's clients; they wouldn't go after our clients. We always kind of stayed over in the NBA and NHL, and they're over in football and baseball. So when we won the Olympic Stadium, the gloves came off. It was going to be a big deal to either Ron or me. One of the two of us was going to win that stadium, that's just the way it was, and I never thought that much about it because we weren't that heavy into baseball anyway and weren't interested in doing the nostalgic kind of stuff, so I didn't worry about it that much.

"But then when Bunky called and we put together a concept that really captured Ted's interest, and then ultimately won the thing, I think Ron was pretty shocked. They then started pursuing the arena side of things, beginning with Denver and the United Center."

On the heels of their Olympic Stadium success, Turner, Hallmark, and Dan Meis soon departed Ellerbe Becket with another idea in mind: combining sports architecture with entertainment architecture (think performing arts centers, concert halls, amphitheatres, and clubs) outright. Ellerbe Becket executives were reportedly not keen on the idea, so the three colleagues shopped the concept around to other architecture firms until they found a receptive ear: NBBJ, based in Los Angeles. "Where else?" Meis was quoted as saying at the time. "Los Angeles is the entertainment capital of the world."

In 1995, NBBJ Sports & Entertainment Architecture was born.

Staples Center and the Downtown L.A. Renaissance

NBBJ Sports & Entertainment, established with a cutting-edge design studio mentality rather than as a cookie-cutter volume shop, had its first significant project in the $260 million Miller Park, home to the Milwaukee Brewers. This led to design contracts with the Cincinnati Bengals and with Philadelphia Eagles owners Jeffrey and Christina Lurie for their new downtown stadium (more on this later). But Meis and Turner's signature achievement at NBBJ was L.A.'s cutting-edge $375 million Staples Center, opened in 1999 in a seedy area of downtown Los Angeles, adjacent to that city's huge convention center complex.

Turner soon moved on to establish the sports and entertainment division of architectural giant RTKL. There, he went on to design the mixed-use L.A. Live district, comprising Staples and the revolutionary Nokia Theatre complex across the street. Together, the projects helped to revitalize a large downtown section of the second biggest city in the country—and created a set piece of venues that takes center stage alongside the biggest entertainment acts in the world.

Staples Center employs an unusually sloped oval roof that, night lit, is a bright blue beacon in the downtown Los Angeles skyline, a high-tech welcome mat to the thousands of flights from all over the world landing at close-by LAX airport each year. Under its novel exterior, it is a carefully thought-out patchwork of square and round sections, combining meeting space with high-end restaurants and lounges and giving the architectural VIP treatment to Jack Nicholson, Denzel Washington, Penny Marshall, Billy Crystal, and the other Hollywood luminaries who spend much of their leisure time inside.

Seeking to create a round-the-clock environment for the mass influx of tourists, conventioneers, and area residents, the Los Angeles Land Company commissioned RTKL to design a comprehensive 33-acre (13 hectare) sports and entertainment district. The plan also included corporate office buildings (including a West Coast studio complex for ESPN) and 4,000 residential units.

The focal point of the massive $2.5 billion L.A. Live retail and entertainment complex is the Nokia Theatre, a 7,100-seat concert venue, and adjacent 40,000-square-foot (3,700 m2) Nokia Plaza. The Emmy Awards, the American Music Awards, the sports ESPY Awards, and the *American Idol* finale now call the Nokia Theatre home, with the Grammy Awards held annually at Staples across the street. Club Nokia at L.A. Live is a tri-level club with a futuristic decor including a timeline wall, where visitors can send text messages, pictures, and videos to the venue's digital mailbox and watch as they appear on giant screens throughout the club. The club is expected to host more than 150 events annually; Usher, the Stone Temple Pilots, and Sarah Silverman were among the acts that performed in the venue's first year.

L.A. Live offers Nokia visitors so many dining, entertainment, and lodging options that there's hardly any need to leave the development—terrific for tenants, not so terrific for the neighborhoods, attractions, and businesses surrounding it.

Meis is now managing director of the Los Angeles offices of international architecture firm Aedas. He is working with billionaire developer Ed Roski to bring NFL football back to Los Angeles in the form of a stadium in the nearby City of Industry that, if the project comes to fruition, will far eclipse Staples in its scope and breadth.

He has competition, however—in late 2010, AEG announced that it is spearheading the development of a $1.3 billion retractable-roof stadium complex adjacent to Staples, L.A. Live, and the Los Angeles Convention Center. What's more, Farmers Insurance announced that it would spend $700 million over 20 years to name the facility Farmers Field, an unheard-of step for an unapproved building with no tenant. Ron Turner, who now heads up the sports and entertainment division of architectural firm Gensler, was tapped to finalize the design.

Now, all that the would-be Los Angeles stadium godfathers need is a team.

Meanwhile, Down in Texas

As the HNTB/HOK and offspring's sports architecture empire spread across western civilization these last three decades, the parent and sibling companies weren't just competing with each other for projects. Down in Dallas, another sports division of a renowned architecture firm was making a name for itself: HKS. Leading the charge in the heart of Texas is Bryan Trubey, a visionary who has solely focused on sports architecture over the course of a 26-year career and has managed to earn the confidence and respect of one of the allegedly most difficult people to please in the industry: Dallas Cowboys owner Jerry Jones.

Trubey, a Texas A&M grad, was named one of the 20 most influential people in sports facility design, architecture, and development by *Sports-Business Journal.* Alongside the iconic Cowboys Stadium, facilities on Trubey's resume include Lone Star Park, American Airlines Center, and MLS Pizza Hut Park complex in Texas and U.S. Cellular Field renovations in Chicago. His international projects include the groundbreaking Liverpool FC Stadium; Territorio Santos Modelo; 2014 FIFA World Cup venues in Rio de Janeiro and Brasilia, Brazil; and cricket stadiums throughout India including Mohali, Delhi, Jaipur, Kolkata, Mumbai, Hyderabad, Chennai, and Bangalore.

A principal with HKS with 26 years' experience, Trubey actively participates in all phases of the architectural design process. His primary role occurs in the initial planning stages where he is responsible for setting the design concept and then maintaining design continuity throughout project development. Like Turner, Trubey's most notable projects effectively integrate a one-of-a-kind sports environment with entertainment, creating timely, memorable mixed-use destinations.

"We are really in a totally different marketplace to some extent than the firms we compete against for projects," Trubey says. "That's how different we are because we've been in a situation quite a few years now where we've solely created completely one-off venues. What owners get, the minute they start working with us, is everything thought through from a custom standpoint. Everything we do is completely unique to that particular client, that particular place, and that particular time.

"The thing that's fascinating about it," he continues, "is linking the look and the function to the particular desires of that client, and so to a

Bryan Trubey (left) discusses blueprints with Dallas Cowboys president Stephen Jones.

Blake Marvin, HKS, Inc.

larger extent, we really don't find ourselves competing on a level playing field with any of the other firms in our industry because we have such a different approach and we tend to get work in a competitive mode. We're five for five in competitions for projects over the last eight years—we've won every single one that we've entered. That's been really phenomenal for us because those are all the new relationships we have. The rest of our work, about 80 percent, is repeat client work—the highest percentage in the industry."

Trubey estimates that about 20 percent of the firm's current workload is overseas—a number that's on par with the international expansion HOK is experiencing since they have merged with London and Sydney–based Lobb Sports Architecture. He loves the work, the challenge of translating cultural nuance into concrete and steel.

"Cultural and ethnic differences are very interesting," he acknowledges. "We're designing a totally different building in Liverpool than we would design in the United States, and a lot of that's based on the cultural differences unique to the U.K.

"The other thing that's a huge influence on us is the sport itself," Trubey continues. "There's a completely different rhythm to soccer than American football. We've got a lot of experience working on MLS venues in the States—but it's still different in the U.K. You've got a 45-minute period, a 15-minute break, and a 45-minute period. People in the U.K. and Europe and most of the soccer world tend to not leave their seats as much during a soccer match, because it's a low-scoring game and you really don't want to miss any of the plays that might make a difference in the outcome of the game.

"What we are finding all over the world is that when you create venues that provide a higher-quality experience all the way around, people trend in different directions. People buy food and beverages at higher levels, they spend more time at the venue both before and after the game. Those tendencies tend to be universal."

And what about the widespread perception that sports facilities elsewhere in the world are years ahead of those in America?

"One thing that we've been pretty surprised about is [that] even the recently built venues in the U.K. like Wembley and Emirates really fall behind what we've been doing here in the U.S., and they shouldn't," says Trubey. "A lot of the U.K. venues traditionally are underdesigned compared to what we would provide here in the U.S. in terms of points of sale for food and beverages, and even restrooms. That's the opposite of what you want in those venues because you've got the same amount of people with access to those facilities for fewer minutes. If you extend that logic, you should provide more points of sale and more facilities because you have a more intense rush period, which means a more intense use period. We've analyzed that very carefully.

"Another thing we're introducing to that marketplace with the Liverpool project," Trubey continues, " is what we've been doing on our venues here in the U.S., which is putting all of our premium seating on the sidelines (what they call laterals in the U.K. and Europe) because we know we're going to achieve the highest value for it. The final big concept that we're implementing that has proven market success is several different-sized suites in different locations and several different types of club seating in club environments. Why? Because we know for a fact that the smaller the increments are from one pricing level to the next, the more likely a fan is going to graduate to that next level."

It is likely, however, that designing the new Dallas Cowboys stadium, which formally opened in September 2009, will be the crowning achievement of Trubey's career—however long he lingers over a blueprint. The $1.2 billion stadium has received critical praise from the international architectural press. David Dillon, architecture critic with the *Dallas Morning News*, calls it "a highly cinematic and futuristic piece of contemporary architecture." (See case study at the end of this chapter.)

Size Does Matter

How do our modern temples of sport stack up to real houses of worship?

World's Largest Stadium

Rungrado May Day Stadium, Pyongyang, North Korea

Capacity: 150,000

World's Largest Racetrack

Indianapolis Motor Speedway, Indianapolis, Indiana

Capacity: 257,325 permanent seats; 400,000 including infield overflow

World's Largest Church

Winners Chapel, Canaanland, Otta, Nigeria

Capacity: Inside seating, 50,000; outside overflow, 250,000

World's Largest Mosque

Shah Faisal Mosque, Islamabad, Pakistan

Capacity: Inside, 35,000; outside overflow, 150,000

What Makes for a Good Stadium Design?

Even when you have sophisticated 3-D computer animation, detailed scale models, and custom graphics in your toolkit, there's no question that designing a stadium is much more complex than designing an office building. For one thing, few office buildings reach icon status in their communities or are so visually tied to a place that someone seeing it on television instantly knows exactly where that broadcast is coming from. You see a giant pirate ship, you know you're about to see the Tampa Bay Buccaneers kick off.

"The beauty of a high-rise, from a design standpoint, is that it's repetitive," says a hard-hatted Chad Sheckel, HKS' project manager on the Lucas Oil Stadium build in Indianapolis, on a hot August day as the stadium was slowly taking shape. "You get one floor and you figure out what you have to do to make that floor work and make the design better. Then it just gets repeated. If I've got one problem solved on this level, that carries all the way up through. I'm done!

"But the volume and the spacing and the complexity of the job with this building," he says, gesturing at the enormous 1920s-era field house—circa 2007—going up around him, "is what makes it so compelling."

So what is it about some stadiums and arenas that make them more memorable than others? That make you want to return to them again and again—even if your favorite team is 13-39 for the season and has zero chance of making the playoffs?

In the minds of the architects, that's a fairly simple question to answer—it's all about what they call the "stadium experience." What you want to take away from that experience, however, is vastly different for a team owner than it is for the fans.

"In stadium design, there are really only four questions you need answered up front by the guys paying the bills, and then we simply deliver what we need to do," Wellner says. "What's your sport? How many seats do you want to have? What's your number of luxury suits? What's your number of club seats? With those answers, you can do an entire building.

"In regard to premium seating," he continues, "there are probably several dozen iterations of that requirement that you can generate. All premium seating on one side, or premium seating on both sides? Do you want any in the end zone? Do you want a breakdown of premium seats tied into more than what is typical? Do you want seats on the field? Do you want field-level club space? It's infinite from that standpoint, so most of our energy during design is spent on the educational process rather than getting a finite vision from the client up front.

"Then, we need to get into operational specifics," Wellner says. "Do you want to hire a concessionaire, or do you want to operate the building yourself? How much additional concert, convention, and special event business do you anticipate soliciting? Are you planning on bidding on a Super Bowl, an All-Star Game, an NCAA basketball tournament? All of those issues have a direct impact on the functionality of the building, its power and storage and point of entry requirements. But all of these issues should be invisible to the fans and other event attendees.

"What matters most up front," he concludes, "is simply doing enough drawings so that a budget can be put to it and you can get financing commitments. Site planning is a critical part of it—we always know the visual images that represent what it's going to look like will be used in community meetings. When we designed Orioles Park, there were neighbors living right across the street, so there was a great deal of discussion positioning the building so it wouldn't disrupt their lives. The biggest hurdle and yet in fact the easiest thing to do is just talk to people. If you talk to people, if they've been heard, there usually isn't a great deal of resistance to our designs because the process has been kind of neat."

"Some clients come to us and they have no idea what they want, or they may have some ideas, and they can't express them," Labinski states in a *SportsBusiness Journal* Q&A. "I think in other cases, they've seen something they like and they want something similar to it. In other cases, they want something that's totally different from anything that's been done. These are the kinds of wishes that the clients generally come to us with. We're kind of the interpreter of those wishes. In the design process that takes place, we try to take the input from all these people and come up with a final design that hopefully satisfies the desires of everyone—the client for a unique building; the city for something that will help in the redevelopment of an urban area; the operator for something that is user friendly; the concessionaire for a building in which his per capita income can be maximized; and not the least of which, the spectator who comes and is thoroughly entertained from the time he reaches the site until he leaves."

Earl Santee, longtime head of HOK Sport's baseball practice, explains the fans' perspective on the design formula this way: "The event is the background," he says in a conversation with Ian Mount of *Business 2.0* magazine. "The foreground is all these other activities. It's 'I need to buy a sweater' or 'There's a beer garden.'"

Trubey, however, sees it a different way. "The essence of a fan's love for his team," he argues, "is based on the total and absolute unique nature of his team as compared to others, and the more unique his team is, the more in love he is with the team. It's the same reason you love your wife or your husband, or you love your children, because they are totally and absolutely unique to you. The essence of that translates to fans and how they feel about their teams.

"As an architect," Trubey continues, "the more you can leverage the very unique nature of a team, the more the fans are in love with it; that's the thing that really motivates us as designers. We know that every corner, every turn, every brick that we can lay in a way that's totally unique to that particular team is going to help fill the stadium up year after year and add value in terms of the way that fans love that team. That's what turns us on—I mean, that's just a huge thing for us as architects."

"There are a lot of different ways to express oneself in the venue," he summarizes, "and that's one thing we do have control over as architects. When you look at our venues from Miller Park to the baseball park in Arlington and to our NFL facilities and arenas such as American Airlines Center, we create a ton of very unique environments from which you can watch the game and a lot of varied environments in the concourses where you can have really unique experiences. Often, those relate to sponsor activation, so they're different ways to leverage not just the sporting event but the ability for others—and this is the big issue with owners—to showcase products in a super-activated environment. We focus on those things a lot."

Turner puts it a little more bluntly. "I always feel as if architects are just way too crazy about themselves thinking that it's all about what *we* do, you know, and it's really not. It's really about the experience. It's really about how that kid comes away from that baseball game, or the circus, and just feels like he's bigger than life. It's all about that, it's not about the architecture. But the architecture can enhance the experience in a big way."

How does all this love and enhancement translate to the bottom line? In San Francisco, according to Mount, the Giants averaged less than two million in annual attendance at 60,000-seat Candlestick Park and lost $97 million between 1995 and 1999. In the team's first three years at 40,000-seat Pac Bell, the team averaged more than three million spectators. Revenue doubled, and the club managed a small profit for the 2002 season—even after making its annual $20 million payment to the investors who put up $140 million for the ballpark.

At the end of the day, owners and the architects themselves aren't shy about looking outside stadium walls for inspiration. Before Chicago Bears president Mike McCaskey embarked on a redesign of Chicago's iconic Soldier Field, he consulted with an Italian architect, AIA and Pritzker Prize recipient Renzo Piano—who had never before seen a game of American football. Likewise, Arizona Cardinals owner Bill Bidwell turned to renowned architect Peter Eisenman—much better known for his groundbreaking House VI and the Memorial to the Murdered Jews in Berlin than any sports facility—for the desert masterpiece: the University of Phoenix Stadium.

Practice [Facility]
Makes Perfect [Community]

Often overlooked in the sports facilities conversation are teams' practice facilities—the players' and front office personnel's true home away from home.

When it opened its doors in 2001, the Philadelphia Eagles' NovaCare training complex instantly set the standard for practice and rehabilitation facilities in the NFL and other leagues. The NovaCare complex was not only the first NFL practice facility to reap the financial benefits of a naming rights deal—in this case, a reported $60 million over 25 years—but also an instant magnet for sought-after free agents wanting to partake of the 8,000-square-foot (750 m^2) weight room, the state-of-the art hydrotherapy system, the stunning locker room and players lounge, and the affiliation with the top-notch NovaCare rehabilitation center.

Long before architect Michael Graves sketched the first rough drawings of the new practice facility, Eagles owner Jeffrey Lurie and his wife Christina were looking well beyond the traditional sports mind-set when they envisioned the complex. "When we designed our practice facility, we didn't want to go to an HOK, someone who focused on sports buildings," Jeffrey Lurie says. "This was going to be a real model for an urban business in a sporting activity, aesthetically attractive, great atmosphere, all woven into a facility that would provide us with a competitive advantage. We didn't want to go with that traditional look we saw when we visited other teams' facilities, so we hired Michael Graves, who had never focused on sports, to do the project."

Christina, who also pioneered many of the "green" initiatives at Lincoln Financial Field immolated throughout pro sports properties today, was the driving force behind the aesthetics. Jeffrey focused on the community in the making. "We were very impressed with the studios in Hollywood, such as the Disney Campus and the Universal Studios lot, the camaraderie and uplifting culture you can get from creating a wonderful campus-like environment," he says. "Even though we were working in an urban environment, we thought we could do the exact same thing.

"When we visited different teams' practice sites, it always felt to me like a factory approach and not really something that brought people together. There weren't centerpieces where people can congregate every day, such as our cafeteria in the center of the main NovaCare building, or the combination auditorium and digital theater where all the interviews are done, where the team meets every day, where we have movie screenings.

"Understand—we were coming from the most depressing building imaginable—the basement of Veterans Stadium. So we really saw the negatives of not having that kind of environment.

"The first day this building opened up, the entire Eagles culture changed from being sort of dreary to very upbeat, optimistic," Lurie adds. "We can compete with anybody and be very proud to be part of this organization. As the players have explained to me, almost instantaneously word got around the league that hey, you're not an Eagle of the basement of Veterans Stadium. You're an Eagle of the NovaCare Complex. It impacted the team more than almost anything."

The Luries and the Eagles staff have also done the little things that mean so much to veterans such as Bill Bergey. The former Eagles linebacker was quoted as saying he felt as if he had "leprosy" when he walked down the hallways of Veterans Stadium when Norman Braman owned the team. But then Bergey saw the dozens of pictures throughout the NovaCare

Complex that paid tribute to the Eagles' past, to players whose hearts and souls carried the organization to where it is today.

"It means everything to me," said Bergey at the NovaCare ribbon cutting. "You know, I always felt like such an outcast before Jeffrey bought the team. I felt as if I didn't belong. I couldn't understand it.

"I told Jeffrey when he bought the team: 'We don't want to be stroked. We don't want to take away from the glory of these players. We just want to be welcomed.' He's made us feel welcomed."

Raising a Roof

How do stadium designers and team owners decide if a new building is going to have a retractable roof—or not? In Chicago, Boston, Cleveland, Kansas City, and the Meadowlands, the public sector rejected overtures by teams to spend public funds for roof additions—even if adding a roof meant adding additional Super Bowl, Final Four, and convention revenues to community coffers.

In other cases, especially in cold-climate cities, common sense says the owner of a team will not be as supportive of a roof as a community might be, because while a community might want Super Bowls, conventions, and other events inside, the owner may want the opportunity to increase the prices for a weatherized part of the stadium. Want to stay warm during a night game in November? Buy a suite.

Wellner disputes this notion. "To date," he says, "I believe that the existence of a roof versus open air has been driven more by the cost of the roof than a philosophy about that, and yet the philosophy about that is really what's over a stadium. Football is for hardy fans. It needs to be played outdoors, and if the fan has been sitting outdoors for all these years, there really isn't a reason to spend $200 million on a roof and enclose your building (and pay the high costs of heating and air conditioning) unless there's a longer view of what else you might be able to do with the building, and if it's controlled by a municipality, the team owner may or may not care about that.

"I have not seen a difference in the pricing of premium spaces because they were in a cold-weather climate. A premium market, I think, is a premium market."

Moving Walls, Moving Forward

When Labinski and HOK began designing stadiums, scoreboards were rudimentary. "There were maybe four shades of gray, and the big development was 16 shades of gray," he says, laughing. "Video boards are now one of the key elements in any stadium design. You have to make sure 100 percent of the spectators can see the boards. With the new formatting for high definition, they're longer and narrower. In a lot of stadiums we're doing double boards, just to increase the number of things we can do."

The Cowboys, of course, have taken HDTV to the max in their stadium, not only with the giant screens hanging above the field but also with more than 3,000 individually controlled screens throughout the building. This would not have been possible had they not partnered with Cisco Systems, the company that not only developed the backbone of the World Wide Web and virtually every backroom telephony in corporate America today but also pioneered StadiumVision and the HAL-esque stadium of the future.

"The new multipurpose Cowboys Stadium will incorporate advanced video technologies from Cisco, improving the fan experience and helping transform the way the Cowboys organization operates the venue," said John T. Chambers, Cisco chairman and chief executive officer. "Cisco is committed to demonstrating the power of the network in maximizing the value of the venue and providing a new look at sports and entertainment experiences for a premier brand, such as the Dallas Cowboys."

Cisco Connected Sports solutions are connecting teams and fans in new ways at sporting venues around the world and at such mega events as the NBA All-Star Game and the Super Bowl, where they have a major imprint in host facilities in Miami (2010), Dallas (2011), and Indianapolis (2012). Cisco's family of innovative products and services are reinventing the fan experience, driving new revenue streams and revolutionizing venue operations.

Cisco recognized early on that with a connected network platform, opportunities abound for teams, leagues, and venues to transform the fan experience with a variety of services that include tickets and upgrades on their mobile devices; customized digital signage; selection of video, camera angles, and replays; merchandise delivered or ready for pick up; and Web access as well as pre- and postgame materials.

Savvy sports owners and general managers were quick to recognize the value of Cisco's sports product offerings. Within the first two years of the Sports and Entertainment business unit's formation, the New York Yankees, Kansas City Royals, Toronto Blue Jays, and Miami Dolphins were showcasing Cisco technology in their stadiums alongside the Cowboys. The NBA has also partnered with the company to use Cisco's TelePresence life-size videoconferencing capabilities to enable a "face-to-face" conversation between athletes and fans at its NBA All-Star celebrations.

"If you . . . want to go out on a limb," Labinski concludes in *SportsBusiness Journal*, "maybe the new stadium or the new venue of the future is one in which we all get in our own levitation vehicle and take our levitation vehicle and position it somewhere inside the stadium bowl and view the game and never leave the comfort of our own levitation vehicle.

"Who knows? I think for the foreseeable future, the bigger question is what is going to happen in sport itself and what kind of changes in the business of sport, what kind of changes will that prompt?"

Cowboys Stadium, Arlington, Texas

"Extraordinary." "Iconic." "Supersonic." "Spectacular." "Stupendous." "Breath-taking."

Somehow, none of these descriptors quite does justice to the $1.2 billion, steel and glass homage to Texas football that Dallas Cowboys owner Jerry Jones and his family conceived, perfected, and presented to the world in September 2009. In February 2011, the facility was back in the global spotlight as the home of Super Bowl XLV, an iconic matchup between the Pittsburgh Steelers and victorious Green Bay Packers.

Cowboys Stadium is one of the largest buildings in the world and certainly the largest NFL venue ever likely to be built. Encasing three million square feet (275,000 m2), the majestic scale of the building measures the length of the Empire State Building; the Statue of Liberty could stand upright inside the structure. It features the most spectacular column-free room in the world, stretching a quarter-mile in length.

Conceptualized by the HKS Sports & Entertainment Group under principal designer Bryan Trubey, who worked side by side with Jones on the project for close to a decade, the venue enhances the international Cowboys brand with its modern, progressive architecture while incorporating such elements of the Cowboys' Texas Stadium heritage as the Ring of Honor and the shape of the opening for the retractable roof.

Jones entrusted Trubey to bring to life his vision of an airy, technology-charged building that would define the future of watching football and compete with pro sports' biggest 21st-century challenge, the big-screen HDTV in front of a fan's own couch. "That's why I spent the money," Jones told the *New York Times*' Richard Sandomir. "It has a chance to be one of the most visible buildings in this country. . . . I could have built this for $850 [million]. And it would have been a fabulous place to play football. But this was such an opportunity for the 'wow factor.'"

Designed to allow every fan a great view of the action, Cowboys Stadium can hold up to 100,000 fans, 10,000 of whom pay only $29 for standing-room-only Party Pass space in the stacked end zone plazas. It offers 350 luxury suites, including 50 on the field level, a variety of concourses and private clubs, the Cowboys Hall of Fame, the NFL's biggest pro shop, and food options created by Legends Hospitality Management, a joint venture of the Cowboys and the New York Yankees. More than 3,000 HD digital displays, using technology deployed by Cisco Systems, give the team and sponsors dynamic billboards and points of sale that maximize revenues while enabling fans to never lose sight of the game.

Visitors whose notion of culture extends way past the gridiron will be mesmerized as well. A museum-worthy collection of 14 site-specific works by world-renowned artists—mobiles, murals, and other contemporary installations—is prominently placed at entranceways and above the concourses. And in the club-level Dee Lincoln's Tasting Room and Bubble Bar, oenophiles who previously despaired inside stadiums can compare tastings of Rudd Vineyards 2005 Napa Valley Cabernet Sauvignon with the 2004 Silver Oak from Alexander Valley or sip a glass of Etoile Rose champagne.

Besides its monumental arches, the signature feature of Cowboys Stadium is its one-of-a-kind center-hung video board. Suspended from the roof structure 90 feet (27 m) above the field, HD video boards facing each sideline span 60 yards (55 m), measuring 72 feet (22 m) tall by 160 feet (49 m) wide. Complementary video boards facing the end zones measure 27 feet (8 m) tall by 48 feet (15 m) wide. It's virtually impossible to take your eyes off the boards, which immerse spectators in such startlingly crystal-clear images that the tiniest of details do not go undetected: a trickle of sweat running down a linebacker's temple, blades of bright green turf, individual silver fringe on a cheerleader's sleeve. The screens create a premium for upper-level seats and present the game, concert, or halftime show in a way never before experienced and never to be forgotten.

The HD scoreboard alone cost $40 million—one and a half times the entire cost to build Texas Stadium in 1971.

Thanks to the new stadium, Jones added that he expects team revenue to rise at least 50 percent this season—a key factor in Trubey's appeal to the dozens of team owners with whom he's worked. "Cowboys Stadium was designed to be America's Stadium," Trubey says. "Its modern style represents power, motion, agility, and the grace of the team, linking architectural form to the primary use of the venue. Our goal was to design the best stadium in the world, with the biggest fan payback and the biggest boost to the team's and the community's bottom line."

According to an economic impact study completed before the venue opened, the city of Arlington can expect to see an annual economic impact of $238 million, with the creation of 807 permanent jobs; surrounding Tarrant County can anticipate a $416 million annual boon and 1,940 new jobs. (The stadium itself employs up to 4,000 workers.) Over 30 years, it was projected that Cowboys Stadium could bring in between $12.5 billion and $27.7 billion to the county.

The stadium—the NFL's biggest venue by far—is designed to host non-football events from the 2010 NBA All-Star Game and the 2014 NCAA Final Four to the biggest acts in entertainment. There's arguably none bigger than the headliner before the stadium's first-ever preseason game, Sir Paul McCartney, former Beatle and cultural icon. It is only fitting that in its first football week, Cowboys Stadium was blessed by entertainment royalty. ∎

5

The Government Gets Into—and Out of—the Game

► Between 1990 and 2007, 260 sports, arts, convention, and entertainment facilities were developed in the United States at a cost of more than $21 billion.

► The growth of sports facilities spending from 2007 and beyond is huge: an additional $13.4 billion has been spent on more than 81 arenas, major and minor league stadiums, and surrounding infrastructure.

► From Pittsburgh to San Diego, stadiums, arenas, and entertainment centers are important economic drivers and branding tools for communities.

► Sports facilities and franchises enhance a region's ability to attract new business and create jobs.

of residential real estate—whether you're building a custom property, purchasing a home in a new development, or buying a gently used home—is fairly straightforward. Either (a) you have the means to pay for the house outright, in cash, or (b) you borrow all or part of the money, usually, of course, from a bank.

Buying a commercial property is more complicated and more expensive, but purchasers often have additional means of assistance via local business subsidies and incentives. Build in a development zone, for example, and you'll usually see relaxed building codes and zoning laws, streamlined permit processes and rebated permit fees, reduced taxes and licensing, low-market- rate loans, technical assistance, referrals, and marketing help.

But what about financing a sports facility? In the olden days, pre-1990s, most local stadiums and arenas were primarily publicly funded, treated no differently from a library or school. Shea Stadium was paid for entirely by the city of New York. Veterans Stadium was paid for entirely by the city of Philadelphia. But the cost for such facilities began to increase at an exponential rate. Needed large tracts of land diminished, and community populations exploded (with their attendant infrastructure needs).

Central to all sports facility deals, says Joseph Leccese, principal at Proskauer Rose LLC in New York City, which handles dozens of major stadium development, naming rights, and franchise placement deals each decade, "is the ground. What piece of ground for this community are we going to be able to get? How quickly can we get it? If there's a piece of ground that is most desirable, it's likely going to take you years to acquire. It might have more community opposition; it might have more regulatory issues.

"You tend to have a relatively narrow window to get these stadium projects done. If you don't hit that window, it's not like you can come back and open it next year. Wellington Mara negotiated a Meadowlands deal with five different New Jersey governors, only the fourth of which was interested. How long have the 49ers been at it? How many places did Jerry Jones look around? It's a very difficult process, so you have to start with the right piece of ground. How much will it cost, who's going to buy it, what can we build there, what's the cost of that, what can we afford, what can the public sector afford, what benefits for the community exist or not, that will justify the public investment? Is the neighborhood acceptable to the location, is it right in the middle of downtown? All of those factors not only drive cost, they drive the core feasibility of the project.

"I know what I need to have when I go to the financial institutions," Leccese continues, "because I know what their expectations are. If I can't deliver to the financial institutions a package and price and the certainty of the price that they will expect, then even if I've gotten a fair deal from a mayor or a governor, I can't build my building. Unless you can see the end at the beginning, you're not going to get off to a very good start."

More and more questions arose as to who was really benefiting from the facilities, the taxpayers—or the fat cat owners and leagues? It became increasingly clear that a new model was needed. The now standard public–private partnership was born, and stand-alone sports facilities were increasingly integrated into downtowns or into mixed-use entertainment zones, more tightly woven into the fabric of the community. For sports fans, this means closer proximity to the homes of their teams, a year-round source of entertainment, and the knowledge that a smaller chunk of the taxes they pay are going toward the funding of such projects.

Tax Increment Financing

Financing public infrastructure through a technique known as tax increment financing has been used for the last three or four decades as a device to tie the growth in tax revenues directly to the project that helped spur that growth.

Identified by different names in different places—tax increment financing, recapture, rebate, empowerment and development districts, and others—this technique assumes that public infrastructure that was built as a result of bonds sold will have a direct impact on the long-term growth of the region.

The formula goes like this: The difference between the tax rate and the estimated growth in taxes attributed to the infrastructure and facilities is used to pay off all or part of the bonds for construction and operation of the facilities.

Originally, tax increment districts were created for basic infrastructure services: roads, bridges, lighting, and the like. Then, downtown developers began using the tax increment districts as part of larger master plans for downtown and regional development, arguing that new arenas and stadiums would expedite the development of the master plans. They argued that not only would the fans, opposing teams, concessionaires, and suite holders spend more money in that area but also the development of the sports and entertainment facilities would speed up the building of residential, commercial, and retail space—increasing the tax base even further.

Politically, the use of this technique has at least two advantages. First, it replaces or supplements a direct increase in other taxes that would burden particular interest groups (restaurateurs, hoteliers, and the like). Second, the funds received are directly tied to the growth spurred by the specific projects, an argument that proponents must make in order to convince skeptical citizens that stadiums and arenas serve a useful public good.

The last 20 years have produced unprecedented development of entertainment infrastructure, both nationally and internationally. Between 1990-2007, considered the golden age of modern sports facility development, 260 sports, arts, convention, and entertainment facilities were developed in the United States at a total cost of more than $21 billion. This is part of the overall $3.5 trillion spent in all infrastructure development since 1990, and, given the rising costs of land and materials, will likely remain the pinnacle of sports facility spending for the next century.

The shift from public money to private in shaping America's cities in all infrastructure initiatives is evident in U.S. government data. By the end of 2007, the beginning of the recession, government outlays on physical infrastructure declined to 2.7 percent of the GDP, from 3.6 percent in the 1960s. Government investment has sagged for several reasons. Tax cuts, largely introduced by the two Bush administrations, have helped to hold down overall government spending. Politics has also intervened, with the oft-criticized earmark process in Congress cited as a prime example of misdirected spending. And frequent voter and taxpayer polls indicate the widespread view that public investment is often wasteful and inept.

In this age of austerity, the Obama administration and state houses across the U.S. have continued the clampdown on spending taxpayer money on infrastructure, and with the exception of a new ballpark for the Florida Marlins, virtually no major sports facilities have broken ground since 2009.

The growth in sports facilities spending from 2007 and beyond is staggering. An additional total of more than $13.4 billion is being spent on more than 81 arenas, major and minor league stadiums, and other infrastructure facilities at least through 2010. Major facility openings include the $276 million Sprint Center in Kansas City; the $130 million Dick's Sporting Goods Park in Commerce City, Colorado (an MLS stadium); the $375 million Prudential Center in Newark, home to the New Jersey Devils; the $1 billion new Yankee Stadium; the $800 million Citi Field for the New York Mets; the $1.2 billion Cowboys Stadium in Arlington, Texas; and the $1.6 billion New Meadowlands Stadium. Minor league facilities will open from Tulsa, Oklahoma, to Bentonville, Arkansas, to Columbia, South Carolina, to Wichita, Kansas, and in between.

FACT **According to an analysis by the *New York Times*, New Jersey taxpayers still owe about $110 million on bonds sold to finance old Giants Stadium. . . .even though it was demolished in 2010.**

The introduction of the American Recovery and Reinvestment Act in 2009 provided additional sports facilities construction possibilities. During the Depression, President Franklin Roosevelt poured about $11 billion, or about $175 billion in today's dollars, into the Works Progress

Administration; not a city or county in America wasn't touched by the WPA in one way or another.

That organization during the 1930s built or refurbished more than 2,500 sports stadiums around the country, with a seating capacity of nearly six million. That includes Doubleday Field in Cooperstown, built in 1939 (where the MLB Hall of Fame Game is held today); Gittone Stadium in New Jersey in 1934; and the Miami Orange Bowl in 1937 (now the site of the under-construction Florida Marlins stadium).

WPA criteria specified that projects had to be locally responsible, be executed by an available supply of workers who met WPA eligibility requirements, be completed by a specific date, and generate general public usefulness. That's where the whole trend of public purpose really started.

WPA rules basically created the predicate for the American Recovery and Reinvestment Act, which committed more than $800 billion toward public infrastructure work in its first phase. Of that, $544 billion in spending is expected to create about four million new jobs and strong economic stimulus; sports and recreation projects nationwide will benefit.

An interesting side note: Cleveland-based international law firm Squire, Sanders & Dempsey aided the government agency that spearheaded the WPA initiative in the 1930s. Today, the firm is still instrumental in advising the U.S. government on American Recovery and Reinvestment Act decisions.

FACT According to Jim Ross, head of sales for the New York Yankees, Yankee Stadium consistently draws 80,000 tourists annually—on nongame days!

Of all of America's pro sports entities, the NFL has led the way in facility development and modernization. Since 1992, 28 facilities have been built or substantially renovated at a cost of over $8 billion. All have been the result of successful public–private partnerships. The average cost for these is $325 million, with an estimated 60 to 70 percent of the costs contributed from public sources.

Now, and looking forward, the price tag of a new NFL stadium is well over $1 billion. Originally estimated to cost $650 million, the construction cost for the new Dallas Cowboys Stadium in Arlington, Texas, was in excess of $1 billion, which makes it one of the most expensive sports venues ever built. (More on this amazing facility in the previous chapter.) The New York Giants and Jets borrowed $650 million each to build their shared stadium, the full cost of which was estimated to exceed $1.6 billion when it opened in August 2010. Fan interest in the new stadium was so high that both the Giants and the Jets sold a handful of their prime suites—priced at $1 million a year—three years before the new stadium was scheduled to open.

Stadium and arena renovations aren't cheap, either. "When considering a major renovation, the first step is to determine how much public assistance is available to your franchise," Joseph Leccese says. "That number rarely, if ever, reaches 100 percent. So where do you go from there? Are you in a position to work directly with the capital markets? Or is your credit access limited? These are the basic questions sports franchise owners and developers have to answer, both for initial builds and for renovations."

Despite the price, cities, regions, and states will continue to invest in stadiums, arenas, and entertainment centers. Why? They're important economic drivers and branding tools for the communities—even for those citizens who aren't sports fans. The 150+ regions of North America that have successfully implemented major and minor league sports, entertainment, and convention infrastructure of all types since 1990, totaling nearly $20 billion in public infrastructure, have been motivated by five specific benefits. These broad conclusions have been reached by a sampling of economists, consultants, chambers of commerce, and other business groups. Their analyses have been widely accepted as important components of the 30 successful public voter referenda and more than 220 other respective public–private partnerships.

Benefit 1

Successful projects have generated substantial development activity, including ancillary business activity, residential development, and infrastructure investment.

- **Pittsburgh**: In the late 1990s, Pittsburgh undertook a huge urban development project to revitalize its North Shore, spurred by the construction of the NFL Heinz Field and baseball PNC Park. The Pittsburgh Stadium Authority created a 25-acre (10 hectare) development zone, defined by the football stadium and baseball park, the Allegheny River, and an elevated highway. Spurred by the overall development, construction began on the $390 million, 1.6-mile (2.6 km) extension of a light rail system linking the North Shore development to the city center. A $47 million promenade, completed in 2001, was built along the river's shore. A $30 million headquarters for Equitable Gas was also completed in the area.

- **Cleveland**: Since Jacobs Field (now Progressive Field) and the nearby 21,000-seat Quicken Loans Arena opened in Cleveland in 1995, more than 50 new restaurants or retail establishments have opened nearby. What's more, more than 85 storefronts in the area have been renovated at a cost of $1.2 million. Both facilities are located in the 28-acre (11 hectare), $362 million minority development–oriented Gateway Project, which has created 6,269 permanent jobs since 1994 and generated $6.5 million in payroll taxes over its first decade. Downtown Cleveland business owners have suggested that the facility complex has provided more than 300 active dates and four million additional annual visitors to Cleveland since the opening of the stadium. The Rock and Roll Hall of Fame and Museum, as well as the Cleveland Browns Stadium, are nearby.

- **Denver**: As a consequence of the 1995 opening of Coors Field in Denver, studies pointed to an increase of more than $40 million in taxable sales from 1994; $20 million in incremental downtown business activity; and more than 25 restaurant openings. Land adjacent to Coors Field, previously assessed at $1.77 per square foot, recently sold for approximately $27 per square foot. Many converted warehouses have loft units selling for $200,000 to $300,000 per unit. One in every three tourists visiting Denver considered attending a Rockies game. Denver's downtown sports complex also includes Invesco Field at Mile High Stadium.

- **Phoenix**: A report by the Phoenix Finance Department demonstrates that fans attracted to Bank One Ballpark (now Chase Field) during its first year of operation helped contribute to a 34.1 percent increase in city sales tax revenue in the downtown area. Retail sales through the summer of 1998 in the Phoenix downtown core were up 93.8 percent over the same period in 1997. Restaurants and bars downtown saw an increase in revenue from $40.3 million to $52.4 million over one year. Hotels and motels in the square mile contiguous area demonstrated a 6.6 percent revenue increase, compared with a 4.3 percent increase citywide.

- **San Diego**: In San Diego, the April 2005 opening of Petco Park signaled the first stage of larger infrastructure development surrounding the downtown Gaslight District. The city provided $143.8 million of the $294.1 million hard cost for the stadium itself. The Center City Development Corp. also invested $60 million for land and infrastructure, helping to transform a 26-block section of the East Village, one of the city's most blighted areas. Neighborhood land values there soared from $35 to $200 per square foot; economists project $3 billion in development by 2020. JMI Realty has coordinated the development of $593.3 million worth of hotel, residential, retail, and parking structures, including the $172 million Omni hotel adjacent to the ballpark; nearly 800 residential units in projects valued at $327 million; and a 1,109 vehicle garage. The ballpark village also contains a square-block "park at the park" and a tree-lined boulevard, all served by four stops on the city's trolley line, which makes it transit-oriented. Beyond that, $479.8 million worth of nonancillary development is planned or under way, including a $120 million library. If the San Diego Chargers and city officials have their way, the East Village neighborhood will soon welcome a new downtown stadium for the Chargers and keep that team from heading out of town, perhaps north to Los Angeles.

Daytona Live!

In May 2007, International Speedway Corporation (ISC), the controlling arm of NASCAR, and the Baltimore-based Cordish Company entered into a 50–50 joint venture for a $250 million renovation of ISC's Speedplex Office Park across from Daytona International Speedway. Plans for the Daytona Live! project include a retail, dining, and entertainment area; a movie theatre; a hotel; residential units; and improved and expanded office space.

Other major entertainment infrastructure and urban development projects are planned around the country. Brooklyn's $2.5 billion Barclays Center development, underwritten by Barclays Bank (via a 20-year, $400 million naming rights deal) and featuring an arena for the NBA New Jersey Nets, is anticipated to spur unprecedented growth. The phased 7.7 million-square-foot (700,000 m2) development contemplates four office towers as tall as 60 stories clustered around the arena. It would also contain 4.4 million square feet (400,000 m2) of affordable, moderate-income, and high-end housing in about 4,500 units; 300,000 square feet (28,000 m2) of retail; and 6 acres (2.5 hectares) of recreational park. Much of the 24-acre (10 hectare) complex would be built over unsightly rail yards.

Benefit 2

Facilities and franchises enhance a region's ability to attract new business and create jobs.

Right after the millennium, Detroit unveiled an ambitious new plan to draw millions more visitors to the region and reverse the city's image as an unsafe place. The 10-year strategic plan is increasing visitor spending in the metro Detroit area by an estimated $3 billion per year and, all told, will see the creation of 31,000 new jobs. This strategy was based in large part on the opening of the new 65,000-seat Ford Field and also on the resurgence of the city's NBA Detroit Pistons in their home, the Palace of Auburn Hills.

"Huge differences in team values have been created in local markets depending on whether or not the team is playing in a new, improved building," Leccese says. "Some people have brand new arenas with great leases. Some people have older arenas with not so great leases. In the first era of modern sports, which for all intents and purposes ended at the millennium, many arenas became antiquated within a short period of time, not only in terms of size and amenities but also in terms of revenue-use ability. That creates a value difference.

"A lot of people see the Palace of Auburn Hills as a benchmark of the modern market, largely because owner Bill Davidson and Palace Sports and Entertainment have done such a great job in both marketing that building and servicing their fans," Leccese continues. "You don't see a lot of unhappy Pistons [fans]—that customer is very well taken care of. I think that that created an enormous recognition of the value one can drive for the in-arena experience.

The aforementioned Pittsburgh North Shore development has spurred at least $240 million of construction, added 1.2 million square feet (110,000 m2) of office and retail space, and created 4,200 permanent jobs, according to that city's Sports and Exposition Authority.

The Jacksonville Sports Development Authority and Chamber of Commerce suggests that the Jacksonville Jaguars enrich the local economy by an estimated $131 million a year from visitors buying game tickets, eating at restaurants, and staying at hotels. Additionally, the Jacksonville chamber believes that the new team and facility have been indirectly responsible for the creation of upwards of 50,000 new jobs by virtue of companies expanding or relocating to Jacksonville as a consequence of a successful marketing campaign around Super Bowl XXXIX, which generated more than $300 million in economic impact.

Benefit 3

Facilities, via their events, generate substantial economic impact during construction.

A recent study by Conventions, Sports & Leisure International (CSLI) suggests that the Tennessee Titans pump more than $108 million in direct spending into the central Tennessee economy annually. The study indicates that the team generates $85 million worth of personal earnings, and 2,100 jobs were generated by direct and indirect spending surrounding the Titans after the team was established there and its stadium completed (now called LP Field) in 1998. CSLI also surveyed fans in five NFL markets and determined that the average fan spends $28 before and after a game in addition to money spent inside the stadium on such things as tickets, concessions, and parking.

Other economic impact studies have told similar stories. A 1990s study by the University of Cincinnati Center for Economic Education estimated the total impact of construction of Great American Ball Park for the Cincinnati Reds and Paul Brown Stadium for the Cincinnati Bengals at $1.1 billion. More than $373 million in earnings and 18,641 jobs were generated as a result of the two projects.

An analysis prepared for the Maryland Stadium Authority suggests that an average Baltimore Orioles season generates $117 million in regional gross sales, $44 million in earnings, and more than 1,500 full-time jobs. Total statewide economic impact amounts to $226 million in gross sales, $77 million in earnings, and 2,340 full-time jobs. The study also suggests that 1.6 million out-of-town fans, or 46 percent of all fans, were attracted to Baltimore from outside the area. These visitors spent $46 million in the Baltimore area, representing new economic growth in that region's economy.

And then there's Los Angeles and that city's constant efforts to once again land an NFL team—the latest of which involves developer Ed Roski Jr. and his plans to put an $800 million privately funded NFL stadium and surrounding mixed-use development in the City of Industry, and surrounding Farmers Field, a competing downtown retractable-roof stadium funded by AEG and named by Farmers Insurance for a record $700 million over 20 years.

Because taxpayer subsidies for stadium construction available elsewhere have become a thing of the past in California, efforts to lure an NFL team there must be accompanied by substantial corporate investment. Construction costs for a new privately funded stadium in California could easily be accompanied by as much as $40 million annually in debt service. With no offsetting tax money available, selling suites, seat licenses, naming rights, and other locally generated revenue is essential.

The final step, of course, is luring an NFL team.

"The [NFL] has always been very interested in coming to Southern California," Roski says, "but it always is a stumbling block because we don't have public funds to do these projects. We had to come up with a way to build a facility that really says 'Los Angeles' but at the same time [find ways] we could save money.

"The amount of support that the project has is just fantastic," he continues. "Every day, we get hundreds and hundreds of people's comments on our Web page, lots of encouragement."

A study by the Anderson School of Business at UCLA put the total annual impact of a new football stadium in the Los Angeles region at $63.8 million, with a one-time construction impact exceeding $376.1 million. This includes more than $2.9 million in annual taxes and $1.6 million of taxes from construction. While the study was done specifically with the Coliseum site in mind, the concept has universal applicability to the Los Angeles region—and the impact clearly increases when Super Bowls figure in.

However, Los Angeles, unlike many other professional sports cities, "doesn't want a team because they need to boost a sagging economy," says Alan Rothenberg, chairman of the Los Angeles Sports Council, as quoted in the *Los Angeles Times*. "We think it would be a nice addition to the city." As proof, the *Times* presented data from a study the Sports Council commissioned. In 1993, before the Rams left for St. Louis and

LA Confidential:
The Legacy of Jack Kent Cooke

"Machiavellian kind of birds" was how the late Jack Kent Cooke described the Los Angeles Coliseum Commission in the mid-1960s.

At the time, the erudite former Los Angeles Lakers owner hoped to add an NHL expansion team to the Sports Arena, then home to the Elgin Baylor and Jerry West–era Lakers. But the commission had already granted exclusive hockey rights to the minor league Los Angeles Blades (whose ownership group was also trying to score an NHL team). Cooke threatened to build an arena of his own for the Lakers and a hockey team that would in time become the Kings. "Ha. Ha. Ha," replied one scornful commissioner in response to the threat.

As told by the book *Winnin' Times* many years later, Cooke recalled, "Now, if he'd only laughed, I would have laughed with him, you see? But he actually said, 'Ha. Ha. Ha.' I said, 'In that case, I *am* going to build my own arena.'

"I've had enough of this balderdash," he declared to an aide, and promptly as possible he built the Great Western Forum. For the next three decades, until the downtown Staples Center opened in 1999, the Inglewood arena was home to the Lakers and Kings, eight league championships between them, as well as every major concert attraction of the era. Led Zeppelin sold out six nights in a row at the Forum in 1977, following the three sold-out shows they'd performed in 1975. The Rolling Stones, the Who, U2, and Bruce Springsteen followed suit.

The Sports Arena, meanwhile, fell into disrepair, suitable only for WrestleMania 2 and VII, high school basketball championships, and low-budget conventions.

the Raiders returned to Oakland (in 1994), the region's "teams, events and venues generated $930,000 in revenue, attracted 19.4 million fans, and employed 1,716 full-time workers and 12,857 part-time." In 2005, after the area had lost two NFL teams but gained a NASCAR facility in the California Speedway, soccer's Home Depot Center in Carson, and the multiteam, multiuse Staples Center, Los Angeles region "sports generated $1.7 billion in revenue, attracted 28.6 million fans and employed 3,135 full-time workers and 13,267 part-time workers."

"We do very well without football," added David Fleming, vice chairman of the Los Angeles Chamber of Commerce. "We can do better with football."

Eagles owner Jeffrey Lurie notes that, while important, a rabid fan base "is simply not what drives the economics that allow you to finance a stadium. What you need," he says, "is corporate support. In the past, you'd have franchises getting 100 percent publicly funded stadiums, and relatively low acquisition costs. Now you have franchises selling for more than $800 million. You're talking about how to finance acquisition debt and stadium debt. You've got to be creative and be a successful marketer."

Benefit 4

Major special events can be attracted to a new facility–Super Bowls, All-Star Games, and Final Fours.

As noted in chapter 1, a significant benefit to the public sector from facility development involves the "new money" generated from major special events. NCAA basketball championship Final Fours now generate more than $50 million in direct economic impact per event as they continue to be played in such large-domed facilities as San Antonio, Minneapolis, Atlanta, St. Louis, Indianapolis, and St. Petersburg. Recently, the MLB World Series has averaged nearly $70 to $100 million in economic impact for its respective communities during the 10-odd days that the Series occurs.

Besides Jacksonville, Super Bowls in Houston, New Orleans, Atlanta, Miami, and North Texas each generated more than $250 million to their respective local economies. A study done by Georgia State University suggests that the 2000 Super Bowl held in Atlanta created more than $292 million of economic impact as well as $5.9 million of direct taxes to the public sector. The Sports Management Research Institute study reported that the 1999 Miami Super Bowl created $396 million of economic impact, $239 million of that from direct expenditures.

A study done by Marketing Information Masters, Inc. for the 2002 Super Bowl XXXVII in San Diego reported more than $366.9 million in direct and indirect impact for the City of San Diego. This includes $193.7 million of direct expenditures and more than $173.1 million in indirect revenues generated by vendors, spectators, and visitors to the area.

By 2011, when Super Bowl XLV was held at Cowboys Stadium in Arlington, Texas, preevent economic impact studies conducted by the North Texas host committee pegged the potential windfall from the game and all the events surrounding it at $600 million. (Unfortunately for local businesses, snow and ice throughout Super Bowl week curtailed people's movement and spending, putting actual economic impact numbers at about half to two-thirds of the original estimates.)

Benefit 5

Many community leaders believe that sports teams and facilities provide such intangible benefits as image enhancement and community pride.

A poll conducted after the construction of Heinz Field and PNC Park in Pittsburgh revealed that 73 percent of the respondents believe that the facilities "will revitalize Pittsburgh and improve the quality of life throughout the region." Pittsburgh mayor Tom Murphy said that the facilities had "done more than anything in the last 25 years to shape an image of Pittsburgh in a different way."

In its May 1997 report, the Economic Analysis Corporation provided a perspective on the 1996 Congressional Research Service study on facility development. It concluded the following:

> "Sports teams provide valuable consumption benefits to a local community. These benefits include the ability of local residents to follow and enjoy a home team, an increase in community spirit, and a potential means to draw people to downtown areas. In many respects, local government support of new stadium construction is similar to local government subsidization of other valuable local consumption activities, such as concert halls, zoos, parks, and golf courses. . . . Sports teams are a unique type of consumption good in that they provide substantial benefits to many local citizens who do not attend the team's games. These citizens in the local community receive valuable consumption benefits merely from the presence of a professional sports team. Since these citizens cannot be charged directly by the team for the benefits they receive, there is a stronger economic rationale for local government subsidization of professional sports teams than for most other publicly subsidized consumption activity."

In fact, the Florida Supreme Court described the public benefits of stadium facility construction in *Poe v. Hillsborough County*, the 1997 case validating the bonds to construct Raymond James Stadium in Tampa). The Court explained:

> "The Court finds that the Buccaneers instill civic pride and camaraderie into the community and that the Buccaneer games and other stadium events also serve a commendable public purpose by enhancing the community image on a nationwide basis and providing recreation, entertainment and cultural activities to its citizens."

Sports teams also provide national and international exposure for communities on a regular basis. It is estimated that, on any given fall weekend, almost 120 million viewers watch NFL football on television, nearly half of the U.S. population. Regular-season games are broadcast to 220 countries, and the NFL regular-season broadcasts last year averaged 15.5 million viewers (the postseason broadcast average reached 30.6 million viewers).

Nearly 3 in 10 Americans who follow at least one sport said that pro football is their favorite sport, according to data from Harris Poll conducted in January 2011. As America's favorite spectator sport, affiliation with an NFL team is a tremendous source of community pride.

Sports-Minded Mayor: Michael Bloomberg

Right now, in the greater New York region, an unprecedented convergence in which seven major sports facilities projects are being completed at the same time is occurring. The Prudential Center is complete (1). New stadiums just opened for the Yankees (2) and the Mets (3). The Red Bulls have their new soccer complex (4), and the Giants and Jets have played their inaugural season at New Meadowlands Stadium (5). The Barclays Center is on the drawing board (6), ground has been broken for a renovated Madison Square Garden (7).

One government representative is at the center of this harmonic sports convergence: New York City mayor Michael Bloomberg.

Michael Rubens Bloomberg was born on February 14, 1942, in Brighton, Massachusetts. Wheeling and dealing was in his blood—his grandfather Elick Bloomberg, a Russian Jewish immigrant, was an early real estate agent.

Bloomberg attended Johns Hopkins University, graduating in 1964 with a bachelor of science degree in electrical engineering, and followed that up with a master of business administration degree from Harvard Business School. Before Johns Hopkins, he earned the rank of Eagle Scout in the Boy Scouts of America—an achievement he would oft refer to when he was campaigning for mayor of America's largest city.

He married Susan Brown in 1975; they divorced in 1993. They have two daughters, Georgina, an Olympic-caliber equestrian, and Emma.

As a general partner at Salomon Brothers, Bloomberg headed equity trading, sales, and system development. Yet it was his financial software service company, Bloomberg LLP, launched in 1981, that made Bloomberg's fortune.

Coming in at number 10 on the 2010 *Forbes* list of America's richest people, Bloomberg's net worth is estimated at $18 billion. Besides creating customized financial information terminals that provide real-time financial data to money managers across the globe, Bloomberg LLP established business radio and television networks and acquired *BusinessWeek* magazine in late 2009. Bloomberg chronicled his success in a best-selling 1997 autobiography, *Bloomberg* by Bloomberg.

His fortune, and a post–September 11 voter desire for a steady hand, helped elect Bloomberg mayor of New York on January 1, 2002. From his first days in office, *The New York Times'* editorial board praised his handling of the city's issues from garbage to homelessness and, especially, crime. The media mogul mayor remained focused on getting things done, not getting headlines.

In the sports realm, Bloomberg's handling of New York's unsuccessful 2012 Olympic bid led some to question his leadership, especially the collapse of his four-year quest to build a $2.2 billion NFL stadium development on Manhattan's West Side. Bloomberg prevailed in his subsequent quest to give the New York Mets a new ballpark, and his pro–stadium complex development stance, with its attendant subsidies and tax credits, paved the way for the seven-project regional sports development boon.

As mayor of New York City, Bloomberg has declined to receive a city salary, accepting a token payment of $1.00 annually for his services. He resides not in Gracie Mansion, the official mayor's residence, but at his own home at 17 East 79th Street, on Manhattan's Upper East Side, between Madison and Fifth Avenue. His home address is listed in the White Pages, and he often rides the subway to his office at City Hall.

A dedicated philanthropist, Bloomberg has pledged to give away the vast majority of his fortune and has established a headquarters for his charitable foundation right around the corner from his 79th Street

New York Mets shortstop Jose Reyes, third baseman David Wright, and Mayor Michael Bloomberg during the ground breaking for the New York Mets new stadium (Citi Field) in 2006.

© David Saffran/Icon SMI

townhouse. Bloomberg's personal network has allowed him to engage in substantial philanthropic endeavors, including a donation of $300 million to Johns Hopkins, where he served as the chairman of the board from 1996 to 2002. He currently serves as an ex officio trustee of the Museum of Modern Art.

In 2008, Bloomberg kept political analysts and reporters guessing for months as they tried to guess whether or not he would jump into the presidential race. He didn't—much to the relief of the New York Yankees and Mets, whose sweetheart deals with the city Bloomberg had championed since his first day in office.

Bloomberg was elected to a third term in office on November 3, 2009. A day later, at the new $1 billion Yankee Stadium in the Bronx, the New York Yankees beat the Philadelphia Phillies 7-3 to clinch the 2009 World Series.

The third time Bloomberg steps up to the plate, he hits a grand slam.

Entertainment Infrastructure— A Blueprint for Success

As we move forward with facility development in the new millennium, the following four guidelines are critical for successful public–private facility development for entertainment infrastructure.

First, with public–private facility partnerships coming under increasing public scrutiny, and with local electorates constantly reassessing priorities, communities must be creative, flexible, and consistent in their facility goals and objectives. Cooperation between and among business, political, and civic leadership is an absolute necessity. A consensus-building process necessarily includes the following interests: business, political, private risk capital, city government, county government, state government, developmental entrepreneurs, and technical analysts.

Second, public facilities in the new millennium will be designed as diverse entertainment and activity centers. As such, these facilities should be viewed as critical components of long-term regional infrastructure development, independent of any desire to satisfy the needs of respective major league teams.

Third, new facilities require developing creative public–private financing partnerships where the public sector often provides investment capital to jump-start the project. In these cases, the tangible linkage between specific public revenue sources and realistic, quantifiable return on the public investment is an absolute political and economic necessity.

Finally, these types of entertainment infrastructure facilities—like any visionary public assets—are inherently controversial and complex. Their implementation requires significant (and potentially unprecedented) regional support from respective business, political, and civic leadership. However, once these facilities are developed, they provide substantial economic, tangible, and psychological benefits for the entire region for years to come.

The Sports Industry on Capitol Hill

Whether it is the president hosting a championship team at the White House or Congress tackling issues such as NBA gambling or the NFL's Spygate, sports and politics are unquestionably intertwined.

As the sports business continues to increase, so will government regulation. Consider that in 2009, representatives protested the Bowl Championship Series (BCS) and the validity of sports marketing initiatives exposed when financial services companies sought TARP funds. And it took bankruptcy courts to facilitate the sales of the Chicago Cubs and Phoenix Coyotes (which remains under the ownership of the National Hockey League). However, while people are quick to point out why the government shouldn't get involved with sports, they frequently overlook the positive reasons it should.

Congress essentially eliminated steroids from baseball, and as recently as November 2010, the U.S. House Judiciary Committee held a hearing to reduce long-term brain injuries in the NFL. State and local governments also deserve credit for often putting up cash to help finance stadiums and prevent their home teams from moving. Of course, it doesn't hurt to have advocates such as Bill Bradley, Steve Largent, and Tom Osborne high up in the government.

Nevertheless, one person against this marriage is Washington Capitals owner Ted Leonsis, who says, "I don't think it is a good idea to mix politics and sports, because half of the fans will disagree with what you say or do." Maybe that's why he donates money to both political parties—so no one feels alienated at Caps games.

While most government involvement in sports properties and development is carried out on the local, regional, and state level, it only takes a quick scan of headlines to see that sports industry issues—steroids, concussions, broadcast carriage issues, and gambling—often journey up Capitol Hill. When they do, league lobbyists are there, ready to make the industry's case.

Based on mandatory filings with the U.S. Senate, the top 10 politically active American sports entities—the NFL, MLB, the NBA, the NHL, NASCAR, the PGA TOUR, and football and baseball players associations, plus the NCAA and the BCS—spent $3 million in federal lobbying efforts in 2006. In 2010, in the midst of labor negotiations that led to a lockout, the NFL and NFLPA spent $3.25 million funding lobbyists, far more than any other U.S. sports league.

According to a *SportsBusiness Journal* analysis, Major League Baseball is the only professional sports league to fund full-time representation on Capitol Hill. Records show that baseball remains the most active among pro sports leagues in defending its interests in Washington. The MLBPA spent $620,000 from 2003 to 2005 alone, the majority coming in the spring of 2005, when Jose Canseco, Rafael Palmeiro, and Mark McGwire infamously testified before the House Committee on Oversight and Government Reform investigating steroid use among players.

Another major issue for which baseball, NFL, and NASCAR representatives lobbied on Capitol Hill is television and radio carriage. Baseball went to bat for its Extra Innings package, while the NFL worked with the FCC to compel cable companies to carry their NFL Network channel. NASCAR, meanwhile, was more concerned with satellite radio carriage issues, urging the FCC to allow Sirius and XM satellite radio entities to merge. (These issues are also covered in chapter 2.)

In 2009, the nonprofit Sports Fan Coalition was founded to organize the diverse body of American sports fans and turn them into a unified political voice. Started by David Goodfriend, a deputy staff secretary during the Clinton administration, the group's primary targets include the NFL's television "blackouts" (especially in cities with taxpayer-funded stadiums), the college football BCS, and the escalating cost of attending sporting events. The Coalition has received financial support from companies including Time Warner Cable and Verizon and has been accused of lacking transparency, as Goodfriend is also a former Dish Network executive (although Dish Network has declined to donate to the organization).

The Sports Fan Coalition also intends to be the voice of the fan on Capitol Hill for as long as the NFL lockout goes on.

In addition to labor and media issues, immigration reform, Internet gambling, air space control over stadiums, antitrust, copyright, and tax exemption are also issues of significant interest to the sports industry in Washington. And sometimes, the lobbyists are sport's own—one of the biggest lobbying firms for sports issues on Capitol Hill, commanding close to $1 million in fees from 2003 on sports-related causes alone, is J.C. Watts Companies, run by J.C. Watts Jr., former congressman . . . and football star.

Oklahoma City, MAPS, the Hornets, the Sonics, and the Thunder

The intricate dance that ends with the SuperSonics reincarnated on the Oklahoma prairie—as culturally and climatically removed from Seattle as you can get—as the Oklahoma City Thunder—really began in the summer of 1993.

As was documented in my previous book, *When the Game Is On the Line,* I worked with Oklahoma City leaders, including the city's visionary mayor at the time, Ron Norick, to create Metropolitan Area Projects Strategies (MAPS), a $500 million facility infrastructure package that bundled nine distinct civic projects into one public facility referendum, the largest in U.S. history. Among those projects were construction of the downtown Ford Center, a 19,675-seat arena, and the Bricktown Ballpark, home to the minor league Oklahoma RedHawks.

Because of MAPS, the Ford Center stood ready to receive the homeless NBA Hornets for 36 home games after Hurricane Katrina devastated the New Orleans Arena. Because of Hornets owner George Shinn's commitment to the rebuilding of New Orleans, as soon as his old arena was playable again, he packed his ball bags and took his team back home. The Hornets had handed Oklahoma City $120 million in economic impact in the two years they'd played in the city, but sports fans were left hungering for more.

Enter Clay Bennett, lifetime resident, local benefactor, successful businessman, and ardent sports fan. The athletic center at Casady School, Bennett's high school alma mater, bears his name. It was at Casady that Bennett met Louise Gaylord—daughter of local media mogul Edward Gaylord, owner of the *Daily Oklahoman*, the state's largest newspaper; the Grand Ole Opry in Nashville; and a web of U.S. television and radio stations. When he died in 2003, Edward Gaylord had an estimated net worth of $2 billion. Bennett married his high school sweetheart; they'll soon be celebrating their 30th wedding anniversary.

Bennett got his first taste of sports team ownership when his father-in-law became a part owner of the MLB Texas Rangers. When he accompanied Gaylord to his first Rangers meeting, Bennett later said, it was then he was able to grasp what had always drawn him to professional sports: not just the competition, but the business side of the games. He is also the first to acknowledge that his professional skill set is a good fit for sports team ownership: "A real interest and love for sports; decent professional background in sports and sports administration; a good background in entrepreneurial-related business; [and a] background in civic-related activities."

Gaylord's Rangers shares were ultimately sold to George W. Bush, which in turn led to the family's buying a 30 percent stake in the San Antonio Spurs in 1992; Bennett served on that team's board. The following year, Bennett headed an investor group that purchased the Oklahoma 89ers from Jeffrey Loria, future owner of the Florida Marlins, for $8 million, the most ever paid for a minor league team. The 89ers, for whom Bennett had served as club president, were renamed the RedHawks and began play in the MAPS-produced Bricktown Ballpark in 1998.

After the Hornets left Oklahoma City and the SuperSonics went up for sale, Bennett reprised his role as investor wrangler and spearheaded the ownership group that in 2006 purchased the Sonics from Starbucks chief Howard Schultz for $350 million. Among his co-owners were longtime friends Jeffrey Records, Aubrey McClendon, and Tom Ward—"a frat house of commerce," as one Washington newspaper put it. From the perspective of Sonics fans, Bennett was either the savior of their beloved first professional sports franchise or Public Enemy Number One for the theft of it.

Soon after finalizing the Sonics purchase in October 2006, Bennett set about persuading the city of Seattle that in order for the franchise to remain there, 44-year-old Key Arena, home to the Sonics, needed to be replaced. He gave Seattle officials a year to make that happen, setting a deadline of October 31, 2007. Since failure to get public financing for a new arena was one of the key reasons Schultz decided to sell the team in the first place, the outsider Bennett was obviously up against a concrete wall. The Halloween deadline came and went, and after repeated failed attempts to arrange arbitration to break the Key Arena lease, on November 2, 2007, Bennett announced to NBA Commissioner Stern his intent to relocate the team to Oklahoma City.

Meanwhile on the prairie, anticipating that the Sonics were soon headed their way, Oklahoma City mayor Mick Cornett announced a March 2008 vote on a temporary penny sales tax to pay for $100 million worth of improvements to bring the $90 million Ford Center up to more fan-friendly NBA standards, including better concession areas, new restaurants, VIP clubs, and a practice facility. And just before Christmas 2007, the city passed the largest general obligation bond issue for infrastructure in its history, at $833 million. The 11 discrete issues all passed with between 75 and 89 percent of the vote, also shattering city records. As Kevin Taylor, an Oklahoma City resident, was quoted in the *Daily Oklahoman* on December 22, 2007, "It's going to create jobs and enhance the national perception of Oklahoma City. It's not something we can buy in any other way. This is the kind of public investment I can get behind."

The vote passed. In time for the 2008-2009 season, the Thunder rolled in. So far, the team is in the NBA's top five teams in attendance figures. It features one of the league's favorite players, Kevin Durant. And they're getting better on the hardwood, too—for the first time ever, in May 2010, the Oklahoma City Thunder advanced beyond the first round of the NBA Playoffs, and they repeated the feat in 2011. ∎

6

So You Wanna Own a Sports Team?

► American professional sports leagues have similar ownership structures but incredibly diverse groups of owners, from all walks of life.

► Sports team "ownership" really means buying the rights to operate an ongoing franchise with specific responsibilities under the operating and franchise agreements provided by the respective league.

► Since 1995, the average value of NFL franchises has increased 550 percent, from $160 million to more than $1 billion.

► Almost all sports franchises are owned by a group of owners in a limited partnership.

► The new breed of sports owners is likely to have diversified holdings of teams in multiple sports and locales.

► Corporate ownership is traditionally not as successful as family ownership.

the last billionaire boys' club left standing in America. Its members gather regularly in luxury resorts in Palm Beach, Scottsdale, and Park City—where its members are rumored to import conference room furnishings just to maintain their status quo. It's protected by federal antitrust exemptions. And very few of its employees ever make it into the group.

The club, of course, is the cadre of roughly 150 majority owners of North American pro sports franchises. Increasingly, these owners enter sports after having been highly successful in other businesses. They're nepotistic, overwhelmingly conservative, and highly selective—and if you want to join them, even as a small minority owner, you'd better have at least $10 million. In cash. To purchase a controlling share of a team, you'll need a net worth of at least $250 million.

Each North American pro sport has similar ownership structures but incredibly diverse groups of owners. With very few exceptions, most made their money outside of sports. (See related charts at the end of this chapter.) And a healthy percentage of these sports owners populate *Forbes*' annual list of the 400 wealthiest Americans—entry to this list is now a minimum net worth of $950 million, down from the $1.3 billion threshold of the prerecession boom years.

So why do successful businessmen and wealthy families pour tens of millions of dollars into the fickle world of sports, when in most cases they would see a much quicker return on their investment through more traditional wealth-building channels? Most frequently, it boils down to sheer passion, either a lifetime love for and support of a particular team or devotion to the surrounding community. Sometimes, it's a vanity play—prestige, fame, the spoils of infighting between members of this elite fraternity. You underbid me on that multinational communications giant I wanted to add to my portfolio? Fine. I'll buy the sports team you've been coveting since you were in kindergarten. Right out from under you.

For a large bloc of owners, however, such as Rocky Wirtz in the NHL, Jim Irsay of the NFL Indianapolis Colts, the New York Yankees' Hank and Hal Steinbrenner, and Jim and Jeannie Buss of the Los Angeles Lakers, it was simply a given. They were born into the game.

Colts owner Irsay was all of 12 when he was first immersed in the family football business in 1972 by father Robert, best remembered as the man who spirited the franchise away from Baltimore in the dead of night. "I always say it's like growing up in the circus where you have the sawdust in your blood," Irsay says. "It's just such a part of your identity when you're around it as a kid; you have so much love for the game, so much passion."

"I was named general manager at 24 years old," Irsay continues, "and I was still the youngest general manager when I became owner at 36. I think my dad wanted to save money; he knew he could fit me in at maybe $8,000. God love Papa."

The endgame is where pro sports ownership really pays off. Owning a sports team is an investment that almost never goes down in value, even in a recession, as a year-to-year comparison of *Forbes'* annual franchise valuations shows. Since there's a large pool of would-be owners and only a finite number of teams available for purchase, demand is always high. Therefore the cost of buying a sports team keeps escalating and keeps pro sports relatively immune to downturns. The *Wall Street Journal* even calls it "one of the last asset bubbles in North America."

Normal business metrics simply don't apply to owning a sports team. For starters, very few of them are held by publicly traded companies, so their financials aren't easy to obtain. Successful sports franchises can be priced at five to six times their annual cash flow, far more than the valuation of more traditional businesses in manufacturing or service. Debt-to-value ratios are often completely out of whack. And struggling teams, with lower ticket sales and sponsorship revenues, can sustain annual operating losses exceeding $10 to 15 million without even taking into account debt service and depreciation.

Principal and minority owners looking to sell always recoup their investments upon the sale of the franchise. In the meantime, operating costs are huge, and they're usually accompanied by substantial losses. Only two franchises in the last 15 years in the four major sports have actually sold for less than they were purchased for.

But capital gains upon a sale are profits—and they're taxed a lot more favorably than regular income. Once they're admitted into the sports club, their teams, and newfound opportunities for deal making at the highest levels, usually make these super-rich richer.

The savviest and most strategic owners diversify their sports portfolios by investing in other teams and complementary business channels. They know that the only way to make money in this game is to own not only the team but also the marketing rights, the concession sales, and the facility in which the team plays. But as the cost of land and stadium and arena construction continues to climb, and public money for such facilities dries up, and as the risk of player unrest grows, team owners are shouldering more debt than ever before to keep a state-of-the-art roof over their teams' and fans' heads. Teams are also shelling out more money to players in an effort to remain competitive, despite some form of salary cap in all leagues save Major League Baseball.

How's an owner to keep up? Does the escalating economics mean that we'll see more corporate team ownership than ever before? As the tide continues to rise, is team ownership even remotely sustainable?

The Cost of Ownership
in Today's Sports Market

Owning a professional sports franchise varies league by league and is a complicated structure worthy of entire legal departments of law firms. While average franchises in many sports exceed $1 billion, and Stephen Ross recently paid $1.1 billion for the purchase of the Miami Dolphins from Wayne Huizenga, the purchaser does not completely "buy" a franchise. Rather, he buys the goodwill, uniforms, player contracts, stadium leases (or, in the Dolphins' case, the actual stadium), and other items necessary to run the pro sports team.

As it relates to each of North America's pro sports leagues, however, the purchaser actually buys the rights to operate an ongoing franchise, with specific duties and responsibilities under the operating agreement and franchise agreement provided by the respective league. In this context, sports ownership looks more like owning a McDonald's franchise, where the owner buys the goodwill, the right to market the logo, the rules of the game (in that case, how to operate a McDonald's), and the like.

The leagues are also allowed to restrict certain behavior, such as a team's arranging its own schedule or forging its own television rights agreement. Leagues can even take a franchise back if certain financial considerations are not met—the core of the Phoenix Coyotes ownership dispute that clouded the beginning of the 2009 NHL season.

Team price tags vary from league to league, largely affected by the size of their facilities and television rights contracts. By the end of 2010, according to *Forbes*, 25 sports franchises throughout the world claimed a value of $1 billion or more, led by Manchester United of the English Premier League ($1.84 billion, owned by American Malcolm Glazer, also steward of the NFL Tampa Bay Buccaneers). With the exception of the New York Yankees ($1.6 billion), most of the other teams in this elite group are NFL franchises, from the Dallas Cowboys ($1.8 billion, largely thanks to their new stadium) and Washington Redskins ($1.55 billion, in 2004 the first team to break the billion-dollar ribbon) to the New England Patriots ($1.36 billion; three Lombardi Trophies certainly don't hurt) and Houston Texans ($1.17 billion, holders of the most lucrative stadium naming rights deal in sports before Farmers Field in L.A. came along).

The National Football League is more than just an American juggernaut; estimated as a $7 billion industry, it is the most lucrative sports property in the world. The NFL consists of two conferences, the AFC and the NFC, and functions as a veritable trade association for the 16 franchises and their ownership groups in each of those conferences. While each team functions as its own business, shared revenue is generated through licensing, merchandising, and the league's all-important broadcast rights agreements. The NFL's revenue-sharing footprint is much larger than that of the other pro sports leagues and has long been the keystone of its competitive balance and business success.

No other professional league comes even close to matching the NFL's unprecedented growth. Since 1995, the average value of franchises has increased an astonishing 550 percent, from a paltry $160 million to just over $1 billion.

All told, 16 out of the NFL's 32 franchises are worth $1 billion or more (out of only 25 franchises in the world valued above $1 billion), and the league is collectively worth more than $33 billion. Not bad for a product mostly consumed on leisurely Sunday afternoons in the fall.

Outside of the NFL, NBA teams range in value from the top-ranked New York Knicks ($655 million) to the $258 million Milwaukee Bucks. NHL franchises are valued from $505 million for the Toronto Maple Leafs to $134 million for the league-owned Phoenix Coyotes. And in baseball, outside of the astronomical Yankees, most MLB franchises are valued in the $400 to $500 million range . . . though the lowly Pittsburgh Pirates are worth only $289 million.

Despite these high market values, when scarce sports franchises change hands, the purchase price is often well beyond their estimated worth. The *Wall Street Journal* notes that when hockey's Edmonton Oilers and Nashville Predators last changed hands, the sales prices were about 30 percent above *Forbes'* most recent valuation levels.

2009 Sports Franchise Sales

With the economy limiting the resources of many owners, more professional sports teams were sold in 2009 than in any year since 2004.

Team	League	Buyer	Price
Phoenix Coyotes	NHL	NHL and Ice Edge Holdings	$140 million
New Jersey Nets	NBA	Mikhail Prokhorov	$200 million
Pittsburgh Steelers	NFL	Dan Rooney	$250 million
San Diego Padres	MLB	Jeff Moorad	$500 million
Miami Dolphins	NFL	Stephen Ross	$550 million
Montreal Canadiens	NHL	Molson Family	$575 million
Chicago Cubs	MLB	Thomas Ricketts	$845 million

To Own the Vandals, It Takes a Village

Even though they're always controlled by a lead owner, almost all sports franchises are owned by a group of investors in a limited partnership. Outside of the exceptionally wealthy on the *Forbes* list, few individuals can bankroll a team on their own. Invest with a group and you still get the glory—even if it's only 10 percent of the glory, and your players and fans have no idea who you are.

As sports franchise values continue to climb, the time-honored model of one individual or family in the owner's box is increasingly rare. With some teams, it's downright crowded up there.

As the *Wall Street Journal* notes, the Boston Celtics ownership group has "18 directors on the board, six managing partners, a nine-member executive committee and one 'governor'" (an NBA requirement). The nine executives who partnered in 2003 to buy the NBA Atlanta Hawks and NHL Atlanta Thrashers have seemingly spent more time in court than courtside, squabbling about everything from player transactions and covering losses to NBA All-Star Game tickets. And when Starbucks magnate Howard Schultz owned the Seattle SuperSonics, before the team became the Oklahoma City Thunder under lead owner Clay Bennett, the team had 58 total investors, split into subgroups with their own advisory boards.

In the fall of 2008, the NFL changed its ownership rules so that a team's lead owner can now control as little as 10 percent of the franchise, as long as other family members own an additional 20 percent. The new requirement is half of the previous 20 percent minimum, which had in turn been reduced from 30 percent in 2004. The most recent change could be considered NFL's second "Rooney Rule," as that family's struggle to retain control of the Pittsburgh Steelers helped spur the revision. (More on the Rooney family to come.) The new regulation is perceived by the league to help succession planning within family ownership blocs.

Going to the Sports Franchise Store

Where do you buy one of these hot properties? Sports Authority doesn't sell them. Neither does eBay. But if you head to Boston's Copley Square and turn right at the Marriott, you're getting close.

Working out of a memorabilia-filled office overlooking Copley Square, Game Plan LLC's Bob Caporale and his partner Randy Vataha are the definitive brokers of buying and selling the biggest professional sports franchises in the United States. Fittingly for many of their clients, the business is also a family-run concern—Vataha's son Collin serves as a senior associate for the firm. Randy Vataha relates how the business, which brokers the transactions of billion-dollar sports franchises, came into its own.

"I played in the NFL for seven years," Vataha begins. "While I was playing, I was the player rep for the Patriots during the strikes in 1974-1975. I ultimately ended up on the executive committee in the NFL Players Association and was involved in years of collective bargaining negotiations. When I retired from the NFL, I started a fitness and racquetball club business back here in Boston, but I stayed active with the Players Association."

Vataha sold his fitness clubs in 1983 and became one of the founders of the United States Football League, owning 50 percent of the Boston Breakers, which soon moved to New Orleans because of stadium issues at home. "We played there for a year," Vataha says, "but then Donald Trump came into the league and convinced everybody we'd play one more year in the spring and then would switch to the fall season. We didn't believe he'd ever take on the NFL, so we sold the franchise to a fellow in New Orleans. They never started the fourth season."

Vataha returned to Boston in 1986 and became CEO of Bob Woolf Associates, one of the pioneers of the agent business. The firm negotiated contracts for such superstars as Larry Bird, Doug Flutie, and Joe Montana (as well as CNN's Larry King), but a few years later, as Vataha puts it, "I was getting kind of tired of representing 22-year-old millionaires." A collaboration with sports attorney and colleague Bob Caporale, who had also been a partner in the Boston Breakers and was now working strictly with sports owners, led to the establishment of Game Plan LLC, the first investment firm that handled nothing but sports, in 1994.

"Our first significant deal was the Pittsburgh Penguins, in 1996," Vataha recalls. "We sold 50 percent of that team for then-owner Howard Baldwin. That transaction probably put a franchise value on the team somewhere around $80 to $90 million."

Game Plan also arranged the high-profile sale of the Boston Celtics in 2002 for $360 million to point man Wycliffe Grousbeck, his father, and Bain Capital managing director Stephen Pagliuca, about a year after Boston parking magnate Frank McCourt and his wife, Jamie, hired the company to represent them in a quest to purchase their beloved Boston Red Sox. When the McCourts' bid fell short of the offer put together by current owners John Henry and the New York Times Company, Vataha immediately got the McCourts thinking about the Los Angeles Dodgers, a for-sale franchise losing owner Rupert Murdoch and his News Corp. Sports a reported $40 million a year.

After what Vataha terms a "long, difficult negotiation," the McCourts purchased the Dodgers in February 2004 for $430 million. (Game Plan may very well be in the mix with the McCourts and Dodgers once again if Frank McCourt is unable to hang on to the franchise after a very costly divorce and MLB's seizure of the team in April 2011.)

"There's a lot of history for people who will look at one team and are unsuccessful in buying it but have made the decision for any number of reasons—financially, their intense love of sports—that they want to be a sports team owner, so they will continue to pursue another team," Vataha says. "I think there's a perception that only crazy people buy sports teams, but if you look at the Standard and Poor Index of these types of investments, and especially when you start looking at downside protection, there's just no history of these things going down in value.

"We get two kinds of clients," he continues, "those who hire us for a specific team and those who hire us for the opportunity. The first surfaces when a particular team is for sale—buying the Pittsburgh Penguins or the Chicago Cubs specifically strikes their interest. Then, we get people who have hired us who say, 'Look, I really do want to buy a sports team.' They may have certain parameters, like they may want something on the West Coast, or no parameters at all. They may prefer basketball or hockey but would consider baseball if no basketball or hockey franchises were for sale."

Vataha estimates that Game Plan's client base is a 60–40 split between the two mind-sets.

Although not a Game Plan transaction, the purchase of the Philadelphia Eagles by Jeffrey and Christina Lurie demonstrates that often things work out swimmingly for the first type of clients, even when they don't get to buy their first-choice team. The Luries bought the Philadelphia Eagles from Norman Braman, after Braman bought them from Leonard Tose, and turned a very unpopular franchise into a popular, successful-on-the-field one. Before he purchased the Eagles, Lurie, a native Bostonian, was outbid by Robert Kraft for the New England Patriots and decided that the Eagles were the franchise on which he would focus.

Via the NFL, the Luries became Philadelphia citizens and top sports mavens almost overnight.

"Over time, I've come to believe that most people who are successful enough financially to afford to buy a team are very big fans but are also incredibly competitive," Vataha says. "A lot of them have a history of playing a sport, and there's something inside that would still like to be back in that arena. An NFL owner can go to a game on a Sunday and have as much or more emotion with winning and losing that game than with deals he works on for months and months. There's a level of excitement and adrenalin involved in on-field competition you can't get any place else."

Besides the Dodgers and the Celtics and their other high-profile team transactions, Vataha and Caporale were also the guys who partnered with

The Spoils of Victory: Why Buy a Luxury Box When You Can Buy an Entire Sport?

Once, you bought:

A luxury box. The Astrodome introduced the skybox for elite fans in 1965. A seat went for $7.90, a major extravagance at the time.

Then you upgraded:

A soccer team. Russian billionaire Roman Abramovich has poured more than $100 million into London-based EPL club Chelsea—but a trophy still eludes him.

Now you buy:

A whole sport. A handful of former Microsoft investors purchased all of professional bowling in 2000 for $5 million. A year later, Walt Disney Co. bought the BASS fishing league for a reported $40 million. (Which makes Game Plan's $4.5 billion bid for the NHL seem like a very fair price.)

Source: *WSJ Magazine* Fall 2008

Bain Capital to offer $4.3 billion to buy the entire NHL during the 2004-2005 lockout. "Unfortunately," laments Vataha, "we weren't able to get that deal done." But they've made out okay as franchise values continue to inflate—on a typical franchise sales transaction, Game Plan earns a retainer for hammering out all the legal and financial details, plus 1 to 3.5 percent of the purchase price.

And Then There's the Arisons

One of the best sports ownership stories around is how the Arison family of South Florida went from not owning a sports team to sports team ownership in less than 30 minutes.

I had a personal involvement with the birthing of the Miami Heat and wrote about it in my book *When the Game Is On the Line.* Bringing basketball to Miami was a daunting task, with South Florida having had more than 30 failures in arena financing and franchise establishment. South Florida had representatives with no money, representatives with fake money (a Saudi Arabian sheik who proposed a major sports complex on South Beach), and representatives fronting other people's money.

This was a real process, however, and, as the executive director of the South Florida Sports Authority, I was in charge with working with David Stern and Gary Bettman (then the number three executive in the NBA). Our Miami contingent—theatrical producer Zev Bufman, former

Philadelphia 76er Billy Cunningham, former New Jersey Nets owner Lew Schaffel, and Carnival Cruise Line magnate (and billionaire) Ted Arison—met with David Stern in January 1987. Stern told us in no uncertain terms that the expansion price was not $24 million (as predicted) but more like $32.5 million. Arison left the meeting, telling Stern, "I'll think about it."

Three weeks later, Stern announced that seven cities (down from nine) were now in the running for a franchise. The others were St. Louis, Pittsburgh, Orlando, Charlotte, Kansas City, and Minneapolis. We immediately met with Arison, indicated that we were very close to an NBA deal, and that we needed to close the deal in New York. On April 21, 1987, the day before the planned franchise announcement, the four of us went to Stern's office at NBA headquarters for a final time.

Arison told Stern that he was committed to a South Florida franchise, but the price seemed "too high." Stern stuck to his $32.5 million price, identifying the other six cities that would "pay what it takes." To my surprise, Arison got up from his chair and left the office. He was gone for only 10 minutes, though it seemed like an eternity. When he came back in, he said "David, let me tell you what I just did. I walked down the street and tried to find another entity that sells NBA franchises. But you know what? There isn't anyone else selling NBA franchises." He extended his hand, and David shook it.

The next day was the formal announcement at the Parker Meridien Hotel. Instead of the expected three franchises that were awarded to Orlando, Minneapolis, and Charlotte, Miami became an official member of the National Basketball Association.

Fast forward to November 2009, as Ted Arison's son Micky, now owner of the Heat and prepping the franchise for his own son, Nick (vice president of basketball operations), tells the *Miami Herald* he has no interest in selling the Heat despite sustaining millions of dollars in annual losses. After coming into the NBA in 1988, the franchise found its stride under the watch of former superstar Los Angeles Laker coach Pat Riley in 1995, became perennial playoff contenders, and won the NBA Championship in 2006. In the summer of 2010 came LeBron James and Chris Bosh, who, combined with Dwyane Wade, once again make the Heat NBA Playoff contenders. The franchise, however, still has yet to turn a profit.

"It's about trying to lose less money," Arison says. "We've never made money here. We're trying to create a climate of fiscal discipline like every other business." Arison also estimated that his primary business, Carnival Cruise Lines, had withstood a $200 million "reduction in operating costs" during the recession—a setback that contributed to the Heat's poor bottom line.

Want in the Club?
Better Not Speak Cuban

"I am constantly amazed that mega-successful billionaire suits lose all business acumen when they buy a professional sports team— with the exception of Mark Cuban."

—Letter to the sports editor in the *Dallas Morning News*

Mark Cuban, the bull-in-a-china-shop owner of the Dallas Mavericks, comes from a technology environment in which out-of-the-box thinking is prized and change is necessary, not dangerous, as it's often been viewed by the world of sports owners. In Cuban's world, the status quo is a business plan for disaster. After all, it wasn't old thinking that inspired the son of an auto upholsterer to create radio feeds of sports broadcasts to the Internet, a simple and inspired idea that earned him more than a billion dollars when he sold his firm to Yahoo! Or that prompted him to push HDNet, the first exclusively high-definition TV channel. Or that landed him on *Dancing With the Stars*.

With Cuban's help, the Mavericks' American Airlines Arena is now state of the art in corporate and sports branding. You can buy airline tickets there, and you can tour the history of the airline. You can also watch Cuban's antics as he blasts referees and otherwise hauls himself before the NBA authorities on charges of Conduct Unbecoming an Owner Who After All Is Supposed to Dress in Something More Formal Than a Black T-Shirt and Must Refrain From Issuing Four-Letter Insults and Other Trash Talk.

Even if you're as well off as Cuban, it smarts to get $1.7 million in fines from the league for infractions ranging from scathing blog entries to leaping onto the court to help break up a fight between players. Still, Cuban prides himself on his rich lines. He was fined half a million for saying of an NBA referee, "I wouldn't hire him to manage a Dairy Queen," and once said of NBA commissioner David Stern, in the middle of a tussle with basketball's front office, "I won't get him in a headlock, but maybe I'll get some tweezers and yank out those nose hairs of his. You know, when you sit next to him, you definitely know which way the wind is blowing."

Despite his antics, Cuban is no sports-owner skinflint. While his free spending earned him the moniker Easy Mark, it's all done with a business purpose. "Everything I do is about taking away excuses," he says. "A player can't get enough sleep because he has a foam pillow? We upgrade the hotel." Even a highly publicized—and ridiculed—luxury locker room towel purchase was a carefully calculated guerilla marketing tactic, a regular reminder for the opposing players who swiped the towels that the Mavericks organization was a nice place to play.

Cuban also actively listens to his fans—he broadcasts his personal e-mail address on the American Airlines Arena JumboTron, answering the bulk of his e-mails himself. "It's been a blast, even with all the stuff with the league," he told the *Dallas Morning News* about his tenure as owner since purchasing the team on January 4, 2000.

Neither business acumen nor attitude, however, benefitted Cuban in his highly publicized quest for Major League Baseball's Chicago Cubs. Under commissioner Bud Selig's reign, the status quo was working out just fine, thank you—MLB revenues jumped 400 percent under Selig, from $1.66 billion when he became acting commissioner in 1992 to $6.5 billion in 2010. Selig seemed much more comfortable with longtime acquaintances and friends in owners' boxes, such as Boston Red Sox owner John Henry and Madison Dearborn Partners CEO John A. Canning Jr., considered the early front-runner to own the Cubs because of his close ties with Selig.

For a while, it looked as if Cuban might have a shot at owning his dream team. "I'm gonna pull out all the stops," he said during a radio interview in the summer of 2008. The Cubs seller, Tribune Company CEO Sam Zell, swiftly eliminated Canning from contention, and Cuban and five other prospective owners made it into the second round. Cuban's reported bid of $1.3 billion for the team, Wrigley Field, and a 25 percent share of Comcast SportsNet was apparently the top offer, but selecting the highest bid certainly wasn't a requirement for the notoriously fickle MLB ownership group. (They had accepted Henry's $700 million bid for the Red Sox, for example, even though the top price offered was $790 million.)

Cuban tried unsuccessfully to lure three deep-pocketed Chicago executives into partnering with him to bolster his bid—Selig had long expressed a preference for local ownership of MLB teams. But none would do business with him, and a source at the MLB owners meetings in the middle of the sales process told the *Chicago Sun-Times* Cuban had "zero chance" at getting the mandatory 75 percent of stodgy MLB owners to vote for him, even if Zell ended up choosing his bid.

The source was correct—Chicago businessman Tom Ricketts and his family got the nod. Now, the sports world is waiting to see if Cuban will once again throw his black hat into the MLB ring and try to buy the Los Angeles Dodgers if they are put up for sale.

Cuban is certainly not alone among high-profile types attempting to buy professional sports franchises. Late summer 2009, controversial radio personality Rush Limbaugh caused an uproar when he announced that he was joining an NFL ownership group, led by MLS Real Salt Lake owner Dave Checketts, attempting to buy the St. Louis Rams. Limbaugh, who had previously alienated tens of thousands of NFL fans when he made disparaging comments about Philadelphia Eagles quarterback Donovan McNabb, was denounced by NFL commissioner Goodell; almost immediately thereafter, Checketts' group severed ties with him. Said Checketts, "It has become clear that [Limbaugh's] involvement in our group has become a complication and a distraction. . . . As such, we have decided to move forward without him."

Echoing the Cuban situation, NFL sources were also cited as saying that Limbaugh's role meant the bid had zero chance of being approved by a necessary three-quarters majority of the league's 32 owners. Like baseball, the NFL contingent is extremely wary of controversial figures that might scare off fans. Or sponsors.

While most owners remained silent on the topic, Colts owner Jim Irsay said, "Sometimes privileges in life do get lost. . . . I've met Rush only once, and he seemed like a nice guy. But when you see the comments that are out there, I would not be comfortable." Miami Dolphins wide receiver Greg Camarillo summed it up well. "The NFL is obviously a diverse workplace," he said, "and you've got to be pretty sensitive to everybody's needs. You can't alienate any group."

Five Most Recent NBA Sales

When Mikhail Prokhorov bought the New Jersey Nets in September 2009, he became the first non–North American to own an NBA team. Here are the prices for the last five NBA teams sold:

Golden State Warriors (2010)	Joe Lacob/Peter Guber, $450 million
New Jersey Nets (2009)	Mikhail Prokhorov, $200 million (80 percent of team, 45 percent of new arena)
Seattle Supersonics (2006)	Clay Bennett, $350 million
Cleveland Cavaliers (2005)	Dan Gilbert, $375 million
Phoenix Suns (2004)	Robert Sarver, $401 million

As Old School as You Get–
The Rooney Family of Pittsburgh

As sportscaster Howard Cosell said on the occasion of the Pittsburgh Steelers' 50th anniversary, "When you play Pittsburgh, you play the entire city." That notion is in no small part a reflection of the philosophy of Art and Dan Rooney and their boisterous extended family. For half a century, the Rooneys have provided a template for sports ownership and are the model upon which hundreds of other sports team owners have bought into the game.

Even though the Steelers failed to defeat the Green Bay Packers in Super Bowl XLV (North Texas, February 6, 2011), the team won Super Bowl XLIII, the franchise's sixth Super Bowl victory out of eight appearances there—the most of any NFL team ever. The victory came despite a season in which chairman Dan Rooney and president Art Rooney II sought to consolidate ownership of the franchise in a protracted family feud that was mostly carried out in the media. The team rose to the challenge Dan Rooney gave them—"Don't worry about this; we will"—according to the Associated Press' Alan Robinson, who wrote under the header, "Amid Ownership Talks, Rooney Stabilized Team."

Says Steelers defensive end Brett Keisel: "They did a wonderful job of not letting it become a distraction, because it was a big deal." Safety Troy Polamalu added that Dan Rooney told the team there was a "situation going on with the ownership right now but . . . if we win, it will take care of everything." Said Polamalu in the *Pittsburgh Post-Gazette*: "And you know, everything's happened the way he predicted."

"They've run a model franchise," says NFL commissioner Roger Goodell. "I think everyone in Pittsburgh recognizes how proud they are of the Steelers. We in the NFL recognize how fortunate we've been to have Dan Rooney's leadership, and now Art's leadership."

In 1933, 32-year-old Art Rooney went to the historic Saratoga Race Course in Saratoga Springs, New York, and placed a parlay bet on a series of long-shot winners. No one could have predicted that the result of that bet would produce one of the most storied and, in recent years, most intriguing ownerships of a franchise in NFL history.

The NFL had always wanted a team in Pittsburgh. So, when the league was able to take advantage of the state of Pennsylvania's relaxing its "blue laws," which prohibited sporting events from taking place on Sunday, Rooney pounced on the opportunity. He took his Saratoga winnings and paid the required $2,500 NFL franchise entrance fee. Although the team was named the Pittsburgh Pirates until 1940 (a tribute to the baseball team that Rooney loved dearly), the Steelers were born.

Following that 1940 season, disenchanted with his team's losing ways, Rooney sold the Steelers to Lex Thompson for $160,000, 64 times the amount he paid for the team eight years prior. With the money he made in the deal, Rooney bought half of the Philadelphia Eagles from good friend, and future NFL commissioner, Bert Bell. Rooney's plan was to turn the Philadelphia Eagles into the Pennsylvania Keystoners, playing half of their games in Philly and the other half in Pittsburgh. However, when team owners struck down that deal, Rooney and Thompson orchestrated one of the most bizarre transactions in NFL history. Since each man wanted to keep his own players and coaching staff, they agreed to trade the city of Philadelphia for the City of Pittsburgh. The tale is particularly noteworthy because it denotes the only time that someone other than a Rooney owned the Steelers.

"I'm nutty when I watch Steelers games. I like to be by myself because I scream and yell," says Pat Rooney Jr., an active third-generation member in the large Rooney clan, who grew up in Philadelphia while his father ran the family's harness track there; Pat Jr. now runs the Palm Beach Kennel Club racetrack operation in South Florida. "I was eight years old when I witnessed the Immaculate Reception. I remember watching it on a black and white TV up in our attic in one of my other sibling's rooms. I had the

NFL Commissioner Roger Goodell hands the Vince Lombardi Trophy to Dan and Art Rooney after Super Bowl XLIII.

© AP Photo/Ben Liebenberg

door closed and I was watching that game by myself up there. I remember crying my eyes out 'cause I thought the Steelers were going to lose and you know, they ended up winning. That was my earliest sports memory."

"Fall, that was football season," he continues. "You put away the golf clubs, you didn't do much on Sundays in the fall. You went to church and came home and if the game wasn't on TV, you tried to get it on the radio. I remember driving around with my dad in Philadelphia, trying to get whatever station in Pittsburgh that the games would be on. There was terrible reception if you could get it at all, but we'd find ourselves sitting in some parking lot somewhere trying to listen to Steelers' games 500 miles away. You ended up doing ridiculous stuff like that to, you know, try to get a score.

"Even though we weren't directly involved in running the team, the entire family was very close. We used to go back to Pittsburgh for Thanksgiving as a whole family while my grandmother and grandfather were alive. There were something like 35 grandkids running around every Thanksgiving. I mean, it was a nuthouse."

Alongside of never losing site of the importance of family, the Rooneys also set out to be among the most fan-friendly, employee-centric owners in pro sports. They're also known as being among the most media-friendly owners in the NFL.

"I remember in the design of Heinz Field in Pittsburgh, we were used to a separation of the media from the players," says architect Dennis Wellner, lead designer of the Steelers' riverfront stadium completed in 2005. "In Pittsburgh, Dan and Art Rooney would say, 'Let's go have lunch.' So we'd walk to their team training room and they would have lunch; the players would be there as would all the media, and you know, Dan Rooney was no different from another person who was having lunch at the team's training table, and the media could say anything or not say anything. It just didn't matter. They were a part of the fabric of the organization. It was just expected. It's the way in which they felt about the media in Pittsburgh."

When Art, the patriarch of the Rooney family, passed away in 1988, his share of the team was divided five ways, with 16 percent of the Steelers going to each of his sons. Dan Rooney was named chairman of the franchise. Still, Art, as detailed in a letter he wrote to his children a year before his death, remained concerned that an ownership squabble would inevitably ensue.

NFL guidelines at the time required that a single person own at least 30 percent of a franchise to be considered the principal owner, so the league was already making an exception for the Rooneys, who individually all fell short of that minimum.

In addition to owning the Steelers, the Rooneys also owned racetracks in New York and Florida that had poker rooms and had recently added video gaming, a move that was inconsistent with the league's gambling policy.

In July 2008, the *Wall Street Journal* reported that the team, which had been with the Rooney family for 75 years, was quietly being shopped to potential buyers, amid a division among the five Rooney brothers and pressure from the league in regard to the Rooneys' involvement with gambling. Dan Rooney and his son, Steelers president Art Rooney II, wanted to consolidate control of the team by buying out Dan's brothers' shares, because some of the brothers wanted to focus their business on the racetracks rather than the Steelers. In the event that the brothers sold their shares to Dan, former commissioner Paul Tagliabue was tapped "to serve as a league representative in discussions with the family in order to reach an agreement on the separation of the gambling interests and on a restructuring of ownership."

Dan, hoping to get a family discount from his brothers, offered a deal that was far below the team's believed market value. Because of their concerns with his offer, the brothers enlisted the help of Goldman Sachs to price the franchise.

At the same time, complicating Dan Rooney's plight, a prospective bidder emerged in Stanley Druckenmiller, the billionaire chairman of Pittsburgh's Duquesne Capital Management. Druckenmiller's offer was for four of the Rooneys' five shares—64 percent—for $550 million. From July to September 2008, it appeared as if Druckenmiller would eventually submit a winning bid and take over the franchise. He even expressed interest in keeping Dan on as managing owner and Art II as team president.

But, when the four Rooney brothers told Druckenmiller that they would not be accepting his offer, he announced that he was removing himself from the process and that the Rooney family needed more time to consider their options about the future of the franchise.

From the *Wall Street Journal* article that broke the story back in July 2008: "The Rooney family's divisions over the future of the Steelers are a classic example of the challenge facing second- and third-generation owners of a family business. Looming estate taxes and diverging interests among the children and grandchildren of the founder raise pressure for a sale, bringing emotional family issues into play."

During the negotiations, Pat Jr. and his father helped keep the Steelers in the family by distancing themselves from the team, since the family's gambling holdings had become an increasingly hot-button issue with the NFL.

"We tried to divest the family owners of the football team from those entities," Rooney says, "and that's when my dad and my Uncle Tim and all the other brothers started giving their stock to the next-generation entities, to try to further isolate themselves from the gambling issues."

The saga was finally resolved in December 2008, when Dan Rooney brought in new investors, two of his brothers sold their full shares of the team, and the other two brothers each sold half of their stakes. Dan ended up with 20 percent of the team and Art II 10 percent, equaling the 30 percent necessary to be considered the principal owner (in this case, the

NFL treats father and son as one owner). To settle the deal, Dan and Art II borrowed about $250 million to buy out the shares. The debt exceeded NFL limits and required a waiver from the league, but NFL commissioner Roger Goodell "gave his blessing to the proposal."

"As I talked to my cousins," Pat Rooney Jr. says, "their concerns were 'Is this a fair deal for everybody?' and 'Is there a way to keep a Rooney involved?' My only issue is the debt that my uncle and my cousin are taking on. We traditionally don't operate any of our businesses with a tremendous amount of debt, and it's a lot. But that's how they want to do this thing."

Dan Rooney brought a diplomatic intelligence to the NFL throughout his entire tenure as steward of the Pittsburgh Steelers, so it certainly made sense when President Obama appointed him to be U.S. Ambassador to Ireland, where he'd also been known for decades of philanthropic work, in 2009. The visionary behind the NFL's so-called Rooney Rule, which mandates each team interview at least one minority candidate when it has a head coach opening, Rooney cherishes his relationship with the president—even though he's been a Republican his entire life.

He had become friendly with Obama, endorsed him, and stumped state to state for him in the presidential campaign, breaking with a long tradition of sports owners maintaining political neutrality, at least publicly, to avoid alienating part of their fan base.

The presidential appointment caused the devoted fan to miss his first regular-season Steelers game in nearly 57 years and to keep him thousands of miles away from NFL proceedings he'd chaired for decades. In fact, conspiracy theorists among sports industry observers speculate

Once a Visitor, Now the Boss

Before he died a decade later, George Steinbrenner, shipping scion who bought the New York Yankees in 1973, reminisced with *New York Times* reporter Richard Sandomir in 2000:

"The first time I came to Yankee Stadium, I drove down from college, and I had a seat two rows from the top. It was overwhelming. You know, Joe D. It was 1952. I went with another friend. We bought the tickets from some guy outside the stadium who said they were good seats. They were way behind home plate. You could see, but there were posts. I remember that. The poor hot dog and beer and Coke guy never came up there. Everything was a climb. . . .

"I bought a Yankee hat and when I got back to school, I remember having to cut it open because it was too small, and a lady at school had to put a patch in it to make it look like it was the regular size. . . .

"I never came to Yankee Stadium again until I bought the team. I saw them play in Cleveland. I had always wanted to go to Yankee Stadium. You heard so damned much about it."

that the timing of the appointment was a deliberate move on the part of other NFL owners to get Rooney out of the picture in order to change the rules on revenue sharing before collective bargaining sessions with the NFLPA began in earnest.

Living la Vida Rossa— Steve Ross and the Glitzing of the Miami Dolphins

With the possible exception of Dr. Jerry Buss with the L.A. Lakers and baseball's legendary Bill Veeck, has any sports owner ever had as much fun as the Miami Dolphins' Stephen M. Ross? No owner of a major pro sports franchise has ever made a more concerted effort to blend big-time sports with big-time pop entertainment, complete with A-list celebrities crowding the owner's suite as limited partners and Jimmy Buffet as the Dolphins' veritable house band.

And this from a low-key man who made his money in real estate, generally perceived as a sexy endeavor only if your last name is Trump.

In his weekday world, Steve Ross is chairman, chief executive officer, and founder of Related Companies, the real estate giant he formed in 1972. Today, Related has developed more than $20 billion in properties and controls a diverse $15 billion portfolio of more than 315 mixed-use residential, commercial, and retail properties across the United States, including the flagship Time Warner Center in midtown Manhattan and an under-construction $3 billion mixed-used development in downtown Los Angeles, designed by Frank Gehry. Last year, *Forbes* ranked Ross as its 78th richest American.

Ross grew up far from the glitz of Manhattan in a modest middle-class home in Detroit and relocated to Miami at the age of 15. He played left tackle at Miami Beach High School and fondly recalls being at the Orange Bowl in 1972, when the hometown Dolphins' perfect season led to a Super Bowl victory and a record that still stands today.

After completing degrees from Michigan (where the business school now bears his name) and Wayne State's law school, Ross practiced tax law briefly in Detroit before moving to New York, where he specialized in real estate and corporate finance at two investment banking firms before founding Related.

Ross at first lived on a $10,000 loan from his mother to get by, and it's likely no coincidence that the company first focused on building and financing affordable housing. And it was in the up-and-down economics of New York real estate that he first began to appreciate the power of cycle and momentum that drives professional sports franchises like no other business.

His Related Group of Florida, developed with partner Jorge Perez, specializes in the construction of high-rise condos at all price levels; time spent in Florida expanding that company led to Ross' purchasing 50 percent of the struggling Miami Dolphins from H. Wayne Huizenga in August 2008. Ross increased his ownership share to 95 percent in January 2009, for a total of 95 percent and a $1.1 billion price tag, the highest price paid for a sports franchise to date—and one that posted a dismal 1-15 record in 2007, sending season ticket sales plummeting from 61,000 to 46,000 in 2008. (Huizenga kept 5 percent of the franchise for which he had originally paid $138 million in 1994.)

When Ross was asked if he thought he had made a sound investment in purchasing the 1-15 team, he replied "Let's put it this way. I wouldn't call it a shrewd investment. I didn't steal it, certainly. Many people would think I overpaid when you look back with 20–20 hindsight, especially in today's market. I'm having more fun in doing something I've always wanted to do, in an environment like this. I don't think a lot of people can say that. I feel really lucky to own the Miami Dolphins. I think there is a lot of opportunity there."

Immediately after he finalized the deal, Ross committed to retooling Dolphin Stadium into a technological showplace and marquee lifestyle destination that invites a level of fan involvement never seen before. A partnership with Cisco Systems is placing their signature StadiumVision interactive HDTV system throughout the facility, increasing sponsorship revenue opportunities via individually controlled video boards, tailored concession offerings, and customized programming in luxury suites. And the Dolphins have worked with Kangaroo TV to introduce Dolphins Mobile Vision, a wireless handheld device allowing on-demand content, customized replays, and fantasy team alerts that's included along with suite leases and club-level season tickets. Ross also took on musician Jimmy Buffett as a business partner; Buffett composed a new anthem for the team based on concert favorite "Fins" and has played gigs at the Fin Zone bar in the stadium, which was temporarily renamed Land Shark Stadium in 2009 to help promote Buffett's Land Shark Lager beer.

But the highest profile part of Ross' strategy with the franchise is bringing in celebrity partners who both reflect the diversity of South Florida and add glitz and glamour to the game-day experience. For starters, Ross had rappers T-Pain and Pitbull rework the Dolphins' fight song. Internationally famed Miami collage artist Romero Britto created new designs for the stadium's exterior gateways. And throughout the 2009 NFL season, Ross turned his owner's suite at Sun Life Stadium into his own Copacabana, coaxing his new celebrity limited partners and their VIP guests into the stadium on a Dolphins "Orange Carpet."

Signed on as team limited partners are Emilio and Gloria Estefan, Marc Anthony (and his wife Jennifer Lopez), the Black Eyed Peas' Fergie, and local girls and international tennis stars Venus and Serena Williams. Together, these diverse celebrities help expand the team's appeal to Latin and African American fans across the globe; attract affluent new customers in a market that has a broad mix of white, Hispanic, and African American residents; and build a sense of pride and ownership among South Florida's Latin-infused communities.

"I wanted to show that the Miami Dolphins were about all of South Florida," Ross says. "It's one of the great diverse areas of our country, very unique. And I wanted everyone to be able to identify with the ownership of the Miami Dolphins. If you look at the celebrity owners, as they have been labeled, you'll feel that. And what they're doing, their excitement in owning part of an NFL team and being actively engaged in the community, seeing it to date, I think it's great."

"It's a great thing for our sport because we know there's so much interest," NFL commissioner Roger Goodell told the *Fort Lauderdale Sun-Sentinel* during an early-season visit to Sun Life Stadium. "It's brought a tremendous energy to the Dolphins and the NFL. Everybody does it their own way. This is obviously unique, and he's done this so that the community feels good about the Dolphins and it reflects the community here."

Knowing that a team's on-field performance means a lot more to its fans than its celebrity owners and A-list entertainment attractions when the final whistle is blown, Ross has also devoted a credible amount of attention to the football side of the business. "All the frills the area has to offer won't fill the stands if the product on the field is sub-par," Ross told the *Miami Herald*. "Everything we're talking about is on the margins, from the fans' standpoint. They really love the Miami Dolphins, but it's all about winning football games."

Owner Power

While the Rooneys depict the wise-old-guard model of sports franchise ownership, their story contrasts heavily with most of the sports owners in the industry today. The new breed of sports owner is much more likely to have diversified team ownership, including international holdings, such as E. Stanley Kroenke (St. Louis Rams, Denver Nuggets, Colorado Avalanche, Arsenal, Dick's Sporting Goods), Tom Hicks (Dallas Stars, Mesquite Championship Rodeo, Liverpool FC), and Malcolm Glazer (Tampa Bay Buccaneers, Manchester United).

Owners also embrace a herd mentality—they yield to key owners as opinion leaders, such as the Dallas Cowboys' Jerry Jones in the NFL and, formerly, Jerry Colangelo in the NBA and MLB. (Making Colangelo's case particularly unique, he helped found three different teams with three different ownership groups.)

Jones is consistently listed among the top 10 of *SportsBusiness Journal*'s annual compilation of the 50 most influential people in sports business. In 2009, as the top-ranked sports owner, he came in at 9, behind MLB commissioner Bud Selig (7) and FOX Sports honcho David Hill, tied at 8. Other owners on the list included the Patriots' Robert Kraft (13); Yankees scion Hal Steinbrenner (24); Red Sox owner John Henry (30); the Broncos' Pat Bowlen (35); NASCAR owner Rick Hendrick (36); and Boston Bruins owner and concession magnate Jeremy Jacobs (41). A common trait among these owner leaders? They largely refuse to stay in the background shelling out cash, instead taking an active role atop franchise management.

And as we've seen in chapters 4 and 5, owners seek to find some perceived edge over their peers in a given sport via a cutting-edge facility that features lucrative corporate entertainment suites, smart cards, and HDTV, in which they can book major entertainment acts and conventions.

Today's owners, finally, seek to control secondary market ticket sales through partnerships with companies such as Ticketmaster and Stub-Hub—an unheard-of notion when Art Rooney bought the Steelers in 1933.

Media as Professional Sports Owners

Can news entities remain impartial if they own a pro sports franchise? These five companies have faced the challenge:

5. **Walt Disney Company:** Disney was the original founder of the Mighty Ducks of Anaheim in 1993 and owned the Los Angeles Angels from 1999 to 2003. Other Disney assets include ABC and ESPN.

4. **Turner (Ted Turner):** In 1976, Turner bought the Atlanta Braves partially to provide programming for WTBS, the precursor to cable channel TBS. Time Warner inherited the Braves after buying TBS in 1996 and sold the team to Liberty Media in 2007.

3. **Tribune Co.:** With the sale to Tom Ricketts, Tribune Co.'s 28-year stewardship of the Cubs came to an end. The multimedia corporation also owns the WGN TV network and a handful of nationally recognized newspapers.

2. *New York Times:* The New York Times Co. holds a 17.5 percent stake in New England Sports Ventures, the company John Henry founded when he bought the Boston Red Sox. It doesn't help that the *Times'* home market is full of Yankees fans.

1. **News Corp. (Rupert Murdoch):** Murdoch's News Corp. bought the Los Angeles Dodgers in 1998 and held the team through 2004. Through its subsidiary, the FOX network, News Corp. also held broadcast rights to Major League Baseball.

League Structures and Committees

"It's all my fault. How did I allow all those years of losing? There's a statement, 'Some people know how to win.' I don't know how to win. I know how to win at everything else, but not at sports. But I'm prepared to do whatever is necessary to win."

–Los Angeles Clippers owner and billionaire real estate tycoon
Donald Sterling, as quoted in the middle of yet another Clippers losing season

Today's sports owners are extremely collaborative off the field, making key decisions as a group. The biggest issues decided by the owners, of course, are voted on at semiannual owners meetings, often held at the most luxurious resorts in the country.

By all accounts from insiders who have attended these meetings, especially in the NFL, seniority and a strict hierarchy rules, with the owners of the oldest (Giants, Steelers) and most powerful franchises (Cowboys, Broncos) getting their issues heard first, with voting following the same pattern. The NFL, in fact, is rumored to ship conference room furniture from its Park Avenue headquarters to whatever resort at which the meetings are being held so that the owners can sit in exactly the same places at the same table that they always do, ensuring a sense of familiarity, continuity, and clout.

In general, the bigger the media market, the higher the team's profile and the more power an owner carries in leagues largely driven by television revenues.

Outside of the semiannual owners meetings, chaired by commissioner Roger Goodell and attended by top NFL executives and general managers, key league decisions are made in highly structured and long-standing committees; chairing the most influential of these subgroups often causes an owner's clout to rise considerably. The NFL is split into four major committees, with competition—establishing rules that govern play—being the foremost. The competition committee comprises a group of eight members chosen from the body of the NFL and includes coaches and team executives along with owners; the Cowboys' Stephen Jones, son of Jerry, is the newest member of that committee, a signal of his rising power within the league.

The other three primary NFL committees are broadcast, finance, and labor, dealing respectively with the league's revenue agreements with broadcast partners, financial outlays, and its players and their union.

Patriots owner Robert Kraft chairs the broadcast committee and is only one of two owners (the Carolina Panthers' Jerry Richardson is the other) serving on a total of three committees; small wonder he consistently makes the top 20 of the industry's annual power rankings. Broncos owner Pat Bowlen, cochairman of the labor committee, will see his considerable share of the spotlight grow even bigger throughout 2011, as negotiations with the NFLPA over a new collective bargaining agreement intensify.

Not having a presence on any of the NFL's four major committees, of course, signals a lack of influence on the league's business issues—it's telling that Arizona Cardinals owner Bill Bidwill, the Bears' Mike McCaskey, and the 49ers' Denise DeBartolo York don't hold any of these seats of power.

Outside of the NFL, the other major pro sports leagues operate in similar structures. Major League Baseball is headlined by its executive council, which maintains the final word on key league decisions. MLB commissioner Bud Selig, former owner of the Milwaukee Brewers, sat atop the executive council as its chairman in 1992. He became the de facto baseball commissioner when former commissioner Fay Vincent resigned; Selig was named outright commissioner in 1998. Other key MLB committees govern player relations, labor policy and long-range labor planning, relocation, equal opportunity, legislative issues, and the all-important schedule.

MLB boards whose members have rising power and clout oversee the Major League Baseball Advanced Media (the league's online operation) and MLB Network properties, key new media components and revenue generators as the league moves forward.

The NBA and NHL are structured similarly. At the top of the pyramid is each league's board of governors, made up of one high-level appointee from each team. Among the NBA's subcommittees are rules, relocation, labor relations, finance, and negotiating. The NHL gets more specific, fronting committees covering such issues as performance-enhancing substances and injury analysis.

"The current mix of ownership in pro sports is a good mix," Game Plan's Randy Vataha says. "Just like in any business, the people who have been around a long time get established in their ways; they're not as interested in changing things necessarily, but some of the things they don't want to change are good things. When Jerry Jones came into the NFL, he was one of the first guys that refocused everybody's attention back on revenues—'Yes, the NFL's successful, but why aren't we getting more per sponsorships? Why aren't we driving premium ticket and suite sales?' New groups that come in frequently apply newer technologies because some owners come from those backgrounds, a Paul Allen or Mark Cuban. Then Dan Snyder, who's a marketing guy, comes in and he starts focusing on how to better market the league. Then you have the Rooneys, who have been around forever. They have really good football operations experience, and they've dealt with the community over the years in a way that's just fabulous; they're synonymous with the game."

Corporate Ownership of Professional Sports Teams—Does it Work?

Outside of most teams' standard limited partnership structures, turning them into de facto corporations, there have been only a handful of corporate owners of sports teams in American history. A few have more than succeeded, such as Philadelphia-based Comcast-Spectacor, which counts the Philadelphia 76ers and Flyers among assets that make it the most vertically integrated organization in sports (divisions include venue management giant Global Spectrum, food service provider Ovation, New Era ticketing, and Front Row Marketing). The purview of team ownership—not taking the teams and their fans for granted—says Comcast-Spectacor CEO Peter Luukko, has raised the level of service provided by all of the company's properties. "We keep the game experience up at a high level," Luukko says.

But most corporate sports owners have been dismal failures—such as News Corp.'s/FOX's disastrous tenure as owner of the Los Angeles Dodgers.

"I think that it is clear major professional sports teams have been better operated by individual interests than by corporate interests," Vataha reasons. "The problem with corporate ownership is that the teams get put in with all the other corporate properties, and they're constantly making trade-offs between those properties. For example, a big company might be much more conscious of their overall corporate brand—in the case of FOX, how's the Dodgers' performance affecting some of our other properties?

"Frank McCourt only cares about the Dodgers," he continues. "He's not worried about anything else but making the Dodgers a success. FOX is worried about a whole bunch of things. Now maybe they say, 'For our corporate image, we'll overspend on players,' or 'We don't want to be in the press having fired Tommy Lasorda.' But there's just so many other influences when the Dodgers are one of many assets, and with entertainment companies especially, very visible assets."

Moreover, "A corporation isn't going to invest $500 million or a billion dollars to build a new stadium just 'cause they're a corporation," adds Eagles owner Jeffrey Lurie. "It's the same economics. They may be able to purchase a team easier, but in terms of the actual operation and the investment in the facility, they're stuck with a bad economic model too."

"Family businesses are more likely than corporations to make decisions on philosophical synergies as opposed to economic ones," Vataha summarizes. "When the Busch family owned the St. Louis Cardinals, they knew that if the Cardinals reflected badly on St. Louis, they would reflect badly on the headquarters of their empire. The Montreal Canadiens are a similar story—they were owned by the Molson family, who ultimately said, 'You know what, we don't want how the Canadiens do to affect our beer.'" (The Canadiens are now owned by Molson once again.)

All in all, once a team is being influenced by other factors within a family, whether corporate or bloodline, it's usually to the detriment of the franchise.

The Colts' Irsay has managed to overcome the dark history of his father's actions in Baltimore and become one of the NFL's top owners, largely because he has put into place a system that ensures continuity from one year to the next—and even one generation to the next. In November 2009, Irsay expanded on the notion of family ownership of sports teams by turning general manager duties over to Chris Polian, son of longtime Colts GM Bill Polian; the two will work together running day-to-day team operations until Bill is ready to step down. (Chris had served as vice president of football operations for many years beforehand.)

"We'll continue to build the team with the same kind of philosophy and core values," Chris Polian told *Sports Illustrated*. "At the same time, we'll look for new ideas to make sure we don't get stale. We have a great

Net Loss

The Nets have had an array of eccentric owners. Here's a look at how much each paid and how the team performed on the court in their tenure.

Owners	Year	Acquired Price	Wins	Price Per Win
Roy Boe	1976	$8 million	46	$173,913
The Secaucus 7	1978	$12 million	683	$17,570
Lewis Katz/ Ray Chambers/ YankeeNets	1998	$150 million	221	$678,733
Bruce Ratner	2004	$300 million	200	$1.5 million
Mikhail Prokhorov	2009	$200 million	12	$16.66 million*

*In Prokhorov's first season as owner
Source: *Wall Street Journal*

situation here. We've always talked about the Rooneys and the Maras as the role models for how an organization should be built."

"I make sure the business is strong through the people I hire, but I try to stay in the sacred and away from the profane in the sense of protecting myself from getting too literal and too weighed down from a business standpoint," Irsay says. "I get my beliefs from the league's founders—Wellington Mara, Lamar Hunt, Art Rooney. Those guys have always said, 'Protect the game.' It's about the game, and it's about the guys who are up in the upper deck and in the end zone. I take those roots with me. You've got to stay humble, you have to give back, and you have to be of service. And you have to be mindful of those things, because I believe if you keep squeezing and squeezing, eventually you're going to take some of the magic away."

Athletes as Owners

Why haven't more athletes ascended to the owner's suite as principal owner of a team? It would seem to be a natural progression for top performers, at least, who come out of their athletic careers as wealthy men and often launch successful businesses in retirement.

John Elway owns a large chain of auto dealerships (as did Hank Aaron). Roger Staubach was the CEO of a multibillion-dollar commercial real estate company. And Magic Johnson, who paid $10 million for a minority stake in the Los Angeles Lakers in 1994 (which he has since sold), sits atop Magic Johnson Enterprises, a $700 million entertainment empire that grew out of Johnson's building of a single movie complex in an underserved, largely African American neighborhood of Los Angeles.

Hockey star Wayne Gretzky, acknowledged as a savvy executive as well as the greatest of all time on ice, was approached by a half-dozen hockey franchises about an ownership role the minute he retired. He bought a 10 percent stake in the Phoenix Coyotes, immediately taking on the role of managing partner and head of hockey operations and becoming head coach a few years later. But perhaps the Great One spread himself too thin—although Gretzky was not the primary reason the Coyotes filed for bankruptcy in 2009 and were subsequently taken over by the NHL.

"Regarding athletes and ownership, I think that owners should be careful," Vataha says. Game Plan has long advised owners that they should be careful about including a former player in their ownership. While the move can add a little marketing value, it's not going to solve a lot of problems and in some cases, it can create some. You're trying to build an organization that's based on business performance, not athletic performance. And sometimes athletes coming in are viewed as getting different treatment than other executives. A little PR value, if the guy turns out to be a really good executive, terrific. But he'll be a good executive because he's a good executive, not because he's a former player."

The man who makes the best case for "athlete as owner" success has to be Jerry Richardson, owner of the Carolina Panthers. A North Carolina native, Richardson built a food service empire after playing wide receiver for the Baltimore Colts, famously catching the winning touchdown pass from Johnny Unitas in the 1959 NFL Championship Game against the New York Giants, a rematch of the 1958 championship, often called the Greatest Game Ever Played.

Richardson is almost single-handedly the reason the NFL agreed to place an expansion franchise in small market Charlotte. Once there, his novel approaches to revenue generation pushed him higher and higher into the NFL hierarchy. The Panthers were one of the first NFL teams not only to obtain the rights to local TV and radio broadcasts and other media channels but also to bring those operations in-house. Other NFL teams soon followed suit.

Richardson also perfected the notion of using seat licenses to fund construction developed in Miami, simultaneously paying for a $185 million stadium and a $206 million NFL franchise fee. Drawing on that experience, he has led the NFL's stadium committee for more than a decade. And until heart issues temporarily sidelined him, he also served as cochairman of the labor executive committee and served on the league's compensation committee. He's well regarded by his peers as a consensus builder and good friend.

And no one could call Richardson nepotistic. At the beginning of the 2009 regular season, Richardson accepted the resignations of sons Jon and Mark from the Panthers' front office and brought in Texas Christian University athletic director Danny Morrison as team president.

Perhaps following in Richardson's footsteps, five-time Pro Bowl selection Curtis Martin has been actively seeking the right NFL ownership situation since his 2007 retirement from the New York Jets. "I've always seen myself as a high-profile owner," he told the *New York Times*. "One of the key differences is that I will be an owner who understands what the player thinks, feels, why he does what he does. I'll be able to empathize, sympathize, and advise athletes in a way that I believe can help out the league as a whole."

A Case for Fan Ownership

Are you a soccer fan with $75 to spare? For about the same price as one premium ticket to an MLS game, you could own a share of Ebbsfleet United. What's more, you can help run the Kent, England–based franchise from anywhere in the world—courtesy of the Internet.

Public ownership in sports is hardly a novel idea—the Green Bay Packers are 100 percent community owned, and public ownership in professional baseball is almost as old as the game itself. According to Jerry Gorman and Kirk Calhoun in *The Name of the Game: The Business of Sports*, the first-ever pro baseball club, the Cincinnati Red Stockings, formed in 1869, were capitalized through a stock offering that raised $15,000. And a handful of minor league baseball franchises through the years have been run by their fans, including the Schaumberg Flyers in Illinois, whose fans develop line-ups as part of Fan Club: Reality Baseball, a Web-based program that takes fantasy baseball leagues to a whole new level.

In February 2008, more than 26,000 soccer fans came together via the www.myfootballclub.co.uk website to purchase Ebbsfleet United, which plays in the Blue Square Premier league (four divisions down from the English Premier League), for £600,000, or about $990,000. For the first time in history, a professional sports team was being run day to day by an online community.

The notion of fan team ownership isn't new—European powerhouses Real Madrid and Barcelona are in part controlled by fans who pay for membership in owning the club, though their responsibilities extend only to voting for club presidents. The myfootballclub ownership model also comprises day-to-day club management. Fan owners vote online to decide match lineups and buy new players. They are also able to watch all matches online, review individual player stats afterward, and get weekly updates on player performances during practice.

Online ownership is yet another means of getting fans deeply involved with a team at a time that most soccer fans are increasingly feeling marginalized by huge player salaries and rising ticket prices. While it's not a solution for all teams—online involvement diminishes in-person attendance, and the mom-and-pop approach will never be able to fund a $1.6 billion Manchester United–level club—for smaller clubs, it's a creative way to keep the team on the pitch.

Just three months after the online community purchased the club, Ebbsfleet United won the FA Trophy at London's Wembley Stadium—the greatest achievement to date by a club founded in 1980.

Team	Main Owner	Income Source
Arizona Cardinals	Bill Bidwill	Football ownership
Atlanta Falcons	Arthur Blank	Home Depot
Baltimore Ravens	Steve Bisciotti	Allegis Group: staffing and outsourcing
Buffalo Bills	Ralph Wilson	Insurance, mines, radio stations, manufacturing
Carolina Panthers	Jerry Richardson	Hardees, Denny's, and El Pollo Loco
Chicago Bears	Michael McCaskey	Football ownership
Cincinnati Bengals	Mike Brown	Football ownership
Cleveland Browns	Randy Lerner	Securities
Dallas Cowboys	Jerry Jones	Oil & gas exploration
Denver Broncos	Pat Bowlen	Regent Oil, real estate development
Detroit Lions	William Clay and Bill Ford Jr.	Ford Motor Company
Green Bay Packers	Green Bay Packers, Inc.	Team is publicly owned
Houston Texans	Bob McNair	Power plants, Cogene Biotech Ventures
Indianapolis Colts	Jim Irsay	Football ownership
Jacksonville Jaguars	Wayne Weaver	Shoe Carnival and Nine West shoe stores
Kansas City Chiefs	Clark Hunt	Shoreline Management Group, oil inheritance
Miami Dolphins	Stephen M. Ross	The Related Companies: real estate development
Minnesota Vikings	Zygi Wilf	Garden Homes residential real estate development
New England Patriots	Robert Kraft	Paper and packaging, real estate development

Team	Main Owner	Income Source
New Orleans Saints	Tom Benson	Automobile dealerships, former owner Benson Financial
	Rita Benson LeBlanc	Football ownership
New York Giants	John Mara	Football ownership
	Jonathan/Steve Tisch	Loews Corp. and Escape Artists Entertainment
New York Jets	Woody Johnson	Johnson & Johnson
Oakland Raiders	Al Davis	Football ownership
Philadelphia Eagles	Jeffrey and Christina Lurie	Motion picture industry
Pittsburgh Steelers	Rooney family	Football ownership
San Diego Chargers	Alex Spanos	Construction services
San Francisco 49ers	Denise DeBartolo York	DeBartolo Corp., real estate development, and retail and restaurants
	John York	DeYor Laboratories, DeBartolo Corp.
Seattle Seahawks	Paul Allen	Microsoft Corp.
St. Louis Rams	E. Stanley Kroenke	Real estate development; wife is a Wal-Mart Walton
Tampa Bay Buccaneers	Malcolm Glazer	First Allied Corp., food processing and real estate development
Tennessee Titans	Bud Adams	Adams Resources: oil & gas; Lincoln–Mercury dealerships
Washington Redskins	Daniel Snyder	Six Flags Inc, Johnny Rockets restaurant chain, magazine publishing and distribution

How They Made Their Money: Major Baseball League

Team	Main Owner	Income Source
Arizona Diamondbacks	Ken Kendrick	Datatel, Inc., Woodforest National Bank
Atlanta Braves	John Malone	Liberty Media
Baltimore Orioles	Peter Angelos	Angelos law firm
Boston Red Sox	John Henry	John Henry & Co. futures and foreign exchange trading
Chicago Cubs	Tom Ricketts	TD Ameritrade
Chicago White Sox	Jerry Reinsdorf	Real estate development
Cincinnati Reds	Bob Castellini	Baseball ownership, Castellini Group of Companies
Cleveland Indians	Larry Dolan	Thrasher, Dinsmore and Dolan LLC, Cablevision
Colorado Rockies	Charlie and Dick Monfort	ConAgra Refrigerated Foods
Detroit Tigers	Mike Ilitch	Little Caesars Pizza
Florida Marlins	Jeffrey Loria	Art dealer
Houston Astros	Drayton McLane Jr.	McLane Company grocery distribution (sold to Wal-Mart)
Kansas City Royals	David Glass	Wal-Mart
Los Angeles Angels	Arte Moreno	Outdoor Systems billboards (sold to Infinity Broadcast)
Los Angeles Dodgers	Frank McCourt	Real estate development and parking
Milwaukee Brewers	Mark Attanasio	Trust Company of the West investment banking
Minnesota Twins	Jim Pohlad	Banking, PepsiAmericas

Team	Main Owner	Income Source
New York Mets	Fred Wilpon	Sterling Equities
New York Yankees	George Steinbrenner	American Shipbuilding Co., Kinsman Shipping
Oakland A's	Lew Wolff	Maritz, Wolff & Co., hotels, real estate
Philadelphia Phillies	David Montgomery	Baseball ownership
Pittsburgh Pirates	Robert Nutting	Ogden Newspapers
San Diego Padres	Jeff Moorad	Moorad Sports Management
San Francisco Giants	William Neukom	K&L Gates LLC, Microsoft Corp.
Seattle Mariners	Howard Lincoln	Nintendo of America
St. Louis Cardinals	William DeWitt	Reynolds, DeWitt & Co. (Harken Energy, Arby's, misc.)
Tampa Bay Rays	Stuart Sternberg	Goldman Sachs, financial services
Texas Rangers	Chuck Greenberg	Sports attorney
	Nolan Ryan	MLB Hall of Famer
Toronto Blue Jays	Rogers Baseball Part.	Rogers Communications
Washington Nationals	Ted Lerner	Real estate development

How They Made Their Money: National Basketball Association

Team	Main Owner	Income Source
Atlanta Hawks	Atlanta Spirit LLC	8 partners
Boston Celtics	Wycliffe Grousbeck	Highland Capital Partners VC
Charlotte Bobcats	Michael Jordan	NBA Hall of Famer
Chicago Bulls	Jerry Reinsdorf	Real estate development
Cleveland Cavaliers	Dan Gilbert	Chairman of Quicken Loans, Inc.
Dallas Mavericks	Mark Cuban	Founder of www.Broadcast.com, HDNet
Denver Nuggets	Josh Kroenke	Son of real estate developer and Wal-Mart heiress
Detroit Pistons	Tom Gores	Platinum Equity
Golden State Warriors	Joe Lacob	Kleiner Perkins Caufield & Byers partner
	Peter Guber	Mandalay Entertainment Group
Houston Rockets	Leslie Alexander	Alexander Group investment and First Marblehead student loan
Indiana Pacers	Simon Family	Real estate development, shopping malls
Los Angeles Clippers	Donald Sterling	Real estate development
Los Angeles Lakers	Jerry Buss	Real estate development
Memphis Grizzlies	Michael Heisley	Heico Companies LLC, manufacturing
Miami Heat	Mickey Arison	Carnival Cruise Lines
Milwaukee Bucks	Senator Herb Kohl	Kohl's (retail)
Minnesota Timberwolves	Glen Taylor	Taylor Corp. printing and electronics

Team	Main Owner	Income Source
New Jersey Nets	Mikhail Prokhorov	Financial sector, precious metals
New Orleans Hornets	NBA	Purchased by the league from previous owner George Shinn
New York Knicks	James Dolan	Cablevision
Oklahoma City Thunder	Clay Bennett	Gaylord media and entertainment
	Aubrey McClendon	Chesapeake Energy Corp.
Orlando Magic	Richard DeVos	Alticor (formerly Amway)
Philadelphia 76ers	Comcast-Spectacor	Sport and property management
Phoenix Suns	Robert Sarver	Former owner National Bank of Arizona
Portland Trail Blazers	Paul Allen	Microsoft Corp.
Sacramento Kings	Gavin/Joe Maloof	Casino, hotel development
San Antonio Spurs	Peter Holt	Caterpillar Tractor
Toronto Raptors	Maple Leaf Sports & Ent.	Sport and property management
Utah Jazz	Miller Family	Prestige Financial, retail, theaters, sports facilities
Washington Wizards	Ted Leonsis	AOL vice chairman emeritus
	Raul Fernandez	ObjectVideo

How They Made Their Money: National Hockey League

Team	Main Owner	Income Source
Anaheim Ducks	Henry Samueli	Broadcom
Atlanta Thrashers	Atlanta Spirit LLC	8 partners
Boston Bruins	Jeremy Jacobs Sr.	Delaware North concessions
Buffalo Sabres	Terry Pegula	East Resources president & CEO
Calgary Flames	Harley Hotchkiss, others	NHL ownership
Carolina Hurricanes	Peter Karmanos	Compuware Corp. CEO
Chicago Blackhawks	Rocky Wirtz	Judge & Dolph liquor distributorship
Colorado Avalanche	Josh Kroenke	Son of real estate developer and Wal-Mart heiress
Columbus Blue Jackets	McConnell Family	Worthington Industries CEO, processed steel
Dallas Stars	Tom Hicks	Hicks, Muse, Tate & Furst investment firm
Detroit Red Wings	Mike Ilitch	Little Caesar's Pizza
Edmonton Oilers	Daryl Katz	Katz Group drugstore & pharmacy conglomerate
Florida Panthers	Cliff Viner	Offshare Advisors investment firm
Los Angeles Kings	Phil Anschutz/AEG	Oil, railroads, telecomm (Quest), and entertainment
Minnesota Wild	Craig Leipold	Ameritel Corp. telemarketing, sold footwear co

Team	Main Owner	Income Source
Montreal Canadiens	Molson Family	Molson Coors Brewing Company
Nashville Predators	David Freeman	Commodore Medical Services, medical waste
New Jersey Devils	Jeff Vanderbeek	Former Lehman Bros. exec
New York Islanders	Charles Wang	Computer Associates founder
New York Rangers	James Dolan, MSG LLP	Cablevision
Ottawa Senators	Eugene Melnyk	Former CEO Biovail Corp., pharmaceutical
Philadelphia Flyers	Comcast-Spectacor	Sport and property management
Phoenix Coyotes	NHL	NHL
Pittsburgh Penguins	Mario Lemieux/Ron Burkle	NHL great and Yucaipa Companies
San Jose Sharks	SJ Sports & Entertainment	8 partners
St. Louis Blues	Dave Checketts	Sports Capital Partners Worldwide
Tampa Bay Lightning	Jeffrey Vinik	Hedge fund manager
Toronto Maple Leafs	Maple Leaf Sports & Ent.	Sport and property management
Vancouver Canucks	Francesco Aquilini	Aquilini Investment Group
Washington Capitals	Ted Leonsis	AOL vice chairman emeritus
	Raul Fernandez	ObjectVideo

Gary Bettman, NHL

Gary Bettman has likely faced many times as NHL commissioner when he wanted to seek shelter behind a hockey goalie's facemask and thick pads. Bettman alone among the current commissioners jumped sports to reach his current spot atop the NHL—he came to hockey in 1993 via the NBA, where he had served as assistant general counsel reporting directly to his mentor, David Stern, since 1981.

The year Bettman took office, the NHL was experiencing its greatest period of growth and popularity in the United States, in part due to the star power of Wayne Gretzky. The growing profile of the sport helped Bettman land a five-year TV contract with FOX and ESPN and oversee a southern expansion into such previously hockey-neutral markets as Tampa Bay, North Carolina, and Phoenix— at the expense, critics said, of traditional hockey towns, especially in Canada.

Bettman's tenure has seen few highlights until recently. He couldn't stave off work stoppages in 1994 and again in 2004 (when the entire season was lost to a lockout). The television deal he orchestrated with Versus at the end of that year was widely panned, resulting in Nielsen ratings of .2 to .3 on average for regular-season games (think *Full House* reruns). Even the 2007 Stanley Cup Finals, usually the high point of the NHL season, earned only a 1.1 for NBC, the lowest in the network's broadcasting history. A Stanley Cup victory that year did, however, build a broader following for the Anaheim Ducks, one of the few bright spots in the league's outlook. And Bettman was widely praised in 2007 for helping to mediate an agreement that kept the old-school Penguins franchise in Pittsburgh.

Gone are the salary issues that precipitated the NHL's work stoppages, as the new salary cap does not allow any player to make more than 20 percent of his team's total payroll. Through the creation of the NHL Winter Classic and Heritage Classic and rule changes promoting goal scoring, the league has placed added emphasis on creating a fan-friendly environment. As such, ticket sales have increased every year since the lockout ended. And in April 2011, Bettman further strengthened the league's financial stability when he signed a 10-year, $2 billion television rights deal to keep the NHL on NBC and Versus.

Finally—the ultimate sign of stability—amongst Kansas City, Seattle, Hamilton, Quebec City, and Winnipeg, there is no shortage of cities itching for an NHL franchise.

Despite all of the NHL's success over the past five years, none of these benchmarks will matter if the league cannot maintain labor peace. The current CBA, which was ratified in 2005, expires in September 2011. Complicating negotiations, the NHLPA is without a permanent executive director after Paul Kelly was fired in late 2009. Although the NHL managed to survive one lost season, another work stoppage would be devastating to the league and commissioner Bettman's reputation.

Q: What teams did you follow when you were a kid?

GB: Growing up in New York, you would have the luxury of picking and choosing your sports and the team within each sport. Growing up in Queens I picked a team in each sport. I tend to gravitate toward the newer or the expansion teams. If Freud were on the phone with us, he would give you the following explanation. In the late 50s, early 60s, I grew up in a single-parent household, which was unusual at the time, so my sport didn't really get passed down from generation to generation in the traditional sense. I focused on being in a place where there was no history. Access to information wasn't as good in those times, so my response was to root for the Jets when they came into the NFL, root for the Mets when they came into MLB, root for the Islanders when they came into the NHL.

Q: Do you remember what was the first professional sports event that you ever attended?

GB: I went to a Rangers game and a Knicks game at the old Madison Square Garden. I went to a Mets game at the Polo Grounds in their first year, and I went to a Giants game at Yankee Stadium.

Q: Coming back to the present, what do you think is the current number one issue in the NHL that you're looking at right now that will have a direct impact on the fans?

GB: First, the game on the ice has to be the best that it can be. We must be absolutely committed day in and day out, night in and night out to make sure our product is as good as it can be.

Second, our competitive balance right now is greatly improved. That's a function of the way we changed the rules in 2004, and it's also a function of the fact that we have an economic system that works so that all teams can afford to be competitive. Your foundation has to be strong.

Q: How critical is your new media strategy to the direction that you're taking the league?

GB: It's important because, as I said, while we were challenged in the traditional media space, our opportunity to make up for lost ground as media reinvents itself will be for us to be cutting-edge in the digital space, because fans want to interact with the content. We've got to do that as well as if not better than anybody else.

Q: How often do the professional sports commissioners in the United States get together and share information? How often are you on the phone with Stern or Goodell comparing notes?

GB: Not as frequently as people would think. You know, we are all friendly and cordial, we see each other at events occasionally. When something

> CONTINUED

happens, good or bad, to one of our sports, we'll call and say hello, but we're not in general consulting with each other.

Q: **What about the franchise owners. How much interaction do you have with each of them?**

GB: Regularly—every couple of weeks at least, one on one. We also have board meetings three or four times a year, as well as executive committee meetings. I make it a point to talk to the owners on the phone on a regular basis.

Q: **The idea of having corporate logos on goalies' and possibly other players' jerseys has come up. Is that something you're considering?**

GB: It's the kind of thing we've considered—there was a report that the goaltenders had gotten together and floated the idea of a goaltenders' club similar to the quarterback club. It would have to go through the Players Association. Well, they can't wear it on the ice unless we approve, but the fact is, nobody's ever proposed it to us. It's all been a function of what somehow got into the media, and you know, I suppose that's a commentary on the fact that anything can get into the media.

Q: **The sports industry is very unique in that so many people in both ownership positions and leadership positions have actually grown up in the sport–it's very much handed down from one generation to another. Which is more important for sustaining a passionate leadership for a sport: growing up in the sport or coming to it with a very strong leadership resume?**

GB: It's not an either-or. You have to have a passion for the sport because when you have one of these jobs, it's totally consuming. It's not a job actually, it's a lifestyle. Whether or not you played the game or whether or not you grew up as a fan, the fact is you must have an all-consuming passion, and you need the skills that will enable you to do the job.

Q: **What are your plans internationally?**

GB: I think China will become an important market for everything and everybody, but just because somebody else goes there, that doesn't mean it's the right place initially for us. We are the most international of the North American sports, and I say that because our players come from 20 countries, and international players from outside of North America represent about 30 percent of the players of the league, and they are some of the best players in the world. So there is already an existing infrastructure for hockey in many countries and an interest in our game because people from those countries want to see how their players are doing playing at the highest level of hockey in the world.

Q: One of the biggest criticisms of pro sports right now, regardless of sport, is that every year pro sports are much less fan friendly, both in terms of the pricing and also because of the attitudes at a game. How family friendly is hockey, and what are some of the steps you're taking to keep the game a great environment for kids?

GB: Well, first of all I think you are generalizing in terms of the problems that sports are having because I don't think that we need to get painted with that brush. We're playing to 93 percent of capacity on a statistical basis. We probably have more women and more kids at our games as a percentage. Our ticket prices aren't a whole lot different than they were five years ago. The inflationary pressure has been ameliorated, which will put us in either third or fourth place in terms of average ticket price. We believe that if you look at our game, we pride ourselves as having a fan-friendly, children-friendly environment for people to see our games in person.

Q: So how much interaction do you have directly with the fans?

GB: I try to go to each market at least once to take in a game, and I let the club set up whatever they want to do in terms of the media and the fans. I was in Nashville about 10 days ago and I addressed a luncheon of 150 sponsors and advertisers, and then I did a ticket holder forum, I think there were 1,000 people there, where I took questions. And you know, the other thing that I do that nobody has done is I have a radio show where I basically take calls and e-mails, and I'll interview somebody on something that I think will be of general interest, which is not something typical that fans would know about. I'm the only commissioner that's ever done that.

I think giving fans a chance to interact is key, because what frequently happens is there is sometimes not a full understanding of why things are the way they are, why we do what we do. I've been at season ticket holder events. I remember one in Florida in particular where somebody asked me a question and then came up to me afterwards and said, 'You know, this was an issue I was very upset about, and now that I hear you explain it in your own words, I get it and thank you for explaining it.'

Q: Does the media get the NHL story right?

GB: I think what's happening is that bloggers are putting pressure on traditional media in terms of what's newsworthy, and so the answer is, I think they will try to get it right and based on the information available, they do a good job, but that doesn't mean that all of the information is available to them to get it right.

> CONTINUED

Q: If there's one single change that you could make to hockey, what would it be?

GB: I believe that our in-person experience is the best in all sports. I don't believe that has to date been the case. What happens in person doesn't translate on television as well as it might, and that's something we continue to work on.

Q: Are we going to see an NHL franchise in Russia?

GB: Don't know. We're playing two games in London, in Prague, and other locations in Europe to respond to the interest in the game. A third of the visits to www.nhl.com come from outside of North America.

Q: How important are the Olympics in helping your NHL marketing efforts?

GB: A mixed bag because we need to disrupt the season to do it. Some of the other major leagues stop because they have the good fortune of either not being an Olympic sport or of having their Olympics in their off-season. When the Olympics are in North America—as in Salt Lake City and more recently Vancouver—removing time zone issues makes the Games more meaningful for us, and it strikes a better balance against the difficulties that are presented.

Growing up, our players have a history and tradition of representing their countries, and this is important to them.

We do it because it's a great platform, and our fans, not all, but a number of our fans, tell us they like it, but that's something that we have to keep evaluating after each Olympics to see if it makes sense because we pay a price for doing it.

Q: Do you think the sport is in good business shape for the foreseeable future, and if so, what's the biggest reason it is?

GB: We went through a number of years that were quite difficult, because the economics were causing teams to struggle, causing some fans in some markets to lose hope because there was a huge disparity in what teams could afford to spend and therefore what talent they could attract. It evolved into a game where less skilled teams were trying to do things to compete with more skilled teams, which we think affected how the game was played.

We now have an economic system, a partnership that works. It means that all teams can afford to be competitive. I don't think any sport has anything close to the competitive balance we have right now. No matter what team you're a fan of, you have hope at the beginning of the season that your team has just as good a chance as any other team of making the playoffs and maybe going all the way.

Q: **Let's talk about your legacy. If you could have a say in how you will be remembered for all of history, what would you want your legacy to look like?**

GB: This question came up on my 15th anniversary of doing this, and I'm not a big one to focus on my legacy. I care about this game, and I care about doing the best job I can for this, game, and I'm not one to be able to focus on what my legacy would be. I leave that to others.

7

One Union Under Center: Athletes, Agents, and Their Deals

- ▶ *Flood v. Kuhn* (early 1970s) dismantled the reserve clause in athlete contracts and paved the way for free agency.

- ▶ Establishing a salary cap in the NFL was a major change agent in all of sports.

- ▶ The key issues in all collective bargaining agreement negotiations are free agency, minimum wage, squad size, the draft, grounds for termination, and suspension.

- ▶ The success of young athletes in the pro world depends on the business savvy and guidance of their agents, who serve as core advisors, tutors, yentas, stylists, dietitians, and confessors.

- ▶ The Sports Agent Responsibility and Trust Act, signed into law by President George W. Bush, strengthens agent regulation.

- ▶ The international athlete endorsement and advertising business is a $350 billion business.

the athlete or the agent? The modern business of sports agency traces its roots to the early 1960s, when representing an athlete was the quickest way into the industry. But sports agents were not really needed before the advent of free agency, and before the mid-1970s, contracts did not have the multimillion-dollar values they do today. It was quite common, in fact, for athletes to find other jobs in the off-season to support themselves.

When they were involved in early player transactions, agents were often persona non grata in teams' front offices. When a Green Bay Packers player brought an agent with him to renegotiate his contract, an oft-told story goes, legendary coach Vince Lombardi left the meeting. When he returned a half hour later, Lombardi told the player and his agent that the player had been traded to the Washington Redskins.

After 1975, the year that saw the end of the sports reserve clause and the advent of free agency, pioneers including Bob Woolf Jr. and IMG founder Mark McCormack helped to pave the way for today's powerful agents. However, there are two sides to every athlete negotiation, and sitting across the table from player agents is a team executive.

While the relationship between agent and executive is often a contentious one, split down player and team lines, together they are charged with a commitment to athletes, without whom the sports industry obviously wouldn't exist. These days, it is more important than ever to have athletes represented by agents who have their clients' best interest at heart. Case in point: A staggering 60 percent of NBA players go bankrupt five years after they retire.

As agents try to get their players the most money possible, executives are asked to turn limited dollars into championships. So teams are asking more and more of their athlete workforce—more playing time for less money and fewer perks. This issue is at the heart of the next round of collective bargaining agreement (CBA) negotiations now ramping up simultaneously in America's top pro sports.

With the CBAs of America's four major professional sports expiring in 2011 and 2012, the onus is on agents and executives, just as much as on players and owners, to find common ground. At the end of the day, responsible management means more money for everyone.

And, more often than not, more shoes.

Percentage of a Sport's Revenue Taken Home by Its Athletes

ATP tennis	26%
MLB	52%
NHL	56%
NBA	57%
NFL	62%

Source: *Tennis Magazine*

Free Agency and the Salary Cap: A League-by-League Comparison

Until only a few decades ago, most U.S. professional sports leagues retained clauses in players' contracts that essentially guaranteed that the players could rarely leave their original teams by choice. Under this so-called reserve clause, the team had a never-ending option to renew a player's contract at a price the player could not control. Reserve clauses were upheld legally because courts continually ruled that sports leagues did not operate in interstate trade or commerce, meaning they did not fall under antitrust laws.

That all changed in 1970, when St. Louis Cardinal outfielder Curt Flood refused to be traded to the Philadelphia Phillies, challenged the use of the reserve clause in arbitration, declared himself a "free agent," and subsequently filed a $4.1 million antitrust lawsuit against Major League Baseball. The league refused to settle, and the case, *Flood v. Kuhn* (MLB commissioner Bowie Kuhn), went all the way to the U.S. Supreme Court. Although the Supreme Court ruled in MLB's favor, the case was later overturned, dismantling the reserve clause. The Flood Act then opened the floodgates to widespread free agency in all pro sports—NBA All-Star Oscar Robinson settled a similar antitrust suit in 1975, doing away with the reserve clause in basketball.

The widespread interpretation of antitrust laws has largely been eroded today. However, MLB still retains limited antitrust exemptions, and the NFL's exemption—for the moment—is even broader. On the other side of the negotiating table, the formation of players unions for the purpose of negotiating contracts with management is exempt from antitrust scrutiny under labor law.

Collective Bargaining Agreement, Key Components (Three Major Sports)

Fundamental differences still remain across professional sports leagues in how athlete compensation is determined, from rookie minimums to up-front and performance bonuses.

Components	NFL	NBA	MLB
Salary cap	Hard cap	Soft cap	No cap
Luxury tax	No	Yes	Yes
Rookie salaries	Fixed contract per draft position	No limitations on rookie contracts	No limitations on rookie contracts
Drug testing	10 players on each team tested weekly during season	Each player can be randomly selected four times during the season	Each player is tested once during season
Revenue sharing	Yes	Yes	Yes

Three decades into free agency, Major League Baseball has come to terms with it—and is even using free agency as a marketing tool. One Hot Stove promotion on www.MLB.com invited subscribers to win tickets for Opening Day if they could correctly predict where free agents would end up.

In other leagues—especially the NFL—one sometimes gets the sense that owners and the league's top executives think that the system worked better in the olden days.

Leigh Steinberg has a different perspective on the issue.

"It wasn't free agency that changed the NFL, it was the salary cap," insists the high-profile sports agent, who for years was particularly famous for his stable of top quarterbacks. "The salary cap breaks up happy marriages. Football players desperately covet structure; they're the most conservative people on the face of the earth. Twenty-five percent are born-again Christians, the next 25 percent are coach's sons. They come from conservative families; they're scared to death about the insecurity of football. They would stay on the same team as long as they weren't starving. They don't want to move, their wives don't want to move, and they don't all want to play in New York. A lot of them like to hunt and fish.

"Football was healthy with set lineups for a long time, without the salary cap pushing players out," Steinberg continues. "Kerry Collins wins a Super Bowl and two years later his salary's too high to buy. The same with Jeff Garcia and a host of other players. It's crazy, and that's not a good thing."

Most sports fans would agree that player salaries are at least a little on the ridiculous side. Observes Steinberg, "The last thing someone struggling to pay their bills making $40,000 or $50,000 or $60,000 wants to hear is someone who complains publicly to say they've only been offered $2 million. It's Marie Antoinette saying, 'Let them eat cake.' It strikes people as insensitive, and it puts an athlete in harm's way in terms of the negative image of greed."

In 1959, the average salary of an NFL player was about $10,000. Today, the rookie minimum is $310,000, with star players making much more. But since player compensation in every sport save baseball is allocated as a percentage of actual revenue, a drop in player pay is inevitable in a recession, and more players could be forced to accept league-minimum salaries. (Not that the minimums are insubstantial.)

The player compensation system is hardly arbitrary—what happens on the field almost always dictates pay. "If NFL rookies miss the window of opportunity in training camp to get repetitions, they fall behind," Steinberg says. "Their contracts have incentives and escalator clauses that are dependent on their playing time, so that if they miss that window, then their ability to catch up compensation-wise diminishes. Escalators in contracts dictate that in year four, if in the first three years the player has played 75 percent of the downs and thrown X percent of passes, a substantial sum will be added onto the core compensation." In other words, if they don't get the reps, they don't get the raise.

Most leagues argue that setting a salary cap provides competitive balance, ensures profitability at the team level, and promotes widespread sharing by players of the sport's total revenues. But there's also support for the MLB model—that clubs with the highest payrolls have a higher likelihood of success on the field. The New York Yankees had a $208 million payroll in 2009, by far the highest in baseball. Was it sheer coincidence the franchise won its 27th World Series title that year?

How Long Does It Take an Athlete to Make $100K?

Courtesy of the *Wall Street Journal*, here's how long it takes a sampling of star athletes to make $100,000, based on the amount of money they earned in 2009:

Athlete and Sport	To Earn $100K
Alex Rodriguez, MLB Yankees	6 pitches
Ben Roethlisberger, NFL Steelers	4 snaps
Tiger Woods, PGA Tour	11 holes
LeBron James, NBA Cavaliers	21 minutes
Roger Federer, ATP tennis	28 games
Tony Stewart, NASCAR driver	125 laps
Norm Duke, Professional Bowlers Assoc.	2,360 frames

Sports Unions and CBAs

In 1967, even before the advent of free agency, the National Labor Relations Board accepted that professional athletes had the right to form unions or players associations alongside employee advocacy groups in other industries. Since then, professional athletes in almost every sport have organized into associations or unions in order to negotiate CBAs with their sport's owners.

Under federal labor law, player representatives and owners must negotiate in good faith mandatory issues: those relating to wages, hours, and working conditions. All other issues are deemed permissive and do not have to be negotiated. Once a CBA is in place, players agree not to strike, and owners promise not to lock out players through the lifetime of the agreement. If the CBA expires without a new agreement in place, chaos often reigns.

In 1982, a 57-day strike shortened the NFL season to nine games. In 1994, Major League Baseball lost half its season and the playoffs because ballplayers went out on strike over the issue of a salary cap. That work stoppage was estimated to cost MLB $374.2 million in lost revenues and cancelled the World Series for the first time in 90 years. The 2004-2005 NHL season was cancelled because of an owners' lockout after the parties' CBA had expired.

Over time, the most controversial issues subject to CBA negotiation are free agency, minimum wage, squad size, the draft, grounds for termination, and suspension. And in nearly all pro sports, limitations on the use of performance-enhancing drugs, or PEDs, have become an integral aspect of CBA negotiations. Counter to what the World Anti-Doping Agency would prefer, drug policies are not uniform for all professional sports. Rather, the CBA negotiated in each sport spells out a policy regarding drug testing, banned substances, violations, penalties, privacy issues, and rights of appeal. Drug violations may lead to suspensions and loss of salary, as we've seen over the last decade with the much-publicized BALCO case and individual incidents involving players such as a group of Minnesota Vikings and the Dodgers' Manny Ramirez.

The PED issue has died down somewhat over the last year, and replacing it front-of-mind with sports industry executives are the simultaneous CBA negotiations going on in America's four major sports leagues.

So far, the NHL has stayed relatively quiet about its yet-to-come CBA talks. In the NBA, where the current CBA is set to expire after the 2010-2011 season, team owners plan to "go for the jugular and drop the players' salaries immensely" during negotiations with the National Basketball Players Association (NBPA) for a new CBA, according to sources cited by ESPN and elsewhere. An anonymous general manager added, "Player salaries are definitely going to take a hit. . . . [Owners are] looking to shorten the maximum length of a contract to four or five years." The source added that owners have "actually discussed trying to guarantee only the first two years of a four-year deal, and that the third and fourth years would be guaranteed only if a player reached certain performance-based incentives." If that were to happen, the labor scenario in the NBA would look much more like that in the NFL.

Also likely to be challenged in the next round of NBA CBA talks: the league's age limit, which effectively prohibits a player from going straight to the league from high school and creates the despised "one and done" scenario on college basketball rosters.

Longtime NBPA executive director Billy Hunter has freely stated that athletes, and teams, are already saving up money for a strike. However, NBA commissioner David Stern is a veteran of three lockouts, only one of which cost the league any lost games.

In baseball, without a salary cap, MLB salaries seem particularly out of whack at a time when the national unemployment hovers around 10 percent. Even the greenest rookies in the majors are guaranteed a $400,000 minimum salary—the same salary paid President Barack Obama. What's more, top players are lured by lavish, creative perks, including bonuses for staying in shape, country club memberships, equestrian training, language classes, and private jets. Yet MLB, facing the same down economy as everyone else, has slowly but surely begun to rationalize its pay structure. The winter before the 2007 season, baseball spent about $1.7 billion in free-agent contract commitments. Before the 2008 season, free-agent commitments dropped to $1.1 billion, and that number continues to shrink. Salary structures look to be the crux of upcoming baseball labor talks.

It's the NFL's CBA talks that really have sports industry execs doubling up on their blood pressure medication. First, a new deal wasn't consummated by commissioner Roger Goodell and NFLPA head DeMaurice Smith by March 2010, so the 2010-2011 season operated without a salary cap. Then, despite a series of formal collective bargaining sessions, it was unclear whether the 2011 season would even take place, as the league and its players' union failed to reach an agreement by March 3, 2011, the date the existing CBA expired.

Despite extending the negotiations for an additional week as the two sides attempted to come to terms, the players' union walked away from the negotiating table on March 10 and decertified, an extreme measure that eliminated its collective bargaining powers and threw the next NFL labor agreements into the arms of a federal judge. The owners responded by locking the players out—as this book was going to print, the matter was still making its way through the federal court system.

Immediately after decertifying, a group of players that included three of the NFL's most popular and influential quarterbacks—Peyton Manning, Tom Brady, and Drew Brees—filed an antitrust lawsuit against the league to attempt to prevent a lockout. Addressing the NFL CBA talk with the media, Brady, months before, had said, "We're all way overpaid." He added, "As a player rep now, I realize all the issues that our league faces. It's a really unique time in our league. As a team player, I don't sit here and say, 'What about me? What about me?' I'm under contract. I'll go out there and play and play my butt off."

FACT **$562.8 million: The amount of money that drinking establishments alone stand to lose during the 2011-2012 season if there is an NFL work stoppage.**
Source: IBISWorld

Representing the Professional Athlete

Maybe LeBron James had been following the HBO hit series *Entourage* a little too closely. In a startling moment in 2005, the NBA superstar fired his agent of two years Aaron Goodwin—who negotiated more than $135 million in endorsement deals for the 20-year-old phenom, including a $90 million deal with Nike. James turned over his representation duties to three longtime friends, rising star Maverick Carter among them, who together call themselves the Four Horsemen.

As in *Entourage*, which follows the trajectory of a 20-something movie star and the three buddies from Queens who oversee his career, the odd man out is the agent. As life imitates art, so does sport imitate Hollywood.

Consider the much-vaunted 2005 NFL Draft class, a handful of years after the fact, as athletes' contracts and roles in the NFL are beginning to mature. Did players live up to expectations? Some did—Green Bay Packers starting quarterback Aaron Rogers not only came into his own but also helped sore Packers fans lick their wounds after the departure of Brett Favre.

On the other hand, quarterback Alex Smith doesn't remind San Francisco 49ers fans of Joe Montana and Steve Young. Running back Ronnie Brown not only failed to make Miami Dolphins fans forget Ricky Williams, the franchise eventually bit the bullet and brought back the troubled Williams.

And what about controversial Ohio State and would-be NFL running back Maurice Clarett? He's in prison.

The success of young athletes in their tough new professional world also depends on the business savvy and guidance provided by their respective agents, who serve as core advisors, tutors, yentas, stylists, dietitians, and confessors.

A traditional knock on sports agencies used to be that any schmo off the street could be an agent. In fact, the only qualification for someone to be a sports agent was that he had some sort of athlete who referred to him as such!

"Most agents will not confront their players when they think they're making mistakes," Leigh Steinberg—the inspiration behind *Jerry Maguire*—points out. "They're afraid they'll get fired. I used to say that if a player was standing on the ledge of a 90-story building and was about to jump, he'd be surrounded by a posse and an agent who would say, 'Son—gravity, that doesn't apply to you. Live out your destiny. Live out your truths. You can fly.'"

Steinberg continues, "What I say to players is, I expect you to be a role model. You have extra responsibilities because you're part of a public entertainment that relies heavily on fan approval and fan willingness to watch and attend games. They're economic resources for tickets, for sponsored products, for memorabilia, for kids' leagues. Your responsibility is to give peak performance, graciously give interviews to the press that enable fans to follow the game, interact with fans in a warm and friendly way, and conduct yourself publicly with dignity and self-respect. If you're not interested in doing that and you feel that it's unfair to be judged by those standards, there are easy alternatives. Go play in the sandlot."

Clearly, as contracts and endorsement deals get richer, sports agents continue to go to greater and greater lengths to win clients. Last year, the NFLPA reported that there were more than 2,000 certified agents. Once certified, player agents negotiate individual player contracts, respecting their fiduciary duty to act in the player's best interest at all times when negotiating.

Who are the biggest agents in the business today? While the specific sport has a lot of bearing on the answer, there's no doubt that the biggest magnet in the athlete representation business is Creative Artists Agency (CAA). CAA has long been among the top talent representation firms in Hollywood, representing the likes of Jennifer Aniston and Tom Cruise. A half-dozen years ago, it caused the sports industry to sit up and take notice when it jumped into sports representation with two cleated feet, signing uberfootball agents Tom Condon and Ken Kremer (clients include Peyton and Eli Manning and LaDainian Tomlinson) and being front and center during the transaction that brought international soccer god David Beckham to Los Angeles. According to insiders familiar with the company's vision, the agency sees sports as a subset of the larger entertainment stage and employs many of the same image-building strategies with its sports clients as those with which it has built movie stardom.

Then there's Scott Boras, the Darth Vader of baseball contracts. Often nervously viewed as the smartest guy in the room at baseball's winter meetings and other gatherings, Boras built his baseball empire on the $252 million deal he negotiated for Alex Rodriguez with the Texas Rangers—the largest contract ever in sports, until his new 10-year, $275 million contract was signed in 2007. All in all, the Newport Beach, California–based Boras told the *Los Angeles Times* his company has negotiated about $4 billion in contracts. He represents close to 100 MLB players and another 75 or more minor leaguers; the Boras Corp. also has a personal management and marketing division along with the Boras Sports Training Institute.

The week before the 2005 NFL Draft, the NFL signed television deals guaranteeing that more than $3.735 billion annually would be added to NFL coffers for the next six to eight years. That big number represents more national TV money than is being spent on the NBA, MLB, NASCAR, the PGA Tour, NCAA basketball, and the Olympics combined. Agents see at least two-thirds of that money going to players . . . and two to five percent of it to their representation.

While *Jerry Maguire* and *Arli$$* popularized the profession, the NFL, the courts, the federal government, and some states have attempted to regulate it. However, while the American Bar Association regulates lawyers and the American Medical Association sets standards for doctors, there is no direct control on entering the sports agency business.

Protecting Professional Athletes' Interest While Negotiating Top Dollar

Sports contracts have obviously become more lucrative, and they will only increase in the future. Total compensation for NFL players exceeded $2.5 billion in 2004, up 20 percent since 2002—and it's increased exponentially since then. When they signed him, the Cincinnati Bengals paid top draft pick Carson Palmer a $10 million signing bonus and a $4 million option bonus. Agent David Dunn's take from the Palmer bonuses alone exceeded $420,000. Compare that to the 1983 signing of first draft pick John Elway—where agent Marv Demoff received $40,000 for Elway's $1 million bonus.

Competition among agents for high NFL Draft picks is fierce. Though agent-lawyers are regulated by the American Bar Association and state canons of ethics, solicitation is commonplace for nonlawyer agents. One agent noted that a second- or third-round draft pick might be provided a six-figure "marketing guarantee" to sign with a respective agent, even if many of the players would never earn enough endorsements to pay these agents off.

On the other hand, high competitive pressures and high economic stakes often cause high visibility problems. The NFL Players Association Disciplinary Committee voted to suspend agent Jerome Stanley for one year, after Stanley "failed to give notice" to the Cleveland Browns that wide receiver Dennis Northcutt wanted to void his contract in 2004— costing him substantial free-agent clout. And in 2005, former Chicago Bulls star Scottie Pippen filed a multimillion-dollar lawsuit against his financial advisor Robert Lunn. Pippen won an $11.8 million judgment against Lunn (who lost at least $7 million of Pippen's money in real estate ventures and $1.7 million in a poorly structured deal to invest in a small jet, according to allegations contained in the lawsuit).

David Falk's Three Keys to Negotiating Success

David Falk has represented more number one NBA Draft picks than any other sports agent in history. He also negotiated professional sport's first $100 million contract, for Miami Heat center Alonzo Mourning. At the height of his power in the 1990s, Falk was often considered the second-most powerful person in the NBA behind commissioner David Stern. The Mourning contract was part of an unprecedented free-agency period, during which his company, FAME, changed the entire salary structure of the NBA, negotiating more than $400 million in contracts for its free-agent clients in a six-day period.

© AP Photo/Duane Burleson

Falk has one other major claim to agent fame: He represented Michael Jordan for the Hall of Fame athlete's entire career. Falk shares his keys for negotiating success.

1. **Identify the strengths or weaknesses of your opponent's position.** It's not enough to sell your position. A great trial lawyer knows his opponent's case as well as he knows his own. Not enough agents prepare well for negotiations; they also don't prepare enough when planning for a client's career.

2. **It's not a zero-sum game.** This is not a situation where one side wins a negotiation and the other side loses. If both sides don't win, then both sides really lose. And you're going to have to deal with these people again. So you have to find a way to get most of what you need and let the other side get enough of what they need to maintain their dignity.

3. **You have to have a great insight into human nature.** This is not a business of rules and guidelines, it's a feel business, about people and understanding the psychology of what makes people tick. I often find it amusing when I look at the rules of the NBA and how they've changed over time. Oftentimes, the owners don't have a sense of the players' psychology and what it really takes to manage them in a good way—they get replaced by a very mechanical set of rules.

Cleaning Up the Agency Business

In the cleanup process, players' unions are first attempting to clean their own houses. The NFL Players Association has taken action against at least 100 agents during the past decade. The most visible, messy case involved agent David Dunn—suspended by the NFLPA after he left former partner Leigh Steinberg in 2001 to start Athletes First and took 50 clients with him. Steinberg's firm spent more than $12 million litigating the case and was awarded $44.6 million in damages in November 2002. The case was later overturned by a federal appeals court, and Dunn's personal bankruptcy again postponed his two-year suspension by the NFLPA.

In basketball, NBA Players Association executive director Billy Hunter formed a "coaching committee" of agents to try to deal with this issue and has actively advocated.

As a last resort, if necessary, states and the federal government stand ready to clean the business up. Over the past years, states including Florida and Pennsylvania have passed legislation that requires agent regulation, and more than half the states in the United States currently have some means of regulating the activities of player agents in addition to oversight the unions provide. While enforcement has definitely increased, state regulation has been uneven and unpredictable—and 13 states have no regulation at all.

On the federal level, the Sports Agent Responsibility and Trust Act was signed into law by President Bush in his final term. Agents who now sign college-eligible players are required to tell their players that they will lose their eligibility by signing with an agent. Agents are also required to inform the athletic director at the player's school within 72 hours of signing. Agents are also prohibited from soliciting a student-athlete and from signing them by giving them false or misleading information or providing anything of value to their families or friends (the central issue in the NCAA investigation of former USC, now New Orleans Saints, running back Reggie Bush). Though enforcement may be difficult, all agree that this is a step in the right direction in cleaning up a business that is increasingly difficult to control.

Growing a Different Kind of Agent: Sports Management Worldwide

For any fan who's ever dreamed of representing the next Michael Jordan or Michelle Wie but has no idea what it takes to break into that highly competitive market, spending some time with Sports Management Worldwide (SMWW) will help you understand exactly what it takes and provide you the skills to get your sneaker in the door.

SMWW's eight-week sports business training programs can be taken via the Internet from anywhere in the world and include live interactive audio chats with seasoned practitioners in your chosen field of interest, whether it's player representation or a position with a team. "We offer each student the 'what you know' and the 'who you know' to advance in sports business," explains founder and CEO Dr. Lynn Lashbrook, a sports agent himself for more than 35 years.

SMWW's intensive training is designed for people wanting to enhance their chances of gaining job placement in professional sports management. SMWW has assisted with sports careers in a huge range of sports worldwide including hockey, soccer, football, basketball, baseball, motorsports, cricket, rugby, lacrosse, mixed martial arts, and track and field.

The company also practices what it preaches—SMWW is an international full-service *sports agency* with an extensive network of agent advisors serving athletes throughout the world. The *sports agent advisor program* makes SMWW unique because it strives to develop a more personal relationship with the athlete, taking a fully integrated approach to their clients' wealth, personal life, career, and postcareer challenges.

"The paradigm of the more clients you have, the more influence you have on and off the field is broken," Lashbrook says. "We have a hypothesis that if you get people with integrity and an ethical compass and skill sets and they keep their day jobs, they are more likely to mentor a player than the super agency with hundreds of clients. The agent advisor can make some money, the player gets more attention, even after their playing days are over, when they sometimes need an agent or advisor more than ever before."

The chaos that typically surrounds a high-profile athlete suits the company just fine. "Almost every day, there's an issue with an athlete somewhere, whether it's a DUI, or domestic violence, or financial problems," Lashbrook points out. "We really feel that the chaos plays nicely into our model because a lot of people would like to be agents given the opportunity, and we really think they're better suited to giving a player the little bit of extra attention they need to manage all the craziness.

"We're getting a larger, more diverse audience than ever before," Lashbrook continues. "We're taking a whole generation of people who are passionate about sports. They can complete our program online and keep their day job while they're doing it, because we can't guarantee a job, although we've been very successful in getting our students placed. I always tell them, 'You have to have a ticket to the game to catch a foul ball,' and by that I mean you have no chance of being a general manager unless you get in the organization, usually via front office and the sales department because that's where there's the most turnover. SMWW can give you a ticket to the game."

The Agent as Owner:
Jeff Moorad Looks Back
From the Other Side of the Table

Jeff Moorad, now majority owner of the San Diego Padres, came to sports ownership with the Arizona Diamondbacks after a long and successful career as an agent. His partnership with Leigh Steinberg produced some of the most innovative—and lucrative—contracts of the 1980s and 1990s. Amazingly enough, when Moorad crossed over in August 2004, baseball's elitist fraternity of owners didn't call a squeeze play. They embraced him.

In his last season in Arizona, Moorad compared his life as an agent to the other side of the owner's desk.

"On the agent side, brokering trades was probably the most exhilarating experience I had," Moorad says. "You're navigating amongst a lot of egos; not just the players but the owners in different cities present quite a challenge, as do the general managers. There's a lot of self-professed expertise when it comes to evaluating a player's worth. But it's the ultimate challenge for a representative, if they're able to get to that point, and I was particularly able to enjoy that position on the football side of the business."

One of Moorad's favorite deals involved quarterback Steve Young's trade from Tampa Bay to San Francisco. "Steve had been traded to the St. Louis Cardinals when the Cardinals were still in St. Louis," Moorad recalls. "At the last minute, we were able to convince Hugh Culverhouse, then the owner of the Bucs, to change the deal and send Steve to San Francisco, so he had a chance to play with Bill Walsh. Being a part of that transaction was really fun—especially when Steve went on to win two Super Bowls as starting quarterback with the 49ers."

Moorad's Arizona baptism was navigating the intricate acquisition of ace Randy Johnson. "Before he came here, Randy was really only open to going to two or three teams, the Dodgers, or maybe the Angels, but he really wanted to be with the Yankees," Moorad says. "Randy and I had known each other casually for over 20 years. I had sat down for a cup of coffee with him in 1984 when he was a junior at USC. We were both northern California kids; he was from Livermore, I was from Modesto. I could never figure out an agent relationship with him, but we'd occasionally stay in touch.

"Randy had two agents, Al Nero and Barry Meister, both of whom I knew over the years, so I rolled up my sleeves and along with Joe Garagiola Jr., then our GM, we worked out a deal with the Yankees that I think worked well for all," Moorad says. "I worked on the player's side with Randy and worked on the financial side with Randy's agent. It was a lot like what I'd done on the agent side for years."

The Johnson deal and most of the acquisitions and trades that Moorad has navigated come with lots of zeros attached. But he claims he's less sensitive to players' salaries than are most team executives because he's lived with them day to day for more than 20 years. "The reality is," Moorad explains, "our players got paid as much money as we could convince an owner to pay, but there was always some semblance of market that dictated the compensation packages. Today, from the other side of the table, it doesn't look any different. The Diamondbacks won a World Series in 2001, faster than any other expansion team had ever won one. The bad news is that in the act of paying players to get there, they've mortgaged the future of the franchise. While we're paying $65 million to players who played for our team this season, we'll cut checks for another $29 million that are part of deferred payments to players who are no longer with our organization.

"So effectively," Moorad concludes, "we're maintaining a $94 million payroll even though we can only show $65 million of it. Until we burn through that past debt, we're not going to be able to advance our team as quickly and significantly as we'd like to be able to."

The Diamondbacks are far from the only ball club to fall victim to sacrificing long-term stability to a short-term trophy—and it's certainly not restricted to baseball. After a decade of cheering himself hoarse courtside, billionaire owner of the Portland Trail Blazers Paul Allen ignored the rafts of data and draft prospectus he'd grown accustomed to poring over—his Microsoft data-processing roots showing—and gave in to his checkbook in a transparent attempt to buy an NBA championship. Always benevolent, Allen lavished on contracts, as *Sports Illustrated* put it, "wildly disproportionate to the players' value." Unknowingly ushering in Portland's "Jail Blazer" era, Allen paid "an out-of-shape, drug-addled" Shawn Kemp $12.7 million a year. Damon Stoudamire signed a deal for $12.4 million. And a past-his-prime Scottie Pippen was awarded a four-year $54 million contract. Despite the league's highest payroll, and a luxury tax that would give pause to even a multibillionaire, Allen walked away trophyless. While the Trail Blazers are now once again conference contenders, it's taken them more than a decade to rebound.

And what of Boras' client Manny Ramirez? Despite a 50-game suspension for a banned substance—in Ramirez' case, female fertility drugs as opposed to steroids—his 2009 season with new team Los Angeles Dodgers was played under a two-year $18 million contract, meaning his per-game salary was $170,000. According to *Los Angeles Times* columnist Steve Lopez, Ramirez' two-year pay could cover the annual salaries of 100 L.A. policemen, 100 firefighters, and 250 teachers. It would take four years for a United States Forest Service firefighter, his life on the line every time he combats a California foothill blaze, to earn $170K.

Karma exists—Ramirez is a Dodger no more, and after a brief stint with the Tampa Bay Rays that involved more allegations of banned performance enhancing drugs, he decided to retire.

If the Shoe Fits: Impact of the "Shoe Wars" on Athlete Endorsements

Teams sign athletes to lucrative contracts because they can play. Agents also sign athletes because they can sell. We have Michael Jordan to thank for this dynamic. And behind him, Sonny Vaccaro.

Vaccaro, John Paul, if you check his birth certificate, is the former Nike marketing executive who signed Michael Jordan to his first sneaker deal and advised dozens of other top prep basketball players, LeBron James and Kobe Bryant among them. After cementing a lifelong relationship with Nike, Vaccaro went to adidas and then on to Reebok—leaving a string of highly paid athlete endorsers in his wake.

From 1984 to 2007, Vaccaro also ran the ABCD All America Camp, a regular summer showcase of elite high school basketball stars that along the way showcased the likes of Bryant and James. During ABCD camp exhibition games, sports agents came running. So did the corporate marketers.

There's no business like shoe business. Just ask Vaccaro—thanks to his camps, he also became one of the lynchpins of the $17 billion sports shoe market.

More money is available for the athlete apparel endorser—though not as much for the nonsuperstar. Nike is prepared to pay more than $1.6 billion for long-term endorsements. Reebok is committed to spend $200.5 million.

Yet corporate America seems to be more carefully targeting endorsements by emphasizing quality over quantity. As a result, many midlevel athletes are being squeezed out.

Clearly, the high-dollar endorsement deals given to Tiger Woods, James, Derek Jeter, Adrian Peterson, former WNBA standout Lisa Leslie, and (the king) Michael Jordan will continue. And the guys and gals who are able to sell shoes often reign supreme.

The launch of James' Nike Air Zoom Generation shoes during the 2006 holiday retail season produced a sale of 33 percent of the retail stock on the first day. The Allen Iverson lifetime contract with the Reebok footwear line was largely responsible for the 25 percent increase in Reebok footwear revenue a few years earlier. And these companies are expanding into other entertainment channels: Reebok's commitment to rappers 50 Cent and Jay-Z produced a 350 percent increase in their Reebok-related products the summer of 2007 alone.

As the competition becomes more intense, athletic shoe and apparel companies continue to expand their horizons. First, the focus is clearly on international expansion. In 2008, before the Beijing Olympic Games, Nike's sales increased 66 percent to an estimated $300 million in China; at the same time, the company was opening an average of 1.5 new stores a day in the country. Companies are continuing to compete in a number of ways for the international basketball dollar—Yao Ming signed with Reebok for an estimated $100 million, and the Reebok NBA deal is keyed to a long-term global affiliation with Wal-Mart.

The international soccer marketplace is also a battleground. In 2007, Nike captured 34 percent of the European soccer market, compared to adidas at 30.2 percent. Nike has doubled its soccer business since the 2002 World Cup, totaling $1 billion in annual sales.

FACTS
- **1.8: Number of pairs of athletic shoes the average American adult buys per year. That's triple the number for Europeans.**
- **70: Percentage of the $1.7 billion worth of basketball shoes purchased each year by American men that never touch a basketball court.**

Source: NPD Group, Inc.

Athletic shoe companies don't just focus on male fans. In 2006, Reebok signed actress Scarlett Johansson to a multiyear contract to develop Scarlett "Hearts" Reebok, a "fashion-forward, athletic-inspired footwear and apparel signature collection." The apparel line, designed by Johansson in collaboration with a team of two young Reebok designers, debuted in spring 2007 at high-end department stores and boutiques worldwide.

"Scarlett embodies the pulse points of our brand—individuality, authenticity and a life lived to the fullest in perpetual motion," Paul Harrington, president and CEO of Canton, Massachusetts–based Reebok, said in a statement about the young actress. "These characteristics make her the perfect fit for our new women's footwear and apparel collection and also for our exciting new women's campaign."

In 2009, Reebok was no more immune to the economic downturn than any other company. The latest in a string of companies forced to let go of workers, Reebok eliminated 310 jobs. Meanwhile, Nike's athletic footwear market in the United States has increased 4 percent over the last four years.

Outside of shoe sales, the sports merchandising and licensing business is healthy. In 2006, before the recession slowly began to take a toll, sports licensing revenue topped $826 million, according to the international Licensing Industry Merchandisers' Association, while retail sales for the NFL and MLB each topped $3.2 billion. (Women's merchandise accounted for slightly more than 5 percent of that total, largely thanks to a new generation of merchandise tailored to women's frames and a profusion of pink hats and T-shirts for every sport.)

Endorsable You

When a company is downsizing, people in the marketing department are often the first ones to get nervous—they don't design or manufacture the product, they're not a profit center, and it's often difficult for them to justify return on investment. The same dynamic applies to sports sponsorship and endorsement contracts at the end of the first decade of the new, poorer millennium.

In 2009, according to *Forbes*, sports sponsorship outlays shrank by $100 million, to $11.3 billion, after sports sponsorship spending had risen annually by more than 10 percent a year for more than a decade.

Yet, substantial funds remain available for athletic endorsements. American companies are regularly shelling out $900 million annually on endorsement contracts, and Nike now has $4.2 billion in total endorsement deals. Because there is so much money at stake, the question for corporate marketers and agency brand managers alike is, which athlete? Dozens of potential candidates join the pro ranks every year, from up-and-coming rookies to college fan favorites to surefire superstars. Which player really embodies a company's brand? Will she work hard for us? Will he behave himself off the field? Can we trust him?

"The ability to choose the right athlete," says Adam Fusfeld, writing for the *Bloomberg BusinessWeek* Power 100, "is the difference between millions of dollars and a metaphorical cleat in the face."

Where events are concerned, sports marketing agencies and their corporate clients adopt a metric commonly used in advertising: cost per thousand views, or CPM, of a sponsor's brand. But when individual athletes are tainted by scandal or alleged drug use, it can also ruin the reputation, and appeal as a marketing platform, of the event in which they're competing.

Clearly, the name of the corporate game is risk avoidance. Sports marketers cannot guarantee against injuries—such as those that caused a major loss of marketing brand identity during Emmitt Smith's twilight with the Arizona Cardinals. Before he joined the New York Yankees, center fielder Johnny Damon was rejected by Disney for a commercial (because of his long hair, he said). Reebok withdrew a commercial featuring rapper 50 Cent from British television after viewers complained that it glamorized guns. Facebook pages, Twitter accounts, and cell phone cameras have turned everyone into a would-be tabloid tattler—just ask swimmer and bong handler Michael Phelps and Portland Trail Blazers center Greg Oden, literally caught with his pants down.

Steroids, especially within baseball, have also hurt athletes' reputations and their ability to sign lucrative endorsement deals. Before he was exposed as an alleged performance-enhancing drug user, pitcher Roger Clemens earned about $3 million annually in endorsement deals, including agreements with AT&T, AutoNation, and Coca-Cola. Now? The Rocket has burned out—and he's facing federal perjury charges.

Corporate America has wizened up and now emphasizes quality over quantity—endorsement contracts are now on average smaller, shorter, and easier to terminate. But corporate America still knows that the superstar moves product. Tiger Woods (pre–Thanksgiving hydrant encounter), Michael Jordan, Peyton Manning, and LeBron James have caused a major upward spike in their respective endorsement products. And such top NFL jersey sellers on www.NFLShop.com as quarterback Tom Brady and linebackers Brian Urlacher and Ray Lewis seem to have two things in common—proven on-field performance coupled with charisma and visibility.

NASCAR drivers and owners are also a wellspring of endorsement potential for corporate partners and perhaps sum up the appeal to mainstream consumers. "People want to buy from someone they like," Kansas automobile dealer Scott Davies told the *Wall Street Journal*. "A lot of customers won't buy a car from GM, but they will buy a car from Roger Penske."

For most team sport athletes, endorsements require patience. While certain first-rounders in any year's draft may be prime candidates for the big endorsement pot of gold, most athletes will not receive substantial marketing money until they make All Pro . . . and stay out of trouble.

It's a little easier for athletes who play individual sports. Before the Thanksgiving 2009 mishap that blew the lid off his carefully controlled image, Tiger Woods dominated his sport, and the endorsement business, like few others in history. On his way to attempting to break Jack Nicklaus' record 18 major wins, the 34-year-old Woods inked deals with companies ranging from Accenture and American Express to Nike and Gillette that totaled $92 million in 2009 alone. Indeed, before his fall from grace, Woods was expected to be the first athlete to have reached the $1 billion in career earnings mark.

FACTS

- The international athlete endorsement and advertising business is a $350 billion business.
- Corporate ad spending on sports exceeded $12.4 billion in 2006 alone.
- Sports-specific spending rose to $61.6 billion by 2010.

Looking at "LeBrand"

At the ripe old age of 20, former Cleveland Cavaliers phenom LeBron James, now one of the Miami Heat Big Three, took an unconventional approach to representation, firing his respected agent and putting a group of trusted friends in his place. This wasn't the first time James had ignored common wisdom. Straight out of high school and NBA bound, he refused to accept a mere $25 million for a shoe deal, much to his eventual benefit.

At age 18, James knew a lot more about the game than what it takes on the court. He knew that he had to create competition and wait for the right time to strike.

The inside view of the LeBron James business story reveals the tactics used to fetch more money for a teenager from sports marketing than ever before. Even at 18, James was a prodigy at more than stuffing the ball in the hoop or feeding teammates. He was a savvy businessman then and is even more so in his mid-20s. With expert advice, he has defined his brand as selective while others are grabbing everything on the block, diluting their names and capital.

"LeBron has a bookkeeper who's a professional and has experience with a major international firm. He has independent investment advisors, he has me as his lawyer, and we help him through his company, which is called LRMR Sports Management Inc.," says Cleveland superlawyer Fred Nance, regional managing partner of Squire, Sanders & Dempsey LLC, whose legal practice focuses on sports and entertainment law and who has provided counsel on a wide range of matters to James since he was a teenager. "He's got a couple of subsidiaries, and we help him make decisions—but ultimately, it's his decision. The thing I love most about LeBron is his intellectual curiosity, his quest for knowledge and understanding. If we say something is a bad idea, he'll ask why."

When James first thought about declaring himself NBA eligible, there wasn't a major sports agent who hadn't found Akron, Ohio, on the map and tried the thick steaks at the Diamond Grill or stayed at the Radisson City Center. After his senior year at St. Vincent–Saint Mary, it was commonly written that James, the most promising hoop prodigy since Michael Jordan, could earn a fortune in a sneaker endorsement alone. Some people were suggesting that it might even be in the neighborhood of $25 million. Members of James' inner circle argued that he should listen to the sneaker pitches and decide on one before he picked an agent—an agent would only take a huge cut from what seemed like an enormously valuable deal already.

One potential agent who knew otherwise worked just 35 miles (56 km) north of Akron. A partner in IMG, started by Clevelander Mark

Mark McCormack: The Original Super Agent

Mark McCormack, who died too young in 2003, was the founder and chairman of International Management Group (IMG). Along with Bob Woolf, McCormack wrote the book on what a sports agent actually does for a living and glamorized the profession through his dazzling client Rolodex.

Born in 1930, McCormack suffered a fractured skull when he was hit by a car at the age of six. Sports such as football and baseball were out, so golf became a passion—he qualified for the U.S. Golf Championship in 1958, and the golf ranking points system he developed morphed into the official World Golf Ranking system in the 1980s.

After attending Yale Law School and serving in the U.S. Army for a short time, McCormack joined the firm of Arter & Hadden, where he soon realized the potential of sports as a corporate communications medium and reasoned that the athletes he represented could earn extra money from endorsements and sponsorships.

In 1960, McCormack offered to sign a young American golfer named Arnold Palmer, and the deal was sealed with a simple handshake. Palmer became IMG's first client, and soon, McCormack was negotiating a $5,000 annual deal for Palmer to endorse Wilson sporting goods—big money at the time.

The next golfer McCormack signed was a talented South African newcomer named Gary Player, followed by American professional Jack Nicklaus. With incredible foresight, McCormack had cornered the Big Three who would dominate the golf world for decades and transcend borders. The athletes he managed were the first to endorse clothing, watches, and motor oil.

In 1968, McCormack branched out into tennis, signing Australian Rod Laver. Later, he added Bjorn Borg, John McEnroe, Ivan Lendl, Chris Evert-Lloyd, and Martina Navratilova to his growing stable of tennis champions.

By 1985, IMG's roster spanned the full spectrum of sports, including the likes of soccer's Pele; skier Jean-Claude Killy; runners Sebastian Coe, Bill Rodgers, and Mary Decker Slaney; baseball star Jim Rice; and football player Herschel Walker.

McCormack and known as the country's largest sports marketing firm, lobbied for what could fast become the most lucrative representation in sports. In the end, however, a man who lived nearly 3,000 miles (4,800 km) away got the job.

Aaron Goodwin, from the Pacific Northwest, specializes in the NBA. Goodwin, who had come regularly to Akron for three years as an investment in James, took over the negotiations with the sneaker companies and soon proved that it's wise to pay a big chunk of your royalties to someone who knows what he's doing. In Goodwin's hands, that "neighborhood of

IMG managed every aspect of the athletes' professional lives, from negotiating with team owners to investing athletes' money and ensuring they got to appointments on time. IMG's athletes knew they stood an excellent chance of earning just as much off the playing field as on, thanks to McCormack and his staff's creative vision.

Early on, McCormack also created a broadcasting arm, Trans World International (TWI), to produce a handful of golf events. Today, TWI produces approximately 9,000 hours of sports programming each year, and IMG runs an average of eight or nine sporting events around the world each day. For TWI, McCormack invented made-for-TV sports events such as golf's skins games, celebrity challenger events, and *American Gladiators*.

McCormack also published numerous books, including the bestselling *What They Don't Teach You at Harvard Business School*. In 1990, *Sports Illustrated* voted McCormack the most powerful man in sports." He was inducted into the World Golf Hall of Fame posthumously in 2006.

The head of IMG's global golf division, Mark Steinberg, negotiated Tiger Woods' $800 million contract with Nike as well as the multimillion-dollar deals with Gillette, Accenture, EA Sports, and Tag Heuer that allowed Woods to become the first athlete ever to approach the $1 billion mark.

Steinberg also did his best to deflect damage to Woods since November 2009, when the golfer became fodder for global tabloids and gossip sites after it was revealed that he'd kept a secret string of mistresses across the United States. Woods took a leave of absence from golf to try and save his marriage, divorced, and hasn't won a tournament since.

As for Steinberg, he was fired by IMG in May, 2011 when he became too expensive to keep after Woods lost several lucrative endorsement deals in the wake of the scandal. Steinberg's salary far outstripped the commission revenue he was bringing in.

$25 million" deal blossomed into $90 million—the richest shoe contract ever given an 18-year-old.

And Nike's end of the deal proved sweet. The morning the first LeBron James sneaker specials emerged at retail outlets, there were long lines at shopping malls around the country. And there are still record sales every time a new version of his signature shoe is released. Goodwin and James' coterie of advisors have added great dimension to his portfolio. James' popularity with kids was evidenced by his four-year multimillion deal with Bubblicious bubble gum. He has also signed on to promote State

Farm, McDonald's, and Coca-Cola's youth-oriented brands including Sprite and Powerade. Jeff Dunn, a Coke executive, said, "LeBron James has brought more excitement and anticipation to the game of basketball than any player in recent history, and we think he's just getting started." Indeed, in 2009, *Forbes* estimated that James made more than $40 million in salary and endorsements. And in Miami, the skyhook's the limit.

8

Sports Sponsorship 101

► The role of sports in overall integrated marketing communications strategy is always evolving.

► Dealmaking between clients and agencies is a complex process.

► Sports properties and sports media have converged; media are often used to create the perception of sponsorship.

► Top brands and marketers in sports sponsorship offer best practices.

► ROI increasingly dictates every move in sports sponsorship relationships.

► Strategic activation on air, on line, and on site is critical to make sponsorship dollars work harder.

a universal source of community pride and a multibillion-dollar industry, sports are a source of fan passion with the power to drive significant consumer brand affinity. Over time, a growing number of marketers who command multimillion-dollar budgets couldn't help but take notice.

A common denominator that transcends cultural and societal differences, sports are an enormous and growing business that delivers a massive and highly engaged audience game after game. As the last Alamo of a time-shifted, TiVo-ed consumption—and with a nearly infinite supply of regularly generated content, storylines, and statistics—sports are perfectly suited for the new multiscreen world, with the rise of technology creating a virtual sports bar for 'round-the-clock content and engagement. Americans love entertainment, and sports—the original reality television—are nothing short of synonymous with everyday theater.

Although the modern business of sports marketing, and specifically sports sponsorship, remains a relatively fledgling industry (remember when the BCS games didn't have a sponsor attached?), it's a vastly different one in the 21st century than it was some 50 years ago. Much has changed in sports sponsorship since the inaugural corporate stadium naming rights deal, sold in 1973 to the Buffalo, New York–based food service company Rich Foods, Inc., for a now-paltry total sum of $1.5 million. At $100,000 per year, this could barely cover the annual cost of a sign in a professional or major college stadium today, even adjusted for inflation.

An evolving understanding of sports marketing as the gold standard of integrated marketing communications has accelerated sports marketing's rise in importance within the broad discipline of marketing. As such, sports command gargantuan budgets for both media and sponsorship and premier consideration within the corporate marketing elite. What began, in many cases, as a way for CEOs to get close to their favorite athletes and pastimes has become a behemoth of an industry: *Sports Industry Almanac 2011* estimates the annual spending for sports marketing and advertising in the United States is more than $27 billion.

Sports Ad Spending in a Recession: Up or Down?

Corporation	2009 sports ad spending (in millions)	Pct. change	Pct. of total advertiser spending (in 2008)
Anheuser-Busch	$309.20	−6%	76%
Verizon	$228.10	−2%	20%
Sprint Nextel	$204.90	10%	36%
Ford	$197.30	10%	33%
AT&T Wireless	$180.90	−32%	24%
Geico	$171.30	26%	40%
Toyota	$166.80	−25%	33%
DirecTV	$166.70	9%	44%
Chevrolet	$160.30	30%	36%
McDonald's	$155.40	9%	22%

Primary Source: *Sports Industry Almanac 2011*

The global financial crisis in 2008 demonstrated that the sports sponsorship industry is far from recession-proof: Marketing purse strings were universally tightened in corporations large and small, and the emphasis on the bottom line renewed with gusto. This "new normal" birthed a new catchphrase: return on investment, or ROI, frequently referred to at leading industry conferences as the holy grail of sports marketing. The recession helped accelerate a new era of accountability in which CFOs and procurement officers call the shots or, at the least, hold corporate marketing officers under the gun to prove tangible returns against business metrics and objectives. No longer would multimillion-dollar sponsorship deals be hatched on a cocktail napkin and executed on the whim of a personal indulgence by a C-level executive whose favorite team had just won a divisional championship.

A fundamental shift in power from marketer to consumer and the onslaught of digital and mobile technologies have driven the migration of consumers to new screens for information and entertainment and changed the very notion of what advertising is and how it is measured. Vanilla deals have become a thing of the past, replaced by increasingly complex sports marketing platforms that include sponsorships that must be activated in new mediums. This continues to challenge the way properties structure partnerships and demonstrate value, and it requires a full understanding of the myriad of consumer touch points. Understanding the new sports marketing landscape, and sponsorship's ever-changing position in it, is crucial for optimizing brand impact with regard to business and advertising metrics, sponsorship, and related media buys, as well as protecting brands from ambush efforts by competition.

Anatomy of Sports Sponsorship

Simply put, corporate sponsorship as it relates to sports is the endorsement of a product or brand by an individual, team, or event.

Corporations, domestically and globally, invest billions of dollars every year to build their images, generate brand awareness, drive consideration, and ultimately inspire purchases via sports sponsorship. Reaching mass audiences with traditional 30-second commercial units and other forms of paid advertising has become increasingly difficult because of the continued fragmentation of viewers and readers and the proliferation of media touch points and content distribution vehicles. Given this, an intimate knowledge of digital media—and mobile and social media, for that matter—and a true understanding of the national and local marketplaces are requisite skill sets for sports marketing executives in order to claim true sports marketing and media mastery. Yet, regardless of this increasing complexity, one truism remains: As a means of plugging into consumer passion, sports know no rival, and the growing understanding of the power of sports to leverage fan avidity and equity transfer from leagues, teams, and properties has catapulted sports marketing and sponsorship to the forefront of nearly every corporate marketing mix in America.

Within the sports marketing mix, sponsorship is an integrated vehicle with which to activate the various advertising and promotional elements wrapped into the platform. In corporations, these are created, activated, and evaluated by different key players within the decision-making process. Given the complexity and scale of sports sponsorship, and the proliferation of properties and media in the marketplace, decisions undergo a rigorous and increasingly scientific process conducted collaboratively by corporate clients, advertising agencies (both media and creative), sports activation agencies, and consulting agencies as well as sponsorship and media sales agencies. Each constituent plays a key role within the marketing and sponsorship life cycle.

Step One: Identifying Objectives

When investigating a sponsorship purchase, brand and agency alike must work to first identify the budget, marketing objectives, and target audiences to be addressed. Possible sports and opportunities within them must be identified and a full audit performed on the marketing ecosystem of these possible sports. In doing so, corporations are able to identify the sports that work best within their budgets and in fact determine whether or not sponsorship is the right vehicle to help satisfy business and marketing objectives. In truth, as indicated later in this chapter, these steps are best taken by the property and sponsorship sellers as well, inserting themselves squarely in the shoes of the sponsorship buying brand and agency.

The general objectives of sponsorship can be broken down into five categories that may vary in importance given a company's product line, brand positioning, and key performance indicators (KPIs).

1. **Direct sales development** is vital because directly attributable sales, leads, or customers acquired are often the ultimate objective and ultimate measure of sponsorship success.

2. **Brand awareness and preference** drive brand selection or retention among a defined consumer base.

3. **External corporate awareness** helps position or reposition community relations and social responsibility for credibility and brand affinity.

4. **Internal relations development** increases employee involvement and distribution channel participation (as often seen with agent, bottler, or franchisee groups).

5. **Competitive advantage** is the ability to shut out the opposition and create preference for a company's brand above others within the same category (think Ford over Chevy; Coke over Pepsi; State Farm over Geico).

For each of these objectives, there may be a combination of industry- and brand-specific metrics by which to assess ROI, a pillar of sponsorship that we'll visit later in the chapter. All possible sponsorships should be evaluated against a rating system that ranks and measures the value and efficacy of both tangible and intangible sponsorship assets. Consideration must be given to a sponsorship's alignment with brand identity, level of prestige and relevance with core and noncore fans, provision of intellectual property, category exclusivity and protection from category ambush, ability to meet business objectives and metrics, and geographic and demographic alignment. These will vary in importance within the sponsorship evaluation, depending on the brand and unique brand objectives, but must all be given close consideration and analyzed fully in order to secure a successful sponsorship.

A consideration that is largely undervalued during most decision-making processes is ownership, the value of which is universally recognized by smart marketers. A dominant sponsor position for leading Fortune 100 brands, or a meaningful position for a challenger or niche brand, has tremendous value; sponsorship (ideally) creates equity transfer, and without ownership there are only so many pieces of the equity pie to go around. Yet, that's not to say that ownership is always the best value proposition. Opinion leaders such as Subway have trended toward intelligent and selective sponsorship with a focus on ownership opportunities, either an entire equity or a specific and highly relevant equity slice of a sports pie.

Step Two: Research, Research, and More Research

Although you'd think at heart it would be an emotionally driven decision to sign an MVP quarterback to endorse your brand, sponsorship demands a sophisticated and calculated approach to planning and research. Sufficient marketing research can mean the difference between a successful sponsorship and a colossal marketing failure. The purpose of research is multifold: to evaluate brand and consumer characteristics, identify measurable objectives, determine which sports align best with the target audience and assess the market health of those sports, determine the sponsorship scope, and help allocate budget.

Marketing research begins with defining and establishing business and marketing objectives in order to develop an advertising and sponsorship plan, as the two can no longer be cleanly segmented and must be planned and executed in tandem. Simultaneously, a brand needs to generate a holistic profile of the target consumer based on analytic research, identifying demographic and lifestyle factors that influence product assessment and purchase, as well as evaluating statistical and numerical market data, including sales figures, proprietary survey results, econometric modeling, and perceptual mapping. These considerations help form marketing and sponsorship strategy to win out in category competition and engage consumer passions in a way that translates into ROI.

A deep dive into the research and analytics provides numerous benefits: It allows for sufficient time for entry and exit strategies of the current sponsorship portfolio; shrinks the list of properties to only those within core sponsorship objectives and strategy; creates a road map to multiyear approaches to sponsorship; allows for tracking of currently unavailable properties for future acquisition; and expedites evaluation of unexpected opportunities based on these long-term objectives. If that's not enough, brands must also continually monitor the ever-evolving mobile and digital media landscapes that require of marketers extraordinary agility and creativity to consistently drive value.

Step Three: Sponsorship Activation

An effective corporate sponsorship has several key components. For one, a sponsorship must allow a brand to tap into a key target audience's personal passions in a relevant and meaningful way.

Tony Pace, chief marketing officer of sandwich giant Subway, one of the true mover-and-shaker brands in sports sponsorship, is particularly vigilant that sponsorship proposals submitted to Subway be customized with much more thought than "just change the brand name. Rather, Subway seeks to build tailor-made platforms around sports by selectively choosing assets inherent in the property and its controlled media and further customizing a marketing program with other traditional and emerging media, endorsements, and marketing assets and relationships. Athletes we use are fans of the brand, and we don't choose celebrities. We happen to choose genuine fans of Subway who happen to be famous . . . customers to speak spontaneously and naturally about brand and how they use it."

Pace puts it this way: "The problem with many sponsorship salespeople is that they reach on the shelf and sell you the same box of assets whether you're marketing soft drinks, QSRs [quick-service restaurants], or automobiles. This doesn't make sense to me, because the whole point of marketing is to differentiate your brand. Subway is anything but a 'me too' brand; therefore, any proposal for Subway should be specific to Subway's business, brand positioning, product mix, and marketing assets, and any program that is not brand specific is sublimating your brand."

It is equally important to remember that sponsorship must be integrated with other marketing communication vehicles—such as broadcast, digital, direct, and in-store materials—in order to provide consumers with a consistent brand experience and sense of continuity. Often, sponsorships that don't work fail not only because the property is misaligned with the brand—think 20-something Tiger Woods driving a stodgy Buick sedan—but also because the particular initiative has nothing to do with a larger integrated marketing plan or the company's overall business objectives.

Sponsorship in the 21st century is driven by an "everything is sponsorable"—and thus, everything must be activated—mantra in which sponsorship assets are broken down into small increments to maximize revenue and value for sponsors. Marketing dollars must work harder, and they also must deliver more value.

The heightened scrutiny placed on sports sponsorship and media investments, along with the nonnegotiable insistence for tangible ROI, has antiquated passive sponsorship and calls for activation of every

7-Eleven

In an interesting local promotion in place from 2007 through 2009, the Chicago White Sox started weeknight home games at 7:11 p.m., moved from 7:07 as part of a sponsorship deal with the 7-Eleven convenience store chain.

The deal, which was purported to be in the $500,000 range annually, included team and ballpark assets. In all likelihood, the largest value received was the secondary media buzz about this creative sponsorship, crafted by a combination of Dan Migala, Brooks Boyer, and Jim Muno, all White Sox executives at the time.

Additionally, Margaret Chabris, a 7-Eleven spokesperson, was quoted as follows: "Every time the media announces the game's start time it will be a gentle reminder of our sponsorship." When this deal was not renewed, the start time was adjusted to 7:10, not returned to 7:07, because the national practice of increasingly lengthy pregame shows (also sponsored) has been fully extended into the local sports marketplace.

sponsorship asset. No longer are sponsorships undertaken without plans to properly monetize and activate the various elements of the deal; rather, activation plans must be put in motion in advance of purchase.

Mike Reisman, principal and founding partner of Velocity Sports & Entertainment, underscores this reality. "I think maybe 10 years ago you might purchase a sponsorship and inherent benefits and figure out how to activate those after the fact," Reisman says. "However, circumstances have become such that you can't justify such a risk. Most companies, or at least the sports marketers, are developing the activation programs first so that they truly understand what they're negotiating for when they sit down at the negotiation table with the property or rights holder to make their dollars work much harder and much more efficiently."

Step 4: Measurement and ROI, the Holy Grail of Marketing

Return on investment, or ROI, is often referred to as the holy grail of sponsorship and the sports marketing industry in general. In the current economic climate, the old adage "Half of my ads work; I just don't know which half" is sooner met with a severance package than a chuckle. This paradigm shift has engendered a new way of looking at sports sponsorship, one in which tickets, signage, suites, and special events ring hollow in the face of achieving true business objectives with tangible results.

All the players in the sponsorship industry—companies, properties, and agencies—have a stake in the execution of effective ROI measurement and analysis. Corporate marketing departments have an obligation to pin down decisive marketing and brand objectives; properties need to track sponsor performance, tabulate data, and generate case studies; and agencies must counsel intelligently and expertly to formulate measurement and postanalysis criteria. In short, ROI looms at every stage of the sports sponsorship pipeline.

ROI, in simplest terms, is a measure of a sponsorship's efficiency. Although no single measurement is universally applicable, ROI can be seen as a combination of direct product or service sales, hard asset value, on-screen and in-media brand exposure, and movement in key brand metrics, whether those are brand or corporate awareness, consumer preference, or other proprietary measures (see figure 8.1). Standards and asset values have become fairly uniform, allowing sponsorships to be measured and benchmarked by research companies using state-of-the-art measurement technology.

Of increasing importance to ROI discussions is the topic of consumer engagement and how to measure it—and, along these lines, the degree to which fan avidity translates to propensity for positive consideration and ultimately purchase. Intuitively, consumers engage with specific television programs or specific sports rather than with television or sports in general. This understanding, as Tom McGovern of OMD's Optimum Sports explains, can have a profound effect on sponsorship consideration. "The ready accessibility of sports and multitude of platforms by which fans consume them pose a challenge to marketers seeking to tap into fan engagement," he says. "A broadcast audience viewing a 'crown jewel'

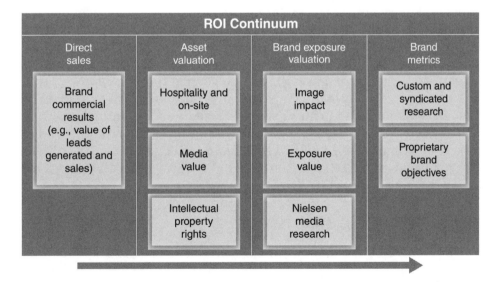

Figure 8.1 ROI continuum.

event is fairly broad, but as you drill down to other mediums, you lose the casual viewer who has less of a vested interest.

"The people who seek out content—who seek out video on demand or proprietary content—are at the highest level of engagement," McGovern continues. "It's these most avid fans who are most receptive to sponsorship, and sponsors need to be cognizant of the fan experience and how it affects the economics of sponsorship."

National Versus Local

Equally important in formulating a sponsorship and activation plan is true understanding of the myriad ways a brand's consumers interact with and associate with the product, service, and brand identity. Although budget is an obvious factor in deciding between an overarching league sponsorship and a more local, team-specific one, even more important is seamless alignment with demographic targets and priority markets.

Steve Bass, director of global integration and development at Rapp Collins, points out, "You don't root for the NFL shield or for the league, but for your local team." There are few exceptions—NASCAR being one of them. "NASCAR is an exception to emotional detachment from league entities; it's one [league] that seems to transcend this," he says. "You'll see the NASCAR logo on the back of pickup truck windows, but you won't see an MLB sticker and you won't see an NFL sticker."

Tom McGovern, managing director of OMD's Optimum Sports (a hybrid sports media consultancy group), agrees as it pertains to the local versus national nature of MLB: "If you look at a sport such as baseball, it's a local sport. You watch your local team on your local TV station, watch your local news that covers your local team, and read your local newspaper that covers your local team." When it comes to finding and tapping into fan avidity and consumer passions, as Bass puts it, local and team sponsorships are a much smarter marketing direction for many brands: "It's the logo that resonates with people. People root for the [New York] Jets, and they're going to buy Pepsi because Pepsi supports the New York Jets. They're not going to buy Pepsi because Pepsi supports the NFL."

However, making a team investment introduces the risk of a brand's perceived strength and identity rising and falling with the tide of wins and losses, a variable that's eliminated at the league level. Just ask any brand that's ever linked itself with the Chicago Cubs.

Sell-Side Considerations

If you have a sponsorship to sell, looking at the sports sponsorship world from the buyer's perspective is an exceptional foundation from which to build property and sales strategy and ultimately close the deal. Prospective sellers need to pay close attention to all the considerations that corporations and their partner agencies must look at in order to incent purchase and, down the road, renewal. Given the myriad opportunities that exist within the sports ecosystem, it's essential to find and strengthen the differentiating factors that will inspire the imaginations of senior marketing executives and their million-dollar budgets.

Customizing the sponsorship package is critical to the sales process, as we've seen with Subway, as is looking at common attributes between the property and the brand. Are they high end or everyman? Regional or international? Old and established or avant-garde? The seller should also consider activation ideas and try to understand how the sponsorship returns an investment to the brand. Properties (usually teams, leagues, or facilities) should also consider whether they should take on sponsorship sales themselves or whether they should hire an outside agency. In most cases, this is best determined by the size of the property and its internal sales staff and the complexity of distributing and packaging the sponsorships at hand.

The Agencies: How Deals Get Done

The marketing buck ultimately begins and ends with the corporations that flaunt advertising budgets and support sponsorship campaigns, but the gatekeepers of the sports marketing world are in many cases the agencies that facilitate sponsorship and media spending. Although companies are responsible for creating a clear vision and direction for business goals and marketing objectives, after absorbing these goals and strategies the agency is left to build the blueprint and execute against it. These agencies, by virtue of their representation of multiple clients, can provide valuable insight and perspective regarding best-in-class negotiation, marketplace pricing, planning against objectives, and activation of a sponsorship and media investment. Increasingly, these agencies must be fluent in all elements of a sports marketing ecosystem in order to truly leverage a sport or sponsorship for the benefit of their corporate clients, and they must have a clear understanding of all media embedded in a given sponsorship.

First, however, an effective outside agency will judge whether or not the sponsorship is salable at all and whether the business model and potential audience justify possible sponsor investment. Sports properties and sponsorships are often undercut by detractions:

- Vague domestic or global distribution results in a lack of ability to project audience numbers and demographics on air and online.
- Production costs are too high relative to possible TV ratings, decreasing the ability to pay for time buys based on return on commercial media inventory.

- The sport or event itself is not attractive to desirable demographic groups.
- There is no consideration of a digital strategy up front and a poor understanding of how the target demographic consumes media in the first place.

The Agency World

The agency world is characterized by global conglomerates that have become synonymous with the Madison Avenue world of advertising, behemoths that call to mind a Marlon Brando–esque gathering of the families. With arms and constituents that span the globe, represent the biggest and best corporations and marketing budgets, and constantly stay abreast of market and consumer trends, the four main players commanded more than $37.5 billion in combined business in 2010 according to *Ad Age*: WPP ($13.60 billion), Omnicom Group ($11.72 billion), Publicis Groupe ($6.29 billion), and Interpublic Group ($6.03 billion).

Within these vast ownership groups is a spectrum of agencies that interface with corporate clients to address the range of needs and tactical approaches that govern both advertising and sponsorship. Media agencies such as OMD, Starcom MediaVest, and Mindshare—figureheads of Madison Avenue—plan and purchase broadcast media across networks and programming. Hybrid sports consultancy agencies such as Optimum Sports, GroupM, and Horizon Media work to combine media and sponsorship expertise to deliver integrated multiplatform approaches. Strategy and activation specialists such as Omnicom's GMR and Marketing Arm help brands devise and execute holistic strategies that encompass experiential and promotional marketing against lifestyle, entertainment, and sports objectives.

As all these functions have become increasingly convergent within sports and entertainment, forward-thinking agency groups have sought to create cross-discipline task forces that unite executive client teams and their agency managements. In 2009, the Omnicom Group assembled an Olympic task force to enable best practices for their Olympic-sponsor clients, including GE, McDonald's, Visa, and Anheuser-Busch. Primarily looking ahead to the 2014 Winter Olympics in Sochi, Russia, this advisory board was able to identify "best-in-class" practices for negotiating, activating, planning, and executing sponsorship and related advertising investment. Inherent in this ambitious undertaking, headed by vice chairman Bruce Nelson and assisted by Ray Katz, now Leverage Agency president of sports properties and media, was streamlining planning timelines for in-market and media activation; isolating public affairs issues stemming from the political and economic landscape in host-country

Russia; and idea sharing and implementation of the research, analytics, and ROI considerations that would allow each sponsor to best utilize their investments.

The Corporate Side of the Coin

As mentioned earlier, today's corporate sponsorship environment is vastly different from the one that existed before ROI became common marketing parlance, and certainly before the emergence of new media. Today, the bulwarks of sponsorship—the NFL, the NBA, MLB, and NASCAR—while still the big men on campus, must work much harder to maintain their stronghold in the sponsorship marketplace, as a multitude of niche growth sports and sponsorship platforms have sprung up about them.

Are You Smarter Than a Fifth Grader: Sports Marketer Edition?

In a modern-day chicken-or-egg scenario, the evolution of marketing and sponsorship has fashioned smarter consumers who are now able to dictate when, how, and where they will accept and engage with brand messaging. The longstanding implicit agreement between marketer and consumer—*you advertise, I'll buy*—has been stricken down by the empowered consumer for whom everything is an option and information is nearly infinite and readily on demand.

Superintelligent consumers, awash in choices, demand personal relevance on their own time, choosing how, when, and where they will allow brands and sponsors to court their interests and passions. The vast proliferation of media and content distribution alternatives that have overhauled the very notion of what advertising is and how it is deployed is a double-edged sword: Although it gives marketers a much richer arsenal of weapons with which to deepen consumer engagement and brand experience, it also creates a huge shift in the ways consumers perceive and interact with marketing messages, making it absolutely essential for brands to engage in increasingly personalized ways. To reach consumers beyond the on-site experience and, dually, to reach enough consumers to actually pay back sponsorship investments, you really have to understand how media has evolved since the fourth quarter of the 20th century.

The 1970s (in sports as in every other programming genre) were a one-screen world and a supply chain of three in the United States—ABC, CBS, and NBC. But that quickly expanded with the rise of dedicated sports television, led, as we covered in chapter 2, by game-changer ESPN and other industry pioneers such as Turner Sports and FOX Sports. That, in turn, begat specialty cable channels such as Speed and the Golf Channel, creating a broadcast world no longer dominated by the major networks but characterized by a preponderance of specific sports programming offerings.

The advent of the digital age sparked a massive change in availability and consumption of content, and even generation of content, by audiences that have driven new content and promotional concepts and divergent marketing strategies. The Internet not only has democratized the flow and accessibility of information and revolutionized the ways consumers interact with brands but also has accelerated the migration of consumers to multiple screens for information and entertainment. Smart phones and social media only add to the litany of media and content alternatives, powerful new channels through which marketers can reach consumers and through which consumers can in turn reach marketers.

The Ultimate in Entertainment

In many ways the current sports marketing landscape, encompassing both sports media and sports sponsorship (which have all but converged), has been shaped by sport's becoming synonymous with entertainment. As a global stage upon which advertisers play and to which consumers flock in droves, sport is at once a multigenre theater: a mix of comedy, tragedy, and drama befitting the great William Shakespeare. As pointed out by NBA commissioner David Stern in the introduction, "[The NBA is] an enterprise that is the largest provider of reality programming in the world." LeBron James' overhyped decision to leave Cleveland, broadcast on a national stage courtesy of ESPN, only reinforced the now symbiotic relationship between sports and entertainment and won him the status of most despised public sports figure in Cleveland this side of Art Modell.

The Super Bowl, in all its glory, encapsulates the transformation: It has expanded from a single championship game into a weeklong on-site, on-air, and online extravaganza and de facto American holiday that ignites a host city with a fervor seldom seen otherwise. As referenced in chapter 1, other sports have followed suit, recognizing the immense value (read: revenue) to be found in embracing sport's status as the big top of big tops. Although most weeks we're a far cry from Bill and Mike Veeck's 1979 Disco Demolition Night, sport has undoubtedly become a spectacle of the highest order.

The Convergence of Sports Properties and Media

As sport and entertainment have become synonymous, the prevailing trend of the past two decades has been the convergence of sports properties and media, a marriage of two formerly near-separate entities. Multiple-screen consumption, exponentially increased channel selection, and time-shifted viewing have all contributed to an audience fragmentation that necessitates the union. Helping also is that sports are inherently suited for the transition: the literally boundless statistics, highlights, and opinions, as well as sport's profound "water cooler effect" and "Monday morning quarterbacking," create on-demand content to feed both emergent media and this larger trend in general.

In essence, sports properties and media companies alike have responded by blurring the lines between media and property. The NFL and NBA, for example, have evolved from pure sports leagues into media companies by virtue of their respective creations of the NFL Network and NBATV, recognizing that ownership of proprietary media creates and enhances additional revenue streams that allow properties to exercise complete control over the production, packaging, and distribution of content. MLB in particular has followed this path effectively and successfully, with the added distinction of creating a standalone and standout digital company, MLB Advanced Media.

Conversely, media companies have created properties and gained control of property rights: ESPN's X Games and NBC's Dew Tour are perfect examples of the former, and FOX Sports' control of the BCS and CBS Sports' ownership of NCAA basketball rights evidence the latter. Additionally, teams are increasingly retaining their own broadcast rights and originating regional sports networks; look no farther than the New York Yankees' YES Network or the rival Boston Red Sox's New England Sports Network (NESN) for examples.

The trend has been fueled by TV, a parallel evolution of fan consumption patterns and the knowledge by sports properties and leagues that significant revenue can be generated through the sale of TV rights. The NFL alone commands more than $4 billion in annual rights fees from its TV partners, a combination of per annum payouts from ESPN (nearly $2 billion), FOX ($720 million), CBS ($620 million), NBC ($603 million), and DirecTV (almost $1 billion). This convergence of properties and media has made it absolutely critical for marketers and agencies to be intelligent about both property and media assets and has engendered an evolution in media buying. In the convergence paradigm, media activates sponsorship and as such entails much more beyond "spots and dots," including on-air features and enhancements, brand integration, and online and in-media extensions of these features.

Multiplatform Sports Marketing

The ever-increasing challenge of engaging consumers, and the proliferation of media, strategies, and sponsorship opportunities, makes it absolutely essential to understand the complexities of multiplatform sports marketing. With the quaint days of single sponsorships long behind us, marketers have to use multiple sponsorship and media vehicles to optimize brand impact and fully ensure proper activation—the lack of which is a veritable death knell for any modern sports sponsorship. As sponsorship and its role as an integrated marketing communications tool have ascended in the corporate marketing mix, sponsorable properties have settled into what are essentially two distinct categories: rights-driven and vertically integrated properties.

Rights-Driven Properties

A rights-driven property is one that commands rights fees for assets such as broadcast networks, digital and mobile distribution networks, players, teams, apparel, and pieces of the whole that can earn usage and ownership fees from sponsors. Properties that have traditionally followed this model are the NFL, the NBA, NASCAR, and MLB, all of which offer a multitude of entry points for sponsors and ambushers and, as such, can be extremely difficult for a sponsor to fully integrate without enormous budgets.

Additionally, these property rights are essentially worthless without a well-laid activation plan, which may double or even triple the total cost of sponsorship of a rights-driven property. Take the NFL, for example. Rights to the NFL marks and logo, and requisite category designations, may cost a brand anywhere from $5 to $10 million; however, the broadcast and digital media commitment (including media and enhancements), participation in NFL events, and creation of additional brand initiatives to properly activate NFL rights in order to avoid category ambush may send the total sponsorship cost upwards of $20 million.

On the flip side of the rights coin, the cost of securing property rights is typically a fraction of the cost of the total true costs of sponsorship, which may allow brands to cherry-pick the rights to assets that are most valuable. As we discussed earlier, a major consideration for brands seeking entry into the major professional leagues is the concept of local versus national: Does fan avidity—and thus the level of engagement that translates into brand and sponsorship impact—resonate most with a specific team, or does it extend to a league? For a brand without multibillion-dollar budgets, purchasing only local team rights may be the soundest approach and the best means of achieving ROI.

Dovetailing out of this is the consideration of how fans consume the sport at hand. MLB fans, for example, may consume content via national TV, local TV, radio, www.MLB.com, or any combination of these. Drilling down into the consumption behavior of core consumers, and sequencing platform asset acquisition accordingly, will allow a brand to execute a sports-spend intelligently and efficiently.

In the case of longtime MLB sponsor State Farm, acquiring exclusive positions on www.MLB.com and on 26 of the 30 team websites was a strategy based on knowing that most insurance quotes are generated online. Additionally, State Farm's procurement of more than 90 percent of MLB-related digital traffic effectively eliminated category competitors Geico and Progressive from MLB consideration and resulted in an approximate 150 percent lift in fan identification of State Farm as the official insurance company of MLB.

Vertically Integrated Properties

Conversely, vertically integrated properties feature a single all-encompassing body that regulates all points of entry and controls all assets, making sponsorship far more ambush-proof and activation far more turnkey for a sponsor.

In contrast to a rights-driven property, for which rights must be purchased separately from media and other assets, vertically integrated properties offer a holistic package in which a sponsor receives full integration across the sport with respect to rights, media, in-venue signage and activation, and players and teams. Vertically integrated properties provide category-exclusive media built into the sponsorship costs as well as venue signage and possibly athlete and activation funds—unlike rights-driven properties, for which real costs are a multiple of the rights fee paid to the league. Entities such as the LPGA, the PBA, and the various national governing bodies (NGBs) control the full suite of property assets in-house and thus are able to provide sponsors with one-stop shopping.

However, vertically integrated properties are generally forced to do time-buy deals to receive broadcast exposure because unlike their rights-driven brethren, these sports are typically not established enough within the marketplace to command a rights deal with a network. These time-buys are often in poorly rated and inconsistent time periods and lack network promotion (a major factor in driving viewership of any genre programming), making it exceptionally difficult to fully monetize broadcast assets and justify top-tier sponsor spending. With media not as much of a factor, having a quality product is a key to success: athletes who are marketable, accessible, and cooperative; strong live attendance; venue and signage control; and a strong TV production.

Activation is especially important with vertically integrated properties, from both the sponsor and property standpoint. Given that vertically integrated properties are often smaller in stature and do not (yet) command significant brand equity with a mass audience, brands that fully activate their sponsorships can create a much greater brand equity transfer than would be the case with the NFL or NASCAR, for example, and can positively influence the partnership for both parties.

Finding a Niche

Embedded in the sponsor consideration of rights-driven versus vertically integrated properties is recognition of brand identity and objectives and how those are best served by the sport at hand. Brand objectives may vary widely between category leaders and challenger brands, and as such it's important to consider the efficacy of large-scale sports properties. Although the juggernaut entities of sports sponsorship—the NFL, NBA, NASCAR, and MLB—may best serve Fortune 500 corporations, for the up-and-comers of the corporate sponsorship space, dominance of a growth sport featuring impassioned fans and participants may be a better use of a finite budget than being a lesser sponsor of a major network or property. Some outstanding efforts in this area have included Paul Mitchell (hair care) and its leadership position in lifestyle sports such as snowboarding and beach volleyball; Xyience's (energy drinks and supplements) affiliation with UFC mixed martial arts; and Corona's presence in boxing, through which the brand has achieved impressive brand preference metrics against a rising Hispanic audience.

Branding and Brand Alignment

Fundamental to the success of sports sponsorship is an understanding of a brand's relationship to the sport it sponsors and to the athletes and fans, along with the ability to forge a strategic connection between sponsor and consumer in dynamic, meaningful ways. An intimate knowledge of what makes both brands and consumers tick is vital for forging the deep business-to-consumer connection that corporations covet and leverage for success. It is exceedingly important to maintain a sense of authenticity; corporate branding is often the deciding factor in beating out the competitive set in consideration and, ultimately, product and service sales. To do otherwise is to invite a failed sponsorship or, worse, the loss of brand preference and market share within the targeted audience.

State Farm, a perennial insurance category power, has exemplified the nuanced elements of brand alignment within sports in many of its sponsorship commitments. Recognizing that sports represents a powerful way to engage consumers, State Farm has endeavored—to the tune of continued success—to align its brand identity with sports properties such as MLB and the NCAA as the official insurance company and corporate partner, respectively. State Farm prides itself on "being there" (like a good neighbor) and aligns itself with the values of community, leadership, trustworthiness, and excellence, and both sponsorships reflect and reinforce those values. State Farm has successfully utilized fully integrated sponsorships to positively affect key brand metrics in meaningful ways, specifically those that serve as close proxies for leads generated and, ultimately, consumers acquired.

The sponsorship was activated locally by strategic team deals with marquee franchises such as the New York Yankees and Chicago Cubs to capitalize on local team avidity. Most importantly, the State Farm baseball platform features ownership of the MLB All-Star break Home Run Derby—a crown jewel event that both reinforced State Farm's excellence and allowed it to further a compelling community initiative with the Boys & Girls Clubs of America via the Gold Ball donation program.

As an NCAA corporate partner, State Farm strategically activates the sponsorship in media by aligning itself with premium collegiate properties such as ESPN's *College GameDay*, March Madness on Demand (a premier live streaming video service), the NABC/WABC All-American teams, and coaches such as Mike Krzyzewski (Duke University) and Pat Summitt (Tennessee)—two pillars of the college basketball community who personify State Farm's brand identity.

A Stadium by Any Other Name

Stadium naming rights are by no means a new endeavor, dating all the way back to 1926 when Chicago chewing gum magnate and owner of the Chicago Cubs, William Wrigley, stuck his name on his team's ballpark. In the first half of the 20th century, most stadiums and arenas bore the names of the team owners who assumed the brunt of construction costs, such as Comiskey Park and Ebbets Field, or were named for their locations, such as Three Rivers Stadium in Pittsburgh.

What's in a Name?

The ballooning of the naming rights market has been driven by the dual need to improve and diversify team revenue streams as well as finance the refurbishment of old stadiums or build new state-of-the-art facilities. In addition, corporations found they could derive immense benefit from entering into such an agreement: As a tool for branding and creating competitive advantage, naming rights are a highly effective means of placing companies in front of a mass of consumers. In the best of scenarios, naming rights can even establish brands as part of the regional and even national vernacular, much in the same vein as using the term *Googling* when conducting an Internet search. In the true spirit of everything is sponsorable, even municipalities have and are selling naming rights: In New York, Barclays bought naming rights to the Atlantic Avenue–Pacific Street subway stop in Brooklyn, an extension of its 20-year $400 million branding of the Barclays Center, home of the soon-to-be Brooklyn Nets.

The benefits of naming rights are well documented. They enable a corporation to establish or expand brand visibility in a new or priority market, and they can also forge important connections with famous stadium tenants—who can facilitate the hosting of ancillary events, such as All-Star and championship games, that increase impact exponentially throughout the lifetime of the deal. External signage creates value both through local market consumption and on-screen and in-media exposure. In addition to the direct economic benefit inherent in financial business for banks or pouring rights for beer and soft drinks, stadium naming rights provide the less tangible benefit of creating community goodwill and enhancing corporate civic responsibility.

Yet, there's also a historically high correlation between naming rights deals and corporate financial troubles. A number of corporations have lost the feather in their caps because of bankruptcy or financial losses—remember, Minute Maid Park in Houston used to be Enron Field—underscoring that this element of sponsorship can deliver a questionable return. It's a reality that has led some pundits to refer to the "stadium sponsorship curse" and encourages a well-thought marketing plan before taking the leap.

Changing in-stadium demographics also make an interesting case for the value of naming rights deals and in-venue activation. Over the course of the last 20 years, the proliferation of preferred seat licenses and season tickets has contributed to the decrease in attendance by Joe Fan, as has the general rise in ticket prices. Coupled with the fact that big-screen TVs and multiscreen consumption now make an in-home experience just as desirable as viewing a game live, this has created what Barrett Davie, founder of InStadium, calls a "hyper-consumer."

"It's all about the folks that are walking in and out of these facilities," Davie says. "They're tough to reach, on the go, and don't have the patience to engage with the messages brands want to deliver, usually through traditional advertising. But when they're in these facilities, they stop; the clock is off."

Citi Field

Although the phrase itself denotes only signage, naming rights deals have evolved into much more than a corporate logo above an entranceway. A naming rights deal typically represents an integrated sponsorship agreement and therefore delivers an extensive asset package and attendant benefits.

In New York, valued at $400 million spread out over the next 20 years, and negotiated by GroupM's MEC Sport & Entertainment, headed up by Greg Luckman, the Citi Field deal is one of the most lucrative stadium naming rights agreements in history. It's also a deal that has provoked considerable controversy: As the recipient of billions of dollars in taxpayer-funded bailout money, Citi has come under the public ire for lavish sponsorship spending and the prudence of paying vast sums of money for corporate branding.

However, the multiple sources of ROI inherent in naming the home of the New York Mets make the deal much more than an exercise in vanity. Citi, as the financier of the stadium construction itself, stands to reap the benefits of exposure to a local fan base and recoup a not insignificant amount of the $400 million total on interest payments alone; additionally, the behind-the-scenes banking relationship that allows Citi to handle the Mets' payroll and place ATMs throughout the stadium, among other things, is an additional source of revenue generated through the investment. With Citi Field being located in the world's biggest media market, and because of the ubiquitous brand placement in the stadium, Citi receives continual exposure in all telecasts and ancillary coverage. The stadium's location makes it visible from the Grand Central Parkway, from the Van Wyck Expressway, and to every arrival and departure from LaGuardia Airport, resulting in untold millions of consumer impressions each year.

Top 10 Sports Facility Naming Rights Deals

If the proposed NFL stadium in downtown Los Angeles goes ahead as planned, the Farmers Field sports naming rights deal ($700 million for 20 years) will be the biggest of all time. For the moment, these stadium naming rights deals top the revenue charts.

Stadium name	City	Sponsor	League	Home teams	Cost	Expires
Citi Field	New York	Citibank N.A.	MLB	New York Mets	$400 million	2028
Barclays Center	New York	Barclays Bank	NBA	New Jersey Nets	$200 million	2030
Bank of America Stadium	Charlotte	Bank of America	NFL	Carolina Panthers	$140 million	2023
Lincoln Financial Field	Philadelphia	Lincoln Financial	NFL	Philadelphia Eagles	$139.6 million	2022
Invesco Field at Mile High	Denver	Invesco Funds	NFL	Denver Broncos	$120 million	2021
TD Banknorth Garden	Boston	TD Banknorth, Inc.	NBA/NHL	Boston Celtics/ Bruins	$119.1 million	2025
Prudential Center	Newark	Prudential Financial	NHL	New Jersey Devils	$105 million	2027
Citizens Bank Park	Philadelphia	Citizens Bank	MLB	Philadelphia Phillies	$95 million	2029
RBC Center	Raleigh	RBC Centura Banks	NHL	Carolina Hurricanes	$80 million	2022
M&T Bank Stadium	Baltimore	M&T Bank	NFL	Baltimore Ravens	$75 million	2017

Sports Marketing:
To Infinity and Beyond

Sports have uniquely withstood the seismic changes undergone by the marketing landscape in the past several decades. Sponsorship in particular has experienced a radical shift in makeup and activation because of the rise of technology that has both fragmented audiences and placed increasing control of content consumption in the hands of the consumer. Smarter consumers have changed the symbiotic relationship between sports, media, and advertisers in both mass advertising and sponsorship, and the new normal has been dictated by a host of factors: the growing inefficiency of traditional advertising due to hyperfragmented audiences and simultaneous multiscreen content consumption; the convergence of sports properties and media; and the increased proliferation of time-shifted viewing and pervasive use of the DVR.

This parallel evolution of sponsorship and consumer has occurred in large part because sports, more so than any other genre, are perfectly suited to multiscreen consumption. In the United States 35 years ago, Saturday afternoon was a one-screen, three-network world, but with the rise of ESPN (an empire that encompasses print, online, and even mobile) and subsequent proliferation of cable alternatives, online outlets, and digital content, today's world is a "highlight world." The nearly unlimited access to diverse sports programming has drastically changed the look and feel of advertising sponsorship; whereas the marketers of yore needed only to purchase a 30-second commercial on *Monday Night Football*, brands now must contend with fans who consume live games, quarterback their fantasy teams online, and check real-time stats and updates on their phones—all at the same time. Yet, as demonstrated by CBS' March Madness on Demand feature and the NFL's decision to allow Verizon to stream content, marketers realize that multiple content portals have an additive effect to live viewership, and not necessarily a cannibalization effect.

The Internet has democratized how consumers engage with brands; bombarded by commercial messaging at every turn, consumers demand personalization and have reached a threshold of ambivalence for most mass advertising.

Conversely, emergent mobile technologies allow messages to reach people in places that have long been inaccessible. These technologies are another powerful channel through which marketers can reach consumers and through which consumers can reach marketers. The 30-second commercial, long the bastion of the marketing world, has become archaic by comparison to evolving technology.

Looking forward, the new generation of sports marketers must take the helm with even more digital expertise. Properties, now becoming content companies, must further adapt to the call for ROI; brands must select sponsorships that address evolving consumerism; agencies must expand their range of capabilities to meet these convergent demands. One thing is certain: Sports will continue to capture consumer fascination and engagement, but in increasingly diverse and complex ways. Sports marketers, and buyers and sellers of sports sponsorship alike, must rise to meet this challenge.

Brian France, NASCAR

© AP Photo/Kathy Willens

Brian France, a third-generation NASCAR CEO, was born riding shotgun and finally got to move over to the driver's seat. The youngest of this roundtable of pro sports leaders, France ascended to the top of NASCAR after his father, Bill France Jr., handed him the steering wheel in 2003 (just as Bill's father, "Big Bill" France, had done in 1972).

Along with his sister, Lesa France Kennedy (president of International Speedway Corporation, NASCAR's racetrack operations division), France grew up traveling the NASCAR circuit. He managed several smaller tracks, including Tucson Raceway Park in Arizona, and became a link between the sport and the entertainment industry when he managed NASCAR's Los Angeles office in the 1990s. France's most lauded accomplishment before becoming NASCAR CEO was working with his father to establish the Craftsman Truck Series in 1995.

Under France's tenure, NASCAR has added the season-ending 10-race Nextel Chase for the Cup and a record TV contract worth $4.5 billion. The circuit has made aggressive inroads to increase diversity and expand its fan and track base well beyond its Southern roots, even pushing hard to establish a track near New York City.

France has been criticized, however, for taking the sport too far from its heritage. His decision to allow Toyota vehicles to race was met with controversy, as has his push for the Car of Tomorrow.

"In NASCAR you manage from the middle," said three-time NASCAR champion Darrell Waltrip in an April 2006 *Time* article. "That way you can go up or down the ladder, and [France] seems to be pretty good at doing that."

Q: You're in a very different situation than the commissioners of the other sports leagues in that you have grown up in your job. What kind of different perspective do you think you have growing up in that business versus somebody like a Roger Goodell who has spent a lot of time with the NFL but not from birth?

BF: I don't know. I'm not sure that is truly a leg up because most of the time a commissioner has had a long relationship with the game in one form or another. In my case, it was a family business, so maybe it's a little more intimate. I would hope I would know the values of what we're trying to do as an organization better than most because of that perspective, so in light of that I think I've had exposure to certain things quicker than somebody else. But look at the people—David Stern's been in his job 25 years, something like that, you know everybody has had a long relationship. You only reach this position if you have a clear understanding of what is going on in your organization.

Q: When you were a kid, what was the first pro sports event that you remember attending?

BF: Well, you know, I don't even remember, but I'm a big sports fan. I go to a lot of sports on my own and usually buy my own tickets and go into the stands and watch them, you know. I'll go to an NBA game or the Super Bowl; I'll try to do a college basketball game. I'm going to one tonight. I'm going to the Florida–Tennessee game tonight. I love it. Aside from the business side of it, I always try to get something out of that, new stadiums or whatever, but I love it.

Q: As a family business, do you think NASCAR is different from other family businesses, say a manufacturing company that's been in a family for three or four generations? Do you have particular challenges that they don't face?

BF: Well, maybe. We all have stakeholders and a constituency to please. We have team owners, but the relationships are slightly different in how they're constructed. So I would say there's a lot of difference in that. We look at family businesses as usually having a different dynamic. There should be less politics in what I do as opposed to some of the things that happen with other leagues, just because we own the organization outright and it allows us a longer view on things, and hopefully that's a benefit.

Q: The fact that you are distributing prize money makes you a lot more like Tim Finchem, the PGA commissioner. Who are your true peers?

BF: Well, you know, the prize money's a work in progress, like I said, we all have stakeholders, and we all have television partners that we have to have good relationships with. We all have sponsorship partners; we have more of those than anybody else. We all have labor at war, you know, our drivers, their players, that kind of thing. We all have licensees—we all have the same kind of issues. There are just different structures to deal with. We often deal with the same people—Sprint has a major role with the NFL, and it has a huge role with us. Fox, the same; they just cross over all the time. So we have pretty much the same issues with the same people.

Q: We talked to Gary Bettman about a sports commissioner meeting of the minds; Gary commented that he'd like to do it more often. Do you think there should be more communication among all the leagues?

BF: Well, you know, personally it would be fine with me. I have made it a point to meet directly with every one of the commissioners, and we have good relationships with most of the sports, particularly the NFL because we have scheduling things we work through from time to time. We certainly have some governmental concerns that we all can share, so personally it would be fine with us if we had more communication not less.

> CONTINUED

Q: The performance-enhancing drug dilemma seems like much less of an issue in NASCAR than in the stick and ball sports. Would you agree with that?

BF: The reality is we've got drivers down on the track with 43 other guys going 200 miles an hour (320 km/h) with 3,000-pound (1,400 kg) cars, so we need to be aggressive about drugs. We also have a sport that is somewhat self-policing for those obvious reasons.

Q: If I'm looking at NASCAR versus the stick and ball sports, I absolutely say your strongest suit is your dedication to the fans. What are some of the things that you personally do to try to keep in touch with them?

BF: I have the same e-mail as everybody else in the organization, so I actually get a fair amount of e-mails. I respond to not all of them but a number of them. I make fan phone calls sometimes. People get a real surprise when they write a letter and then I'll actually give a phone call, you know, we'll talk through an issue. We try to understand what the fans like and what they don't understand, try to make sure we're doing things that clarify our rules extensions or changes. We've had too many changes in the last few years—a lot of them were out of our control; some of it we instituted. But sport has a culture of continuity, so we beefed up our "back to basics" philosophy, limited change, let what changes we had made settle in, and that's where we are today.

Q: We've heard some rumors lately that there may be a NASCAR Europe starting up. Is globalization an important part of your strategy?

BF: Well, it is. We will have opportunities to export our brand, our style of racing. Auto racing is also accepted culturally all over the world; we are number two to only soccer. Our challenge is to do it with local partners wherever we are, Europe, South America, Asia, with people on the ground who know their markets best.

Another thing about us from an international standpoint is that our events are already distributed all over the world. We sell merchandise; we have some pockets of pretty high interest. We already have the presence, but before we can take full advantage of it, we also have to do it in a certain way so that our industry back home can win: building cars that are going to race and that are going to be built by our team owners, providing promotional advice that can be done by our track owners and operations, wherever it can be. We'll have opportunities, we're just trying to make sure we're doing it in that fashion.

Q: **What about digital media? Is your online strategy an important part of your future growth?**

BF: Everybody is sort of doing it differently, and maybe that's because they've wanted it to be conducive to their own sport. Baseball has a successful media package where they've consolidated all their websites with the teams and are doing lots of video downloads. NASCAR has its own channel that we are trying to get distributed. We've licensed our own channel but also have a relationship with News Corp. and the Speed Channel, so we get a lot of benefit there. We have a robust site with Turner Interactive; we've had a partnership with them for a long time. And then we're building out our own NASCAR Media Group, which is our version of controlling content in the future. So whenever NASCAR content can be monetized, distributed, we don't know what that quite means, does it mean over an iPod, or over your cell phone? Whatever devices have virtual media we'll be looking at. I think most of the sports leagues will want to be in a position to control and distribute that at their discretion. I think that will be the one central thing you will see all the leagues trying to figure out.

Q: **If you could personally bring one major change to NASCAR, what would it be?**

BF: I would say it would be that the sport would get the kind of coverage from traditional media sources that the size of the audience warrants, and we're unique in that. Every other sport has better publicity. They're quite well covered on talk radio and print media, the sports page. In our case, it would not be uncommon for us to not be covered at all.

9

Ticket to the Future

- ▶ The vast majority of tickets sold to sports and entertainment events today are purchased and distributed electronically.

- ▶ Professional sports teams have adopted a wide range of ticketing flexibility and creativity, including all-you-can-eat packages, stored value tickets, and dynamic ticket pricing.

- ▶ Live Nation/Ticketmaster controls the majority of sports ticketing, just as it does in the concert world.

- ▶ Leagues and teams have entered the secondary ticket market to compete for revenue with the likes of StubHub.

BOX OFFICE

your modern definition of *ticketing* is. The ticket process may be the most rapidly changing aspect of sports today—long gone is the era of smiling men in sport coats tearing ticket stubs and of buying last-minute tickets from scalpers on the street. The vast majority of ticketing is done electronically, either primary or secondary e-commerce sales over the Internet or e-mail–driven season ticket renewals.

Ticketing has also gotten a lot more complex than in the days when you walked up to a box office window, stuck out a handful of bucks, and got a piece of paper in return. The NHL Stars in Dallas and the MLB Giants in San Francisco, for example, are among early adapters of dynamic pricing to determine the cost of admission for their hardest-to-sell seats. Dynamic pricing in sports is similar to purchasing airline tickets, as the Stars, Giants, and others use a computerized algorithm to update prices based on availability, the perceived demand for the seat, and the quality of that day's opponent. Just like on a plane, the guy sitting next to you may have paid half—or double—what you paid for your ticket.

What's more, would-be season ticket buyers are often flabbergasted by all the options laid before them. In 2010, the Los Angeles Dodgers offered 67 possible ticketing combinations for full or partial season tickets to games at Dodger Stadium. That's enough to make old-timers who'd been around since the Brooklyn days say "fuhgeddaboudit" and just tune the transistor to Vin Scully. But Dodgers ticketing personnel look like minimalists compared to the Minnesota Twins, who offer 120 single-game ticket variations at Target Field.

The current recession also presents the greatest ticket sales challenge the sports industry has dealt with in years. Facing an oversupply of inventory at inflated prices, teams and leagues are forced to start annual sales cycles sooner, cut pricing, and stress group sales. While most organizations figure out ways to handle the downturn, teams are seeing lower gate revenues across the board. The tight consumer market may also temporarily rein in the exceeding elasticity of high-end pricing, especially in brand new stadiums and arenas.

While paperless tickets account for only one percent of all ticket sales, teams such as the Phoenix Coyotes are growing that trend. Instead of game tickets, the Coyotes give season ticket holders a special card that they scan each game. The process is not only an attractive high-tech platform but also saves the team $15,000 in printing costs.

In the NBA, Veritix, formerly known as Flash Seats, has sold more than two million paperless tickets since its 2006 launch and generated more than half a million dollars in new secondary ticket revenue for the Cleveland Cavaliers, Denver Nuggets, Houston Rockets, and Utah Jazz in the first half of the 2009-2010 season alone. Using the Veritix system, about a third of the Cavs' season ticket holders swipe their driver's license or a credit card when they walk through the turnstiles at Quicken Loans Arena. Veritix users also have access to a secure online marketplace where they can sell their tickets electronically or buy more; the system manages the transactions and keeps buyers and sellers anonymous.

What's the ticket of the future look like? There won't be one. Soon, the whole ticketless ticketing transaction is going to be contained in a device—likely the cell phone—in the palm of your hand.

In a World of $2,650 Baseball Tickets, How's a Fan Supposed to Survive?

When did buying a ticket to a sporting event get so complicated—and so damned expensive? Since when does attending a baseball game amount to a luxury item? Most experts keeping statistics on the situation point to the new wave of stadiums built since 1990 as the culprit. As teams' facilities costs went up, so too did their debt service. Naming rights, sponsorship deals, and corporate suites weren't completely covering the tab, so the teams were "forced," as most of them put it, to transfer some of the costs to their very best customers. Then, even teams with aging facilities and not-so-great records began to take notice of what the market would bear and snuck in yearly ticket increases of their own.

By 2010, the average cost for a family of four to attend a baseball game, according to *Team Marketing Report's* annual Fan Cost Index, was $194.98. That included tickets in general seating for two adults and two kids, two regular-size beers, four hot dogs, four sodas, two programs, two baseball caps, and parking. And that's just baseball, long the most afford-able sports option for families. In the NBA, tickets in the last two decades have generally gone up about 3 to 4 percent a year, even when factoring in the 500 league-mandated $10 seats made available at every NBA game. At Los Angeles' Staples Center, home of the perennially championship-contending Lakers, upper-level tickets in 2008 were raised to $40, while lower-bowl seats were going for $85 to $210. Want to sit courtside with Jack Nicholson? That would cost you $2,500 a game.

But sharing space with Jack is still less expensive than the prices charged by the New York Yankees in 2009. When the Bronx Bombers opened their new stadium, a single Yankees Legends Suite ticket was priced at $2,650. The team cut the price in half midway through the season, after embarrassing nonstop media coverage of the empty seats behind home plate. And while the Yankees testily reminded fans that $5 and $10 bleacher seats were available—a league-wide policy—many

Top Five Creative Ticket Promotionals

5. **American Airlines Arena:** To celebrate its 10th anniversary, the arena hosted a sit-in contest. Participants had 24 hours to sit in every single arena seat for the chance to win the ultimate prize of four tickets to every American Airlines Arena event for one year.

4. **Washington Capitals:** In an effort to keep the Verizon Center "red" for their playoff series against the Pittsburgh Penguins, Capitals owner Ted Leonsis told his sales staff not to sell tickets to Pens fans. The team blocked telephone ticket sales originating from Pittsburgh area codes. Unfortunately for Leonsis, the Penguins took two of four at the Verizon Center, including the decisive game seven.

3. **JetBlue:** To recognize the Dodgers resigning of #99 Manny Ramirez, team sponsor JetBlue offered $99 Manny Fan Fare flights out of Los Angeles. JetBlue creates similar flight promotions every time they sponsor a new sports team.

2. **Memphis Grizzlies:** Mired in futility, the Grizzlies offered 2009-2010 season ticket packages tied to the team's lottery position in the NBA Draft. Because the Grizzlies landed the second pick in the draft, select ticket packages were sold for $2 per game, totaling $82 for the season.

1. **NLL Minnesota Swarm:** After drafting Zack Greer third overall in the National Lacrosse League draft, the Swarm signed their rookie to a unique incentive-based contract. Greer's salary will be tied to ticket sales. The more tickets Greer helps sell in his fan club's section, the more money he makes.

were view-impaired, and they weren't priced that way for every game, such as when the Red Sox came to town.

Across the board, too-high prices and the rising unemployment rate have recently lowered expectations for teams' ticket sales operations. American families whose household income is $75,000 or less, an entertainment industry poll revealed, now have zero dollars of discretionary income—going to a live sporting event has increasingly become out of the question.

What doesn't kill you will make you stronger. Thus, professional sports teams have adopted more ticketing flexibility and creativity to combat the down economy than they have since the Great Depression. All across the United States, ticket packages have begun to include attractive incentives—gas cards, all you can eat, two-for-one deals, a free T-shirt or hat. NASCAR tickets have increasingly been bundled with discount lodging for that sport's itinerant fan base. And corporations in the TARP era are adopting a watchdog stance on employee use of sports tickets as well. In an attempt to curtail extravagant spending, more than 250 companies have purchased the Spotlight Ticket Management Solution, a computer program that allows management to keep statistics on sports ticket use—including how much business those tickets bring into the company over time.

Darth Ducket

Who controls the majority of the sports ticketing empire? That would be Ticketmaster, based in the heart of West Hollywood in L.A.

As the world's leading live entertainment ticketing and marketing company, Ticketmaster operates in 20 global markets, providing ticket sales, marketing, and distribution through approximately 7,100 retail outlets, 17 worldwide call centers, and www.ticketmaster.com, one of the largest e-commerce sites on the Internet.

Established in 1976, Ticketmaster provides exclusive ticketing services for leading arenas, stadiums, professional sports franchises and leagues, college sports teams, performing arts venues, museums, and theaters. In 2008, the company sold more than 141 million tickets valued at more than $8.9 billion. That year, Ticketmaster also acquired a controlling interest in Front Line Management Group, the world's leading artist management company.

For clients, Ticketmaster is a trusted and secure source of access to live entertainment, providing flexibility and convenience. From a consumer perspective, however, Ticketmaster is often the big, trumpeting elephant in the room. People think, "Oh, Ticketmaster. They just exist to rip the fans off. They're the reason that my tickets are so expensive and the system is so convoluted."

Not true, says Mike McGee.

McGee, Ticketmaster senior vice president and a longtime shaper of the industry, puts the market into layman's terms like only a Texan can. McGee started off on the team side of the ticket-selling business; today, he has 9,000 sports and entertainment clients within Ticketmaster's vast system. But the company, he insists, simplifies the ticketing process on a broad scale rather than convolutes it. And he draws on his decades in the ticketing business to put the so-called complexity into perspective.

"First," McGee says about franchises' numerous ticket packages, "you've got to take into consideration the inventory that you're dealing with. Let's say the Dodgers are playing more than 80 games a year and they've got 50,000 tickets available per game, so right there how many tickets are you looking at? And if you're a contending team playing a good opponent and the game that you are currently playing is relevant to the position of a drive for a pennant, like in baseball, well, you can't get into this 'one size fits' all mentality. You've got to come up with many packages—this is really more of a benefit to fans."

About ticket pricing, McGee recalls, "When I first worked in Houston in 1979, the most expensive ticket for a Houston Rockets basketball game was $16. These days, the *tax* on that ticket is now 400 percent of the 1979 face value! Regardless, 40 percent of the tickets that are offered for sale generally, not only sports, are priced too low. The most expensive tickets are not priced high enough, and the lowest priced tickets are overpriced. Where the industry's been challenged is in finding a variable ticket policy model that will meet the demands of the marketplace. It's a tough, tough issue."

The Top Acts of 2010

Over the last 10 years, concert ticket prices have risen 83 percent—while the consumer price index has climbed only 32 percent during the decade. While some concert promoters insist that most acts were undervalued to begin with, others blame Mick Jagger. When the Rolling Stones charged extra for premium seats during their 1994 tour, prices escalated—and other acts began to follow suit. (The Stones' legendary front man did attend the London School of Economics, after all.)

While the Stones sat out the 2010 season, other big names raked in record millions. Here are the top 10 touring acts in North America of 2010:

Rank	Artist	Total gross (in millions)
1.	Bon Jovi	$120.5
2.	Justin Bieber	$103.7
3.	Taylor Swift	$102.1
4.	Lady Gaga	$96.5
5.	"The Beatles"*	$92.7
6.	Michael Buble	$90.6
7.	Roger Waters	$89.6
8.	Black Eyed Peas	$82.5
9.	Dave Matthews Band	$79.2
10.	Eminem	$71.7

*Sir Paul McCartney's and Ringo Starr's combined solo tours.

Source: Pollstar

The Secondary Ticket Market— From Classic Scalpers to Some Guy Named Craig

Like most players in sports ticketing operations, Ticketmaster has jumped into the multibillion-dollar secondary ticket market with all four elephant feet. Secondary ticketing allows both fans and brokers to sell tickets to each other, often at prices far exceeding their face value. What's driving the push? The same thing that drives old-fashioned ticket scalpers standing on the corner with cardboard signs. There's money to be made. A report by Forrester Research in 2008 predicted that by 2012, secondary market ticket sales for sports and entertainment would reach $4.5 billion.

Ticketmaster launched its resale service, called TicketExchange, at the end of 2005 and has since signed hundreds of sports teams and venues on to the service. TicketExchange is the official secondary market resale partner of the NFL, the NBA, the NHL, seven major NASCAR speedways, college athletics departments, and theaters and civic centers nationwide. (TicketExchange's earlier iteration, TicketsNow, was accused of "scalping" by no less a music legend than Bruce Springsteen, who was outraged when the main Ticketmaster site directed Springsteen fans trying to buy tickets to his upcoming summer tour to a TicketsNow page filled with resellers offering seats at up to five times their face value.)

Ticketmaster's desire to get in as deep with top entertainment acts as it is in sports was the main factor behind its controversial merger with Live Nation, the biggest concert promoter in the United States. Announced in early 2009 and finalized in 2010, the Live Nation–Ticketmaster merger, according to Ticketmaster CEO Irving Azoff, enabled the combined companies to bring in more corporate sponsorship dollars, reduce the number of middlemen between artists and fans, and lower ticket prices for concerts.

Critics, however, were adamant a merger of the two entertainment giants would concentrate power in the entertainment industry like never before, creating a monopoly that would drive up ticket prices, tack on even more fees than the 25 to 30 percent now common, and limit fans' choices. Artists such as Springsteen and lawmakers in several states publicly decried the move.

Tickets of America's Michael Lipman has experienced the entire spectrum of ticket resale. "When I first came into the business," Lipman says, "you would call a guy from New York who obtained sports tickets from season ticket holders and would charge you whatever he wanted. Nowadays, people are buying tickets on eBay, Craigslist, StubHub, through presales and fan clubs. The consumer is so much smarter that we have to be able to provide the specialized service they expect. One person in our organization only handles eBay transactions. Another just focuses on Craigslist. I have another person who concentrates on wholesale accounts, and another who specializes in American Express gold and platinum card and fan club special offers. It's really a sophisticated way to buy tickets, versus the old days where you just called Joe the ticket broker in New York City, he would call Benny who had seats on third base, then he'd put A and B together."

Another major difference from the old days is that now, reselling tickets above face value is completely legal in most states, which have done away with antiscalping laws at the behest of powerful teams and companies eager to corner their piece of the rich secondary ticket market.

The final spoke in the secondary ticket market evolution is technology—not just the proliferation of secondhand ticket websites but also the powerful computer programs, commonly called "bots," that allow brokers to swarm a company's website and snap up thousands of tickets almost instantaneously. These programs make it increasingly difficult for consumers to get their hands on tickets the first time around, often driving them to higher-priced secondary ticketing sites.

"Philosophically the market is changing now," McGee continues. "There's a difference between pricing to market and cornering the market. If someone says, 'Okay, I'm going to buy these $500 seats and hold them out,' that's a whole other circumstance than Joe Six-Pack buying four tickets and saying, 'You know what? I don't really need four, I only need two and I'm going to sell them.' The above-board players in the industry are all aiming for legitimacy. Ticketmaster, for example, not only guarantees the money a person puts on a ticket, we also guarantee the legitimacy of the ticket. Because of the volume of our business and our access control devices, nobody else can do that."

In sports, the practice of selling season tickets simplifies the ticketing process. "Generally speaking, between 55 and 85 percent of sports tickets are sold on a season basis," McGee says, "so you've got a smaller pool of the tickets available to the brokers in the first place. And the teams have a continuum of activity, so they're always focused on how they can package and market to their ticket buyers."

Making a ticket exchange available to fans also helps teams guarantee that tickets are actually used. Nothing's worse than a no-show factor.

"When I was with the Rockets when they won back-to-back world championships in 1994-1995," McGee continues, "as hot as they were in the city of Houston, it was not uncommon to have a 15 to 18 percent no-show factor at every game. At the time, the average ticket season holder went to about 14 games, about a third of the 41 total home games. The other tickets were given to the neighbors, or Charlie down in the garage. Or worse, they were sitting in a desk drawer.

"And that was a champion team. If you've got a dog of a team, you leave four tickets on your dashboard, somebody breaks into your car . . . and there's eight."

More Ticket Tech

Bots may be bad for fans, but most ticketing technology is to consumers' benefit, providing ease of use, eliminating the need to carry cash, and allowing exclusive offers to be customized just for them.

Peter Luukko is president and chief operating officer of Comcast-Spectacor, the Philadelphia-based sports and entertainment firm that includes the Philadelphia Flyers hockey team, the Philadelphia 76ers basketball team, and Wells Fargo Center. Comcast-Spectacor also runs Front Row Marketing and New Era Tickets, giving Luukko a bird's-eye view on how the technology behind today's ticketing process effectively pulls all the pieces together for fans, in the form of advanced data mining and stored-value technology, aka smart cards.

"Data collection starts with tickets," Luukko emphasizes. "When a fan orders a ticket, that's your first opportunity to get all of his or her relevant information, which we enter into a database that allows us to notice individual preferences. For example, Comcast-Spectacor manages Citizens Bank Park, where the Phillies play. When we had Jimmy Buffett there a couple years ago, we practically sold out one whole show just on database marketing, which is almost cost-free. We targeted our season ticket holders, the Phillies' season ticket holders, our Cyber Club. We presold 42,000 seats this way and still left more than 2,000 seats for sale to the general public. It's very effective and is the future of our business."

The advent of bar coding made a huge difference in being able to market individually to customers. "Now, you have stored-value tickets that function much like debit cards," Luukko explains. "That ticket not only gets you in the building, it first gets you into the parking lot, and holds credit to let you buy concessions and merchandise when you're inside."

Industry studies indicate that fans holding stored-value tickets spend 40 to 60 percent more on concessions that those without them. The stored-value smart card also gives fans special deals on events that matter to them and products they prefer.

"If a fan consistently orders two Pepsis and a hot dog, you know he's a Pepsi drinker," Luukko continues. "Pepsi's a huge sponsor of ours. When we have data on a Pepsi drinker, not only can we send him an exclusive offer for something here, perhaps a Pepsi-sponsored show, but Pepsi can now send him a coupon for their products, too."

The technology also gives teams terrific marketing flexibility. "If you're on a three-game winning streak, today's Friday, and you've got a game

Saturday," Luukko says, "you just blast out an e-mail offer to people with last night's results and the standings. You're creating the type of interest you couldn't drive up in the old days. It goes the other way, too—say you've got a Monday game and you're a little slow. You can blast out a last-minute, deep-discount offer, and fill the seats."

Ticketmaster is also adept at e-mail blasts—according to McGee, the company sends out something like 15 million e-mails a week. "But it's a fallacy that everything can be generated from the Internet," he argues. "We're really a vertically integrated entertainment delivery system that is perceived to be a ticket company. We're much more than ticketing, and we'll continue to be more than that as the business evolves, whether it's on the sports side or whether it's on the entertainment side."

Despite the appeal of smart cards and paperless ticket technology, including the next wave of mobile wireless ticket solutions built right into your cell phone, McGee doesn't think paper tickets will ever completely go away, thanks to the souvenir factor. Who among us doesn't have a cache of fading concert and sports ticket stubs tucked away in a shoebox somewhere?

"People leaving a venue want a visible sign that they attended a landmark event," McGee says. "If we go completely with virtual tickets, we don't have that. In the future, if you want a commemorative ticket to a show, that's when the ticket itself will become merchandise. You'll have your basic paperless ticket. For another 15 bucks, I'll give you a commemorative ticket. And if you really want it special, I'll have it autographed by the band. But that's not $15. That's going to be $50."

"Everybody's bought a ticket for something, so most people think they understand what the business is all about," McGee concludes. "I can go to any cocktail party in the world and be told I'm an idiot.

"'Oh, you're in ticketing? Let me tell you what will sell out.' And you feel like saying, 'Well, I've based my whole last 40 years on this business. Don't you think if I knew what would sell out I'd be out buying it and booking it?'

"It's out of sight."

ABOUT THE AUTHORS

Rick Horrow is the leading expert in the business of sport as the architect of over 100 deals worth more than $13 billion. The CEO of Horrow Sports Ventures (HSV) hosts "Beyond the $coreboard" on the *Nightly Business Report* and serves as a sport business analyst for Fox Sports, Bloomberg TV, *Bloomberg Businessweek,* and the BBC. As the leading commentator on sport business and as a well-connected entrepreneur, he has access to many of the top names in sport, including commissioners, owners, general managers, coaches, and athletes. His clients have included some of the biggest organizations and companies in the world of sport and business: NFL, MLB, NASCAR, PGA, Great White Shark Enterprises, Cisco Systems, Golden Bear International, Enterprise Rent-A-Car, LPGA, and MLS. Horrow is nicknamed the Sports Professor thanks to his time spent as a visiting expert on sport law at Harvard Law School.

Courtesy of Monica Hooper

Karla Swatek is vice president of Horrow Sports Ventures. With Horrow, Swatek pens a weekly column on sport business for Bloomberg Businessweek. She has worked on book projects with Ken Blanchard, Peter Ueberroth, former USC football coach John Robinson, and Robert Hagstrom (*The NASCAR Way*), as well as business leaders like Anthony Smith (*The Taboos of Leadership*).

Courtesy of Shirley Olsen